Epics of Sumerian Kings

Society of Biblical Literature

Writings from the Ancient World

Number 20
Epics of Sumerian Kings: The Matter of Aratta
by Herman Vanstiphout
Edited by Jerrold S. Cooper

EPICS OF SUMERIAN KINGS

The Matter of Aratta

by

Herman Vanstiphout

Edited by

Jerrold S. Cooper

Society of Biblical Literature
Atlanta

Library of Congress Cataloging-in-Publication Data

Vanstiphout, H. L. J. (Herman L. J.)
Epics of Sumerian kings : the matter of Aratta / by Herman L. J. Vanstiphout ; edited by Jerrold S. Cooper.
p. cm. — (Writings from the ancient world ; no. 20)
Includes bibliographical references.
ISBN 1-58983-083-0 (paper bdg. : alk. paper)
1. Epic poetry, Sumerian—Translations into English. 2. Epic poetry, Sumerian. I. Cooper, Jerrold S. II. Title. III. Series.
PJ4083 .V36 2003
899'.9510308—dc22 2003018255

11 10 09 08 07 06 05 04 03 5 4 3 2 1

Printed in the United States of America on acid-free, recycled paper conforming to ANSI/NISO Z39.48-1992 (R1997) and ISO 9706:1994 standards for paper permanence.

Contents

Series Editor's Foreword vii
Abbreviations ix
Explanation of Signs and Conventions xi

Introduction 1
- General 1
- The Stories 2
- Time and Space 4
- Actors 6
- Intention and Message 8
- Structure and Style 9
- The Literary Context 11
- Texts, Authors, and Public 13
- Concluding Remarks 15
- About This Book 15

I. Enmerkar and Ensuhgirana 23
- Introduction 23
- Composite Text 28
- Translation 29

II. Enmerkar and the Lord of Aratta 49
- Introduction 49
- Composite Text 56
- Translation 57

III. The Lugalbanda Poems 97
- Introduction 97
- Lugalbanda in the Wilderness 99
  - Introduction 99
  - Composite Text 104
  - Translation 105
- The Return of Lugalbanda 132
  - Introduction 132

Composite Text 136
Translation 137

Bibliography 167
Glossary 173

Series Editor's Foreword

Writings from the Ancient World is designed to provide up-to-date, readable English translations of writings recovered from the ancient Near East.

The series is intended to serve the interests of general readers, students, and educators who wish to explore the ancient Near Eastern roots of Western civilization or to compare these earliest written expressions of human thought and activity with writings from other parts of the world. It should also be useful to scholars in the humanities or social sciences who need clear, reliable translations of ancient Near Eastern materials for comparative purposes. Specialists in particular areas of the ancient Near East who need access to texts in the scripts and languages of other areas will also find these translations helpful. Given the wide range of materials translated in the series, different volumes will appeal to different interests. However, these translations make available to all readers of English the world's earliest traditions as well as valuable sources of information on daily life, history, religion, and the like in the preclassical world.

The translators of the various volumes in this series are specialists in the particular languages and have based their work on the original sources and the most recent research. In their translations they attempt to convey as much as possible of the original texts in fluent, current English. In the introductions, notes, glossaries, maps, and chronological tables, they aim to provide the essential information for an appreciation of these ancient documents.

The ancient Near East reached from Egypt to Iran and, for the purposes of our volumes, ranged in time from the invention of writing (by 3000 B.C.E.) to the conquests of Alexander the Great (ca. 330 B.C.E.). The cultures represented within these limits include especially Egyptian, Sumerian, Babylonian, Assyrian, Hittite, Ugaritic, Aramean, Phoenician, and Israelite. It is hoped that Writings from the Ancient World will eventually produce translations from most of the many different genres attested in these cultures: letters (official and private), myths, diplomatic documents, hymns, law collections, monumental inscriptions, tales, and administrative records, to mention but a few.

Significant funding was made available by the Society of Biblical Literature for the preparation of this volume. In addition, those involved in preparing this volume have received financial and clerical assistance from their respective institutions. Were it not for these expressions of confidence in our work, the arduous tasks of preparation, translation, editing, and publication could not have been accomplished or even undertaken. It is the hope of all who have worked with the Writings from the Ancient World series that our translations will open up new horizons and deepen the humanity of all who read these volumes.

Theodore J. Lewis
The Johns Hopkins University

Abbreviations

AAASH	*Acta Antiqua Academiae Scientiarum Hungaricae*
AF	*Altorientalische Forschungen*
AfO	*Archiv für Orientforschung*
AOAT	Alter Orient und Altes Testament
AS	*Acta Sumerologica*
AS	Assyriological Studies
BASOR	*Bulletin of the American Schools of Oriental Research*
BBVO	Berliner Beiträge zum Vorderen Orient
BCSMS	*Bulletin of the Canadian Society of Mesopotamian Studies*
BO	*Bibliotheca Orientalis*
CANE	*Civilizations of the Ancient Near East*. Edited by Jack Sasson. 4 vols. New York: Scribner, 1995.
COS	*The Context of Scripture*. Edited by W. W. Hallo and K. L. Younger Jr. 3 vols. Leiden: Brill, 1997–2002.
EE	Enmerkar and Ensuhgirana
ELA	Enmerkar and the Lord of Aratta
ETCSL	Electronic Text Corpus of Sumerian Literature
HSS	Harvard Semitic Studies
JAOS	*Journal of the American Oriental Society*
JCS	*Journal of Cuneiform Studies*
JNES	*Journal of Near Eastern Studies*
LB I	Lugalbanda in the Wilderness
LB II	The Return of Lugalbanda
LOT	Library of Oriental Texts
NABU	*Nouvelles assyriologiques brèves et utilitaires*
OBO	Orbis biblicus et orientalis
OLA	Orientalia lovaniensia analecta
OLP	*Orientalia lovaniensia periodica*
Or	*Orientalia*

RA	*Revue d'Assyriologie et d'archéologie orientale*
RHR	*Revue de l'histoire des religions*
RlA	*Reallexikon der Assyriologie.* Edited by Erich Ebeling et al. Berlin: de Gruyter, 1928–.
UrET	Ur Excavations: Texts
WZJ	*Wissenschaftliche Zeitschrift der Friedrich-Schiller-Universität Jena*
ZA	*Zeitschrift für Assyriologie*

Explanation of Signs and Conventions

[ ]	Brackets enclose restorations.
⌜ ⌝	Half-brackets enclose partially destroyed signs.
-ra$_2$	Indices (subscript) are equivalent to sign numbers; they have no phonetic relevance.
-bu^{ki}	Determinatives (superscript) indicate semantic classes; they are not to be read.
/h/	Velar unvoiced fricative, as in loch
/š/	Palatal fricative, as in shall
/ĝ/	Nasalized velar plosive, as in sing
X	An unidentified sign
. . .	A gap in the text or untranslatable word(s)
KEŠ	Capitals indicate that the reading of the sign in context is unknown or uncertain.
< >	Angle brackets enclose signs omitted by the scribe.
italics	An uncertain rendering in the translation
( )	Parentheses enclose additions in the translation.

Introduction

General

The "Matter of Aratta" is the somewhat anachronistic[1] term used for a group of four narrative poems[2] in Sumerian, dealing with the various ways in which King Enmerkar, the legendary ruler of Unug—the Sumerian name for Uruk (biblical Erech, now Warka)—won supremacy over the faraway, fabulous, and fabulously rich legendary city of Aratta. Together with the Sumerian cycle of Gilgamesh tales,[3] the Aratta stories constitute what may be called, anachronistically again, the *Gesta Urukaeorum*—or the Legends of the Kings of Uruk.[4] These kings, who represent just two or three generations, appear in the Sumerian King List—an ideological document probably drawn up in the eighteenth century B.C.E. and purporting to be historical—as the second dynasty after the flood.

The four poems presented here hang together in more ways than one. They share the same *topic* (the manifestation of the superiority of Unug over Aratta); the same period of imagined *time* (the high water mark of Sumerian civilization as they saw it, expressed in the construction and adornment of the great city of Unug); the same *space* (Unug, Aratta, and the wilderness between them); the same *protagonists* (Enmerkar, Lugalbanda, and the Lord of Aratta—and, in a peculiar way, the goddess Inana); and, finally, roughly the same type of *plot:* Aratta is subdued by nonmilitary means.

There is little doubt that the cycle originated in the Ur III period (2112–2004 B.C.E.), but the actual form of the texts and the tablets themselves date almost exclusively[5] from the Isin-Larsa period (2017–1763 B.C.E.) and are products of the scribal schools, predominantly those of Nippur and Ur. Their state of preservation is generally[6] excellent; as a group they are better preserved than most other groups, such as the city laments or the disputations. This may perhaps be interpreted as an indication of the greater popularity of these texts, of greater care spent on them, or of both.

The Stories

In all the stories the topic is the controversy between Unug and Aratta as to which one is the true favorite of Inana. At least in one story, namely, EE, the "favors of Inana" are expressed in sexual terms and are thus a reflection of the ruler's expected performance in the sacred marriage rite.[7] Elsewhere it is merely a matter of Inana's predilection for one city or the other as her main seat. Taken together, these approaches illustrate the concept that the ruler in a way *is* the city. In all cases the controversy is solved by nonviolent means. However, these means are very different, and these different means are the different stories.

Therefore, it is important to distinguish the basically identical *framework* from the individual *plots*.

The framework is quite simple: one of the rulers challenges the other to submit and admit that he (the challenger) is the first favorite and, consequently, that his city is the greatest. This challenge takes the form of an outright verbal challenge (in ELA and in EE) or a military campaign (in LB I and LB II). A battle—of different kinds—ensues. This central part is then the bulk of the poem. At the end the conflict is resolved, either through the submission of Aratta (in EE and LB I + LB II) or through conciliation (in ELA). The central part, therefore, is the identifying feature of the individual stories. The central part is the true plot. These plots are as varied as the framework is identical.

a. In ELA the controversy takes the form of a series of challenges and counterchallenges. Three times the Lord of Aratta claims that he will submit to Unug only on the condition that Enmerkar, ruler of Unug, can fulfill an impossible task. In fact, the technique is that of a contest of riddles, albeit riddles with a material content. All these challenges and solutions have to be carried to and fro between Unug and Aratta by a messenger who is nimble of foot and competent of word. Since there are three challenges and three counterchallenges that the messenger has to carry from Unug to Aratta and back, and since the sequence starts from Unug and ends in Aratta, simple mathematics ordains that he has to make seven voyages in all, and over seven mountain ranges. Yet the outcome is decided by a rainstorm, which breaks the drought that threatened Aratta with famine. In view of this, and since Unug has meanwhile proven its superiority, the enmity ends. Aratta submits to Unug's superior powers, and on a footing of near equality both cities will henceforward entertain friendly and, above all, productive trade relations.

b. EE is a different story. Here the Lord of Aratta claims superiority, since, according to him, he is Inana's favorite sexual partner. Enmerkar replies and argues plausibly that he is mistaken. The controversy is not resolved. Then appears a sorcerer of exotic origin who had had to flee his own city and sought refuge in Aratta. He offers to bring Unug to heel with his evil witchcraft. He bewitches the cattle, large and small, in Sumer so that all life will come to an end. As a Sumerian countermeasure a wise woman challenges the sorcerer to a competition in wizardry. Her (white) magic is based upon the preservation of life and proves superior. The sorcerer forfeits his own vital force, and thus life is restored to Sumer. The Lord of Aratta admits his defeat.

c. As a story LB I and LB II must be taken together. Here Enmerkar undertakes a military campaign to conquer Aratta so that he can use its riches for the embellishment of Unug, particularly of Inana's abode. When the host of Unug is marching through the desolate mountainous wilderness that separates the two states, Lugalbanda, who is the youngest of the eight brothers commanding the army, falls ill and is left for dead in a cavern. Through his prayers to the great luminaries his life is saved. He also realizes—through a dream—that the gods, for whom he arranges a sumptuous feast, apparently have elected him to a special status among humankind. During what appears to be a cosmic battle between the forces of light and the forces of darkness his exaltation to "holiness"[8] seems to be confirmed. Yet he is still all alone in the wilderness, now in the region dominated and protected by the Thunderbird. He tricks the Thunderbird into granting him the power that he wishes for above wealth, comfort, and military prowess: that of magic speed. Thus he suddenly reappears among his comrades, whose siege of Aratta has remained unsuccessful thus far. Enmerkar needs a messenger to travel back to Unug in order to invoke Inana's help—and this as soon as possible. Lugalbanda makes the journey in a single day. Inana tells him that a magic ritual can overcome Aratta. Unug is victorious.

It is quite clear that there is a problem here. Is this the same story told three times and in different ways, or do we have three different stories, somewhat mechanically forced into a single framework? The short answer is, of course, that both readings apply at the same time, for it is obvious that the problem of superiority posited in the identical framework is solved—with an identical outcome—in three different ways. Thus, one might say that the framework common to the three stories is somewhat abstract. On the other hand, the three different plots also are abstract to some degree. In ELA we find three impossible riddles or tasks, a scheme nearly ubiquitous in folk tales. In EE the plot consists mainly of a magical contest. In LB I and LB II the plot takes the form of the election of the least-likely person and his elevation to the level of most importance in the development of the story.

A closer look reveals that this fusion of framework and plotting has been handled with great deftness. First, the seams between framework and plot are almost invisible in all three cases. Second and more important, the plots, notwithstanding their somewhat abstract structure, are welded into the framework as to their substance. The tasks in ELA are not gratuitous or incidental: they derive from the form the framework takes (the grain task and the famine in Aratta, the scepter as a token of overlordship, the champion's fight as a symbol for the controversy as such and as harbinger of the solution). In EE the bewitching of Sumer's livestock and the magical contest are to be connected with the sexual overtones of the first round in the contest, which is purely verbal, since both motifs are expressive of the vital force. In LB the abstract scheme of the youngest and weakest who becomes the greatest is used to make him into a superhuman messenger[9] and thereby the savior-hero of his people.[10] There can be no doubt that these poems have been constructed with great care and consummate skill.

Time and Space

All the stories make a point of setting the happenings in a definite period: the glorious reign of Enmerkar of Unug. According to the Sumerian King List,[11] the dynasty to which he belongs was the second one after the flood, and thus it antedated the presumed composition of our texts by at least some seven thousand years.[12] But more important is the additional notice in that same document: the entry explicitly says that he is "the one who built Unug."[13] The stories themselves point this out in their introductory parts and even in the substance of the story (in ELA) or in some important passages (Enmerkar's plea to Inana at the end of LB II). Thus the stories are set in the greatest of heroic times, when the city was first built. This amounts to saying that, as far as they were concerned, this is where their history starts: *ab urbe condita* ("since the city was founded"; to the Roman historians, this was the point in time where their history, and consequently all relevant history, began).[14] On the other hand, as will be discussed below, the poems show no sense of time perspective: the times of Enmerkar are in many ways pretty much identical to the times of the conception of the stories,[15] yet the passage describing the invention of writing (including its basic economic rationale) suggests remote antiquity.

As to real time, as presented in the narratives, the three stories diverge. Obviously, the series of seven journeys undertaken by Enmerkar's messenger in ELA, not to mention the caravan transporting Unug's wheat to Aratta, must have taken some appreciable time, and the episode of manufacturing a scepter according to Aratta's requirements is said to have taken a very long time—but this is debatable.[16] In EE also one must reckon with some time for the bewitching of Unug's cattle to take effect. On the other hand, both magic episodes happen very quickly; particularly the final one (i.e., the wizardry contest) is presented as being instantaneous, so that there is a marked distinction between real time and narrated time. Most interesting in this respect is the use of time in the Lugalbanda stories. The relation of the campaign starts off sedately and in strictly linear time, but then Lugalbanda's tribulations, as revealed by a close reading of the text, take only three days (two nights) to elevate the hero from the deepest misery, indeed from the jaws of death, to the heights of his status as savior.[17] The practical effect of Lugalbanda's exaltation to sainthood consists of impossible speed anyway: in a single day he travels from Aratta to Unug. Yet the situation of the army encircling Aratta specifically mentions that a long time has passed. Instead of regarding this as narrative clumsiness one might interpret the contradiction as pointing to an important difference between "natural" time and "supernatural" time. After all, the hero's wanderings take place in a region that is not bound by the rules of physics. These regions may therefore be regarded as another kind of space also, and time seems to be relative to the kind of space one inhabits—and vice versa.

Space as such is obviously an important consideration in the development of the stories. The two points of reference, or the two poles, are Unug, which stands for Sumer as a whole, being the known world, and Aratta, which stands for unknown and fabulous wealth. Unug we know, and contrary to the gist of the stories it was already a rich and vast metropolis perhaps even a millennium before the events related in the stories were supposed to have taken place. In fact, it is still there. Aratta, on the other, hand eludes us. There is significant modern literature as to its possible location; the consensus seems to be that is was a region somewhere in central Iran and had an important role in the lapis lazuli trade.[18] Yet for the understanding of our stories this seems totally irrelevant. Aratta belongs to what Michalowski felicitously called mental geography[19] and will never be found on any "real" map. It is known outside the cycle, but the relationship of the rare and stray mentions of Aratta, if any, to the cycle is limited to the use of the term to indicate anything that is proverbially rich or sumptuous—and unknown. The same consideration applies to the intervening wilderness: although the stories give some points of reference to actual places,[20] these seem to be irrelevant to the story as such. The point is much more that it is a dangerous and—in the Lugalbanda stories—a mysterious and even haunted region. This wilderness, moreover, is defined as a mountain area. At considerable odds with the real knowledge most probably available to (and from) merchants and travelers, the mountains are consistently seen and presented as a conceptual non-Sumer. At most one could say that the references to "real" places point to a knowledge—or memory—of Iran as a source for precious stones and metals and of the rugged terrain one has to cross in order to arrive there.[21]

The action space as a literary feature is also illuminating. In ELA and EE the action keeps switching from Unug to Aratta and back, and thus it illustrates, or is caused by, the basic contest character of these two pieces. In LB I and LB II, however, we have a strictly linear move from Unug to Aratta and back to Unug,[22] on the one hand, and Lugalbanda's sojourn in the wilderness, on the other. It appears that this latter space is more important than the former one, since it makes Lugalbanda into what he is. Again, this spatial dimension is as supernatural as is the temporal one. As noted above, Lugalbanda seems to have stepped out of this world for three otherworldly days before returning to the world we and his companions know.

Actors

The main actors in the cycle are Enmerkar, Lugalbanda, and the Lord of Aratta. The first two appear in the Sumerian King List as rulers of Unug. While Lugalbanda[23] was the recipient of a cult, especially in Nippur, from the Ur III period right through the Old Babylonian period (i.e., right through about 1600 B.C.E.), his only literary survival outside the cycle is found in a few royal hymns and a few mentions in the Gilgamesh epic.[24] To be sure, there is a very old[25] text describing how Lugalbanda won his wife Ninsun, but this story is not reflected in our cycle. Enmerkar,[26] however, had more of a literary afterlife. He is mentioned in one of the legends of the Kings of Akkad,[27] in a mythical story about Adapa,[28] and in a so-called chronicle of the earliest times.[29] Furthermore, there is a still enigmatic composition apparently dealing with Enmerkar's construction of a house for Inana.[30] Obviously we know nothing at all about the Lord of Aratta; his name is mentioned only in EE. In fact, the framework common to all compositions recognizes only Enmerkar and the Lord of Aratta as protagonists: the Lugalbanda poems taken together are precisely about his evolution into the saintly intermediary necessary for the solution of the controversy. As such he is functionally, albeit in abstract terms, identical to the messenger in ELA.[31]

This brings us to a second group of lesser actors: in all poems there are some intermediaries. First there is the messenger in ELA and in EE, whose role is taken over by Lugalbanda in LB I and II. Except for Lugalbanda the role of the messenger is secondary though necessary. In EE there are several other second-rank actors who, as it were, fight the rulers' battle by proxy: the sorcerer from Hamazu and the wise woman Sagburu. Still, in ELA the UR figures, whether man or dog, are also proxies for both rulers. Of still lesser importance are the chancellors and the herdsmen in EE: these merely effectuate or/and comment upon the proceedings. Also the gods, conspicuously modest in their actions, have a function to some degree,[32] but the stories are not about them.

There are, of course, two general and important exceptions. First, in the Lugalbanda poems, the hero is almost constantly in close contact with the gods and other supernatural beings, the foremost being Anzud,[33] but there are also the spirits of light-and-darkness.[34] Each of these personages has a clearly defined role to play. The great luminaries save Lugalbanda's life; the god of dreams reveals Lugalbanda's holy status; the gods are feasted by Lugalbanda; Anzud enters into a close connection with Lugalbanda and grants him the critical power of superhuman speed; a precise evaluation of the role of the Jinni still eludes us. But all this is in harmony with the difference, which in this case is also a prime example of a *differance,* between the Lugalbanda epic(s) and the rest of the cycle. As a story, the Lugalbanda poem is, as it were, the received storyline turned inside out: all attention is given to the saintly mediator. This can be seen in a pedestrian manner by comparing the number of verses dealing with him against those that do not. But the end of LB II makes it clear that Lugalbanda, not Enmerkar, is still the main actor even when the story turns back to the framework.

Second, and finally, there is the matter of the status of Inana. In all the stories she is prominently present. But in what way is she an actor? In ELA and EE she appears to be in the first instance the *instigator* of the controversy. Her preference for one of the two contestants may be expressed openly at the beginning of the story, either in a declaration by Enmerkar (in EE[35]) or by her own advice to him (in ELA[36]). However, the point is that the opponent does not accept this for a fact, and Inana only grants the victory to Unug after the story has run its course—and Enmerkar has thus proved his supremacy. In other words, Enmerkar will have to sing for his supper. The same motif—Inana as the instigator of the conflict—is also used in LB II: Enmerkar's repeated passionate plea to Inana,[37] which incidentally is the important message Lugalbanda has to bring to Unug, harks back to the same apparent indecision or fickleness of Inana. This is only to be expected: somewhat contradictory inconstancy is one of the constant features of the goddess. But all this implies that Inana is at the same time the *prize* of the contest: to the victor belongs the favor of Inana. Lastly, she is also an *active participant* in the contest: in ELA she spurs Enmerkar on, and in LB II she decides the outcome. Yet in LB I she appears to be only one of the three great luminaries (Sun, Moon, and Venus) who save the hero's life, and there is nothing to set her apart from the sun or the moon. As always, Inana is hard to define. It should be noted that this sophisticated and variegated treatment of Inana is based first and foremost on her "character" as known from a multitude of sources.[38] But it is just as important to keep in mind that the main temple in Unug, the Eana, is Inana's abode. In this way the final outcome of the struggle enhances Unug's glory, of which the splendors of the Eana will be the material expression. Also, Inana's final preference for Unug justifies Unug's subjection, albeit by "peaceful" means, of Aratta. Being one of Inana's domains—a point that is made repeatedly in the poems—it is but right that Aratta must submit to the domination by Unug, Inana's main seat.

Intention and Message

An explicitly stated aim of the poems is to praise the glorious past of the House of Unug and thereby of Sumer as a whole. In order to do this the pieces all insist on the fact that the result of the controversy everywhere consists in Inana's predilection for Enmerkar and Unug. That is why the construction and adornment of the Eana, Inana's abode, plays such a prominent part. At the same time, the texts unmistakably have in mind the glory of the Ur III state. This is most clearly seen in the famous "Spell of Nudimmud,"[39] which gives a thumbnail sketch of the extent and structure of that state as well as of its ambitions and self-image. Nor is this cause for surprise: the ruling dynasty of the Ur III state traced its origin to Utu-hegal, king of Unug, whose brother (?) Ur-namma founded the House of Ur and the state of Ur in 2112 B.C.E.[40] The ideological reasoning involved runs somewhat like this: in the remote times of the glorious rulers of Unug the foundations were laid for Sumer's preeminence among nations—and this preeminence persists in the present Ur III state.

Yet this preeminence is not a mere matter of military force or divine favor.[41] It is based upon the qualities and properties of Sumerian culture. In other words: Unug/Sumer's supremacy is based on its superiority in some important aspects, and this may be seen as the message of the poems. In this respect the solutions to the riddles in ELA are enlightening. These solutions are not merely clever; they are at the same time arguments of substance. Thus the invention of trade, which concludes ELA, is based upon Sumer's abundant wheat crops with the attendant technology (the first impossible task), its high technology resulting in the fashioning of the scepter from an artificial material (the second task), and the high standard of its textile industry (the last task). These three technological advances represent Unug's favorable position in the balance of trade: in this way they can have at their disposal the "raw material" (precious stones and metals) Aratta has to offer. But there is more: by the globalization of the use of their language (the Spell of Nudimmud!) and by the invention of writing[42] they also control this international trade.[43] But there is also a moral or ethical aspect to Sumer's superiority. In EE Inana's preference for Enmerkar may at first sight seem simply an instance of her unmotivated sexual choice. Yet the story links it with the victory of life-giving sustenance over the dark forces that threaten the food supply of Sumer.[44] In addition, there is a distinct possibility that the wise woman Sagburu is none other than Inana in disguise. In the Lugalbanda poems we also meet with an ethical consideration of sorts, for Lugalbanda's development into the savior hero of his people, that is, of Unug, has brought him into close communion with the gods and supernatural powers. Moreover, his tribulations take him into uncharted waters and even into the realm of the myriads of stars. All this prepares him for his role as the mediator between the earthly sphere of Unug and the divine sphere of Inana, so that Unug is enabled to overcome the foreign power. What is more, during his travels through the most exotic and dangerous places one can imagine he rediscovers and redefines himself as a human being of a superhuman and divinely protected status who can work wondrous things for his people—in short, a savior-saint.[45] All this is in aid of effectuating and securing Unug's position of supremacy over the "uncivilized" regions.[46]

Therefore it is perhaps not really extravagant to state that the intention and message of the cycle is to illustrate that Sumer has a right of supremacy over all foreign countries. In this context it is relevant to quote one of the Middle French heroic poems: Jehan Bodel claims that the purpose of his work, or indeed of the whole genre he is using, and which he calls the *matere de France,* is to show that:

> La coronne de France doit estre si avant,
> Que tout autre roi doivent estre a li apendant
> De la loi chrestienne qui en dieu sont creant.[47]
> (The crown of France shall be so eminent that all other Christian kings that believe in god must be subordinate to it)

The ultimate intention of our cycle is precisely that: the poems illustrate Unug/Sumer's manifest destiny, a destiny that started with Enmerkar's construction and embellishment of Unug.

Structure and Style

To my mind one of the strongest points of classical Sumerian poetry is its strong grasp of formal structures.[48] As to substance our poems are variations upon a single theme. But also structurally they are variations upon a common formula. The abstract framework already illustrates this, yet the structures of the individual poems are far more subtle than that. Thus in ELA the middle part, ostensibly merely a series of voyages carrying the riddles and their solutions forth and back, is itself framed by two passages creating the conditions enabling trade: the common use of a single administrative language, which happens to be Sumerian, and the invention of writing. In addition, the outcome is finally decided not by the straightforward solution to the third riddle; instead, the final contest between the champions is interrupted by the *ex machina* appearance of the god of rain and storms who creates the circumstances in which the happy solution to the quarrel can take place. Quite apart from the important cultural significance of Enmerkar's clever solutions,[49] the handling of the challenges is subtly different. In the first challenge Aratta is to hand over its riches; in return Aratta asks for Unug's wheat; in the second challenge Aratta is required to accept Unug's scepter, but Aratta will do so only on an impossible condition; in the third exchange both powers must agree to await the outcome of a contest of champions. This subtle play runs the gamut of the formal possibilities immanent in the mere formula of riddle-and-solution. In EE the contest is at first stated verbally, and the outcome depends in a way on one's belief in one of the two sides. But then the value of both contestants' claims is put to the test. In the first attack (the sorcerer's spell) Aratta seems to be the victor, but when the two powers really confront each other the outcome is no longer in doubt. Here again we have a play on formal possibilities inherent in a contest. In the Lugalbanda poems, finally, the system of an outer framework of controversy encompassing a series of possible solutions is imploded or turned inside out. Formally the matter of mediation is reduced to the mere finding of the appropriate messenger, while in ELA seven voyages by the messenger were necessary. However, the development of the unlikely Lugalbanda into the preordained messenger and savior now becomes the kernel of the sequence of poems. No riddles have to be solved; no contest is to be fought by middlemen; the tale is about the development of an unlikely candidate into a savior and about the necessity of a savior figure to solve the controversy. This is obvious from the fact that in the last episode, namely, Inana's solution to the problem, we see only Inana and Lugalbanda, and the implied return journey of Lugalbanda to Enmerkar in order to act upon the goddess' advice is not even mentioned.

As is well nigh universal in narrative poetry, the style of the poems is a mixture of several registers. Thus we find hymnic or appellation[50] passages not only at the beginning of the poems, where they are expected,[51] but also at several appropriate points within the development of the stories. There are purely narrative passages in all poems, but sometimes, as in the rendering of the messenger's seven voyages in ELA or in the two bouts of witchcraft in EE, these are somewhat formulaic. In the Lugalbanda poems "pure" narration predominates. Series of speeches, and sometimes even dialogue, are prominent, especially in ELA. A special feature of the Lugalbanda poems consists of relatively isolated passages of medium length (about ten to fifteen verses) that are explanatory to a situation or a motif just described or announced. Repetitions abound; the principle of spoken messages to be carried by a messenger gives much scope to straight repetition of blocks of speech, but here also there is much subtlety: where one might expect straight repetition, as in the seven voyages of the messenger over the same terrain, we find instead a somewhat artificial series of variations. There is much use of imagery of all sorts.[52] As far as we can judge, language use is supple and not really outlandish; there are few scribal conundrums. Within the confines of stylistic or generic base rules—which we hardly understand at this moment in time—the language seems fairly "natural" for poetic Sumerian. All these aspects need much further study; one can only hope that the present publication may act as an incentive for doing just that.

The Literary Context

Especially when compared to the overwhelming mass of hymns and odes, whether "divine" or "royal" or both, the amount of narrative poetry in standard Sumerian seems rather modest. Yet if one takes into account the length of individual pieces, the modesty of the contribution of narrative poetry to the bulk of the literature as we know it[53] appears to be only relative. As a group, the narrative pieces take second place only to the city laments[54] as regards their individual length. Even so, the pieces we recognize as *narrative* can be divided into three subgroups.[55] First there are narratives about the gods.[56] In general one can say that in these pieces, often called "myths," the narrative content and even nature is often slight. Even when there is a dominant narrative content, this is often swamped by hymnal or reflective passages that tend to leave a clear stylistic imprint on the piece; furthermore, the poems are often highly formulaic and static rather than dynamic.[57] As a second group we have the Gilgamesh poems,[58] which obviously are also part of the *Gesta Urukaeorum*. It is probably highly relevant, but provisionally unexplained, that this group is much less structured, less well represented in the school curriculum, and with a pattern of distribution (about which more later on) different from that of the Aratta cycle. The third group is our material.

As noted above, the relationship with the divine narratives is but slight, mainly on account of the peculiar construction system(s) dominating the latter, and perhaps also because generally speaking they tend to deal with a single topic, mostly an aspect of the organization of the world. There are also important differences between the Matter of Aratta and the cycle of Gilgamesh. First, the Gilgamesh stories are serial,[59] while the matter of Aratta consists of a single topic told in three radically different ways. Second, however close the respective heroes are in dynastic terms, they are vastly different otherwise. Enmerkar is the ideal ruler representing the state of Unug and its supremacy from the beginning; Lugalbanda becomes the saintly savior who enables Enmerkar to fulfill this role. On the other hand, the Gilgamesh stories taken as a whole could be read as treating the king's development into an ideal ruler. The different stories mark the sequence of important stages in this development, up to and including the pomp and circumstance of the state burial that enhances the regal stature of the hero but also insists upon his retaining a kind of superior position in the underworld.[60] The Death of Gilgamesh, unthinkable in the Matter of Aratta, also stresses the force of the dynastic principle and the responsibility of any ruler for his predecessors. Though this might be interpreted as an instance of the identification of ruler and state, it is vastly different from that motif in our poems.

Some formal and substantial features of our texts may also be related to comparable features in the *royal odes*.[61] The problem is, on the one hand, that there is no up-to-date treatment of this bulky mass of mostly ad hoc literary products[62] and, on the other, that these hymnic or odelike passages, except the introductory paragraphs, are generally[63] welded into the storyline and but seldom have an independent status.

A kind of text that is explicitly mentioned by the poems themselves is the *disputation*.[64] One of the poems claims in its final lines[65] that the poem is a disputation. The Spell of Nudimmud in ELA claims that the purpose of the spread of Sumerian over the known world is that this will enable the lords, princes, and kings to hold disputations.[66] Indeed, the tripartite structure underlying and defining ELA and EE, and even the Lugalbanda poems if taken as a unit, is identical to the basic structure of all the disputations. These poems[67] always consist of three parts: (1) posing the question or laying down the challenge; (2) the dispute itself, consisting of a series[68] of verbal arguments and counterarguments by both contenders; and (3) the verdict spoken by a god. Modern scholars sometimes take this identification too seriously. The facts remain that our poems are basically narratives, not verbal wrangling,[69] that the outcome is not the result of an arbitrary (aesthetic?) decision by a god, that in the catalogues of the school curriculum the two groups are kept well apart, and, finally, that the victory of Unug over Aratta depends on actions, not words. Still, the hint at a qualification as a "disputation" is there.

Texts, Authors, and Public

The conundrum at the end of the previous section can best be approached in relation to broader questions. Who composed these narratives? Why did they do this, and for whom? There is little or no doubt that the poems are the product of the scribal education in the schools, as is the bulk of standard Sumerian literature. This is not to say that they, and other compositions, were necessarily composed by scribes. But their acceptance, public reception, and tradition seem to have been mainly a matter of the schools—whatever the reasons for their initial conception. What is more, they belong to the core of the Nippur literary curriculum.[70] This is abundantly clear from the material itself, in the material sense. We know the poems from an ordered variety of tablets. These come overwhelmingly from the Nippur e d u b a[71] and in smaller numbers from Ur. Their distribution is that of the core material: in nearly all cases we have a few complete editions on large multicolumn (five to six columns per side) single tablets; a few more complete editions composed of multicolumn (three to four columns per side) editions of half or one third of the text; many single column extract tablets (i m g i d a). The writing is almost always small, regular, and careful. There are few mistakes. There are but few alternative spellings and readings. Obvious exercise tablets belonging to the earlier phases of education are conspicuously absent. Furthermore, all four poems are represented in the curricular catalogs, mostly as a group.[72] It follows that the pieces were meant for the scholars themselves and represented the final and highest step in their scribal education. It also follows that these poems, as is also the case with the other members of the core curriculum, were not studied for life, but for schooling, as the Latin saying went, *non vitae, sed scholae discimus*.[73]

Is this the complete answer? This can be disputed. The message[74] is highly charged with an ideological content of historical and national pride. The legendary rulers have made Unug/Sumer preeminent among the nations and have laid the foundation, materially and ethically, for its supremacy. The reasons advanced for this superiority, technologically as well as ethically and perhaps even theologically (the support of the gods; the attitude of Inana), may reflect an ideal situation, but they are clearly derived from the actual or supposed situation that obtained during the glorious Ur III period. Since the princes of the Ur III state derive their fame and glory from the House of Unug, we may surmise a function of these pieces in the entourage of the royal court as well. This is less strange than it may look at first sight, for we know of king Šulgi's (2094–2047 B.C.E.) pride and lively interest in scribal education. The unabated interest of later kings, particularly Išme-Dagan and Lipit-Eštar (1953–1935 and 1934–1924 B.C.E.) of Isin, in the schools may add an additional argument. In their time

Babylonia was no longer the (supposed) mighty united state of Ur III. It is reasonable to assume that they are harking back to the Ur III period, which itself took the time of the legendary hero-kings of Unug as its shining model and beacon.

But how are we to envisage the role of our poems at the royal court? There is almost no evidence that the rulers (and their entourage) could actually read, although a case could be made for precisely Šulgi, Išme-dagan and Lipit-Eštar. Here the implied and overt link of our narrative poems to the dispute poems may provide an indirect solution. At least one of the dispute poems, the Debate between Ewe and Wheat,[75] is presented on all levels as happening at the occasion of a banquet, which incidentally seems to be taking place simultaneously among the gods in heaven and among humanity on earth. Although precise indications are lacking, it is not impossible that this debate, and others, was actually performed, with different speakers for different parts, during a festive occasion. By the same token it seems not absolutely improbable that our poems also knew some sort of performance.[76] The relatively restricted number of "actors" needed, the sometimes high-flying rhetoric, the manipulated changes of scenery, the many opportunities for fancy stagecraft—these are all features that speak for just such a possibility.[77] Still, one capital difficulty remains: How many in the audience would have been able to understand this sometimes euphuistic Sumerian and to remain spellbound by it for so long? Of course, there are possible ways of countering this objection as well. First, one could suppose a performance only or mainly for an audience of scribes, even within the school or school district—if there ever was such a thing. In early modern Europe the school was a great producer of school drama, mainly in Latin, but not restricted to that language, as the splendid case of Purcell's *Dido and Aeneas* shows. Why would this not be possible in Old Babylonian times? Another possible answer might be that the texts we have represent a secondary, canonized, and perhaps poeticized libretto for a performance that was livelier, more spontaneous, more dependent on stage action, trickery, and mime, and less verbose. This would imply that the texts developed from a somewhat loose and dynamic basic frame text that could be changed, embroidered, and improvised upon into a fixed, congealed *reading* text. European medieval drama, particularly in the realm of low comedy and satire, abounds with instances of just such a development, and it should be noted that this partly grew out of "performances" with different "speakers" or parts of texts that were not especially dramatic in the technical sense. Yet, although the same reasoning applies with even greater force to the debate poems, the main stumbling block remains firmly in place: Who would have understood and appreciated such a performance?

Concluding Remarks

It can no longer be doubted that the Sumerians, after giving humankind the most precious technological and cognitive tool ever invented, namely, writing, by that token gave us the first highly articulated system of literature. The poems translated here, as we have them, are some four thousand years old, and they still impress us with their clever and agile structure, with their consummate mastery of a highly stylized and poeticized language that was already obsolete if not extinct when they were composed, with their lively and multifaceted stylistic tactics, with their deft handling of many-layered imagery, and with their sheer exuberance in rhetoric.

Moreover, their main emphasis may perhaps still be of great importance for us, even after more than four millennia. For all their cultural pretensions and their avowed aspiration to world domination, there is hardly any sign of xenophobia in these tales. Military glory is spurned and even somewhat ridiculed in at least two of the poems.[78] Instead, the emphasis is on cultural and technical prowess, expressed as the highest form of intelligence and, of course, including writing. Furthermore, they overtly prefer their dominant position to be based on peaceful coexistence, even friendly relations with the outer world, to brute strength. Their ethical principles are founded in respect for and the fostering of the vital forces as such and in all their aspects.[79] Their attitude to the gods is practical and far from naïve. Whatever they achieve, they achieve by their own intellect and craftsmanship, whereas the gods at most give their moral support. Even when one of their culture heroes, the saintly Lugalbanda, is nearly assimilated to the superhuman level, he too reaches this high and sacred status mainly through his own insight into what is possible, courage and adroitness in overcoming hardship, cleverness in social relationship, and openness toward even the most outlandish creatures.[80]

The kind of world and society they have envisaged in these poems, in an obviously idealized way, is therefore indeed a kind of fairy-tale, pastoral universe.[81] Their assumption is that their domination of that world will be beneficial to all and that statecraft and rulership should be used to that end.

About This Book

The Sumerian texts are presented here as composite or eclectic texts. This means that the variations between manuscripts—in most cases not very important anyway—are not reflected in this presentation. Neither does the resulting text show a preference for one (group of) manuscript(s) over the others. The principle has been to adopt the best reading, which is not necessarily the most representative. This implies that the choice is of necessity somewhat subjective and personal. In this respect I should stress that my text lays no claim to diplomatic completeness or exactitude.[82] My text is based upon my own manuscripts, themselves based on hand copies of all texts that have been published and on autopsy of all the material in the Babylonian Collection of the University of Pennsylvania Museum and in the British Museum. Therefore I wish to express my gratitude to the keepers and curators of both museums, who were very helpful. Particular thanks must go to Professor Dr. A. W. Sjöberg and the staff of the Tablet Room in Philadelphia for their extraordinary hospitality, unstinting generosity in allowing me to use unpublished material, and, most of all, their constant good cheer and acerbic wit. Those of my manuscript text reconstructions that were more or less complete were sent in an early stage to Dr. Jeremy Black for the Oxford site ETCSL,[83] which has in turn been of great help in writing the present book. Every Sumerologist owes thanks to ETCSL, but in this case special thanks are due: I could not have written the present pages without it.

In my translations I have tried to steer a middle course between philological meticulousness[84] and readability. Still, I thought that fluency in English should not always preponderate over attempts to approach as closely as possible what the Sumerian text actually says. I must leave the reader to decide to what extent these attempts have been successful. As to explanatory notes, I have tried to keep them to a minimum—without much success, some may think. But here I must plead that the texts are so rich and our understanding still so limited that in most cases I felt the text would suffer without some explanation.

The layout of the Sumerian texts and translations is, of course, not to be found on the tablets. It is merely my personal attempt to divide the texts into their constituent parts as I think they should be understood.

Finally, I am very much indebted to Bendt Alster and Jeremy Black, who took the trouble to read my manuscript and sent me an impressive number of corrections, objections, and suggestions—some of which I even adopted—and to Jerry Cooper for his painstaking yet tolerant and gentle editing of the manuscript.

Notes

[1] Anachronistic, since the term clearly derives from Medieval European custom of dividing epic poetry in the "matters" of France, Greece and Rome, Britain/Brittany, and Araby. See lines 6–7 of Jehan Bodel's introduction to his *Chanson des Saisnes:*

> N'en sont que trois materes a nul home entendant:
> De France et de Bretagne et de Romme la grant.

(There are but three subject matters that anyone knows of: that of France, of Britain, and of great Rome.)

2 Identified here by the sigla ELA (Enmerkar and the Lord of Aratta), EE (Enmerkar and Ensuhgirana), LB I (Lugalbanda in the Wilderness), and LB II (The Return of Lugalbanda). Both the sigla and the titles are modern. In Mesopotamian literature compositions are identified by their incipits only.

3 These can be consulted now most easily in George 1999: 141–208 or more fully in Frayne *apud* Foster 2001: 99–154; Vanstiphout 2002a: 159–229.

4 There is a counterpart, predominantly in Akkadian, for the kings of Akkad as well; see now the splendid edition in Westenholz 1997.

5 Intriguing and important exceptions are the very late bilingual versions of LB II.

6 The exception is LB I, particularly the latter third of the poem. However, our understanding of this part of the poem is still weak, so that the relatively poor preservation of this part as presented here may have more to do with our lack of competence than with gaps in the text.

7 The "sacred marriage rite" assumes that the city rulers had to reconfirm the bond between their city and heaven every year at the occasion of the New Year festival by means of ritualized intercourse with the city goddess. There are no indications of this practice outside of literary compositions. See Kramer 1969; Renger 1972–75; Cooper 1972–75.

8 See Vanstiphout 2002b.

9 Linking him to the very important messenger in ELA.

10 This scheme underlies many fairy tales but is found also in many tales about traditional "national" heroes: Joseph, of course, but also quite a large proportion of saints' lives. See Vanstiphout 2002b.

11 This is a so-called historiographic document, drawn up during the Isin-Larsa period (2017–1763 B.C.E.) or possibly during the Ur III period (2112–2004 B.C.E.). It lists all the ruling houses with their capitals, their rulers, and the years of their reigns "since Kingdom descended from Heaven"; the important caesura is the flood. See Jacobsen 1939; Michalowski 1983; and now Glassner 1993: passim and 137–42.

12 According to the reckoning of the King List. Of course, the King List is not a source for third-millennium history, but neither are our poems, and it is more than probable that the authors of our poems may have shared the preconceptions, methods, and biases of the King List. After all, both our poems and the King List were part of the school curriculum.

13 It should be noted that the Gilgamesh traditions from early on also insist on Gilgamesh's building activities in Unug. It is interesting that these traditions nowhere say that Gilgamesh built Unug: he built its stupendous ramparts; Enmerkar had built the city.

14 This point will engage our attention again; see the section on "Intention and Message."

15 The best example is the episode of the "Spell of Nudimmud" in ELA.

16 See ELA lines 429–432.

17 As far as I am aware, this is the first time in the history of literature that someone who is doomed to die reappears on the third day in order effectively to manifest himself as the savior of his people.

[18] See, e.g., Cohen 1973: 55–61; Hansman 1978; Majidzadeh 1976 and 1982; and Wilcke 1969: 39 (who notes correctly that the precise location cannot be found and thus should not be sought).

[19] Michalowski 1988. In this case "poetical" or "mythical" is perhaps an even better adjective.

[20] For which see Cohen 1973: 41–61; Wilcke 1969: 29–40. See also Sauren 1974.

[21] On these points see Black 2002; Michalowski 1988.

[22] Lugalbanda's final journey, which implies but does not mention as such his return to Enmerkar with the saving advice from Inana.

[23] The major facts about Lugalbanda, together with a fine presentation of the two Lugalbanda poems, can be found in Wilcke 1987. See also Wilcke 1969: 49–54.

[24] In the Sumerian cycle of the Gilgamesh stories Lugalbanda is mentioned as Gilgamesh's father. In the Akkadian epic Lugalbanda is called Gilgamesh's (personal) god.

[25] Possibly dating to ca. 2500 B.C.E.

[26] For Enmerkar, see Weissbach 1934; Wilcke 1969: 41–48.

[27] See Westenholz 1997: 294–95.

[28] See Foster 1993: 435.

[29] See Grayson 1970: 147.

[30] Kramer 1990.

[31] And in a lesser way in the first episode of EE.

[32] Thus Enki renders valuable support to Enmerkar in ELA: by his spell and by his wisdom, which provides Enmerkar with the solutions to some of the riddles.

[33] The reading of the name of this supernatural bird is still a matter of controversy among specialists. In our stories it is written consistently as IM.DUGUD "heavy (storm) cloud," so that "Thunderbird" seems an adequate translation. Still, the consensus is now that it was read as Anzud—with no known etymology or explanation. In reading Anzud I bow to the collective wisdom and arguments of the majority, but I remain convinced that the scribes were thinking of a heavy storm cloud every time they wrote the signs.

[34] These "spirits" are ill-defined creatures of the otherworld that haunt the desert and other lonely places. Yet they can also penetrate into the civilized world, preferably in the lonely streets at night. They are neutral in that they can be "good" or "bad." In many ways they are reminiscent of the Jinni of Arab popular tradition.

[35] Lines 78–113.

[36] Lines 69–104.

[37] Lines 294–321 = 360–387.

[38] See Vanstiphout 1984 and now Bahrani 2001: 148–50, 155–60.

[39] See ELA lines 135–155 and Vanstiphout 1994.

[40] See Jacobsen 1939: 120–23; see also Glassner 1993: 94–85, 113–33.

[41] A piece that presents the preeminence of the Ur III state—or Sumer—as being ordained by the gods is the myth (?) How Enki Ordered the World, for which see now Vanstiphout 1997.

[42] We now know that writing was indeed invented for commercial and administrative purposes and that this happened in Unug. For the invention of writing as told in ELA, see Vanstiphout 1990 with earlier literature and now Glassner 2000: 21–44.

[43] In fact, the mechanics of the invention of trade as described in ELA are eerily predictive of the present-day commercial attitude of the technologically advanced countries vis-à-vis the third world.

[44] The sorcerer has cut off the milk yield, one of the two staple foods in Sumer. Sagburu's magic animals feed on the sorcerer's animals, and the sorcerer's own life force is used to restore the life force of Sumer.

[45] Albeit with much less emphasis on semidivine and supernatural status, Gilgamesh's evolution toward wisdom and insight and moral probity is to a certain degree parallel to that of Lugalbanda.

[46] It is striking that the expressed self-image of many of the nineteenth-century explorers—many of whom were of a highly "ethical" persuasion—has an unmistakable similarity to Lugalbanda's self-esteem. Also, ultimately the explorers' heroic adventures have led to a comparable control of these wild and mysterious foreign parts by their respective nations.

[47] See above, note 1. These lines follow almost immediately the couplet quoted there.

[48] Fine examples are Gilgamesh and Aka (see Vanstiphout 1986) and the Nippur Lament (see Tinney 1996; Vanstiphout 1983b).

[49] See the preceding section.

[50] By "appellation" I mean pieces addressed to a person or an entity (gods, kings, temples, cities, etc.) in praise, prayer, and/or appeal.

[51] One might find that the absence of such a hymnic passage at the beginning of LB II constitutes an additional argument for regarding the two poems as a unit.

[52] Black 1998 is an excellent and much-needed analysis of one group of images. His example needs to be followed up.

[53] The best succinct overview of the Sumerian literary system is Michalowski 1995.

[54] For this group see Green 1978 and 1984; Kramer 1940; Michalowski 1989; Tinney 1996.

[55] I make abstraction of the small number of short tales that are either jocular or exemplary (or both). For some examples, see Alster 1975a; 1975b: 90–96; 1993; Civil 1974.

[56] For an overview, see Jacobsen 1987; Vanstiphout 1998a.

[57] Of course there are exceptions, such as the delightful Enlil and Ninlil II (see Civil 1983), the baroque Enki and Ninhursag (see Attinger 1984), or the enigmatic Marriage of Martu (see most recently Klein 1996; Vanstiphout 2000).

[58] See above, note 3.

[59] As we know now, the tablets themselves indicate this.

[60] While it is obvious that the death and funeral of Gilgamesh stood as a model for the death and funeral of Enkidu in the later tradition, I would suggest a close investigation of the relationship between the Death of Gilgamesh and the Death of Ur-Namma. See Veldhuis 2001; Flückiger-Hawker 1999 (especially 93–182).

[61] I insist on a difference—on all points—between "hymn" and "ode." To be sure there is a significant number of pieces that straddle the dividing line. But to my mind a hymn, which is sung to a divine entity or attribute (such as a temple), is basically an appraising statement of unchangeable and eternal values *an sich,* while an ode is a descriptive list of points on which the actual ruler has scored within this value system.

[62] Flückiger-Hawker 1999: 68–91 provides a good starting point. It is interesting that only a few odes made it into the school curriculum. Was the selection based upon the relative fame of the rulers involved, or upon the literary qualities of the pieces themselves, or on both?

[63] Generally, but there are exceptions. See, e.g., ELA lines 180–186, though even this passage can be read as an introduction to the challenge that follows.

[64] See provisionally Vanstiphout 1990b and 1992b for an attempt at a definition and description of this type of text.

[65] EE lines 281–282. These final lines are often referred to as doxologies. This is not an apt characterization. In this case, as in true-type disputations, these lines are part of the composition, since they represent the final result.

[66] ELA lines 147–149. One might interpret this as a self-reference to the perceived typology of the text, thereby reinforcing the "doxology" of EE.

[67] A sample of these texts can be found in Vanstiphout 1996a.

[68] Minimally three speeches.

[69] In fact, only the first episode in EE might somehow qualify as a disputation. However, the argument, which is simply a matter of yea or nay, would probably be unacceptable in a "true" debate poem, since there is hardly any progression in logic or argued rebuttal of evidence.

[70] For this curriculum see Vanstiphout 1995b and 2003; Veldhuis 1997: 12–80; and now Tinney 1998 and forthcoming.

[71] To be taken in the conceptual sense. There is as yet no evidence for a material e d u b a .

[72] In the Philadelphia catalog (see Kramer 1942): LB I as entry 38, LB II as 39, EE as 40, and ELA as 48. In the Louvre catalog (Kramer 1942; Bernhardt and Kramer 1956–57) we find LB I as entry 22, LB II as 23, ELA as 24, and EE as 25. In the Ur catalog (see Kramer 1961; Hallo 1966; Charpin 1986) LB I is entry 37, LB II is 39, and ELA is 40.

[73] Thus the Roman philosopher Seneca. It is usually quoted the other way around, but Seneca actually wrote it this way—as the observation of a regrettable fact.

[74] See above, Intention and Message.

[75] See Alster and Vanstiphout 1987; Vanstiphout 1992a.

[76] This was actually proposed in some detail by Sauren 1972.

[77] In fact, a scenic performance might explain a somewhat bothersome difficulty: the nonrepetition of Inana's decisive advice in LB II. While the repetition of speeches may be used to drive home the respective intentions or to capitalize on flights of choice rhetoric, the actualization of Inana's advice here ends the story and resolves the controversy. In all respects the story is now over, and a repetition would be merely tedious instead of ending with a fine climax.

[78] In EE: the sorcerer's vain promises; in LB II: the inability of the Unug troops to conquer Aratta.

[79] Including overt and enjoyable sexuality; see the first interchange between the contestants in EE but also the sequel of the story.

[80] Although his attitude toward his own kind is less than frank, but that was the condition; as is the case with most saints, he stands apart from common humanity precisely because of his sanctity.

[81] In the sense as defined by William Empson (1935). Another piece that shows this attitude is How Enki Ordered the World (see Vanstiphout 1997).

[82] In this respect one should keep in mind that, diplomatically speaking, completeness and exactitude are far from being synonyms.

[83] See the introductions to the individual poems for the exact web sites.

[84] To my mind it is important to note that "translations" that pretend to incorporate every single grammatical feature of the Sumerian are (1) impossible and (2) no translations, without mentioning that they usually are based on an idiosyncratic view of grammar, Sumerian or otherwise.

I

Enmerkar and Ensuhgirana

Introduction

With about 280 lines, this tale is the shortest of the cycle. It is peculiar in several respects: the lord of Aratta takes the initiative for the conflict, and the substance and the prize of the contest are said to be the sexual favors of Inana. This contest takes the form of a competition in wizardry and is fought by proxy.

1. In the days when Enmerkar rules over the splendid and awesome city of Unug, the lord of Aratta, Ensuhgirana by name, claiming to be the recipient of Inana's favors, demands Enmerkar's submission to Aratta. Enmerkar refuses, pointing out that it is obvious that he himself is Inana's true and constant lover. The lord of Aratta apparently admits that he has been beaten in this part of the game, but, although criticized by his own people, he in turn refuses to submit to Unug. A sorcerer from Hamazi offers his services to break the stalemate: he claims to be able to bring Unug to submission. The lord of Aratta accepts the offer. The wizard travels to the city of Ereš, where he casts a spell on the cattle of the goddess Nisaba. They stop giving milk, and there is famine in Sumer. A cowherd and a shepherd implore the sun god, who sends a wise woman.[1] She catches up with the wizard on the banks of the Euphrates. They start a competition in magic. Five times the wizard throws fish spawn in the river and draws out an animal; five times the wise woman draws out another animal, which catches the wizard's animal and presumably eats it. Then the wise woman accuses the wizard of black magic, since his magic is draining away the life force of Sumer. He admits that he has been beaten at his own game and pleads for his life. She refuses, takes away his vital force, and thus reenlivens the city of Ereš. Upon hearing this, the lord of Aratta admits defeat and submits to Enmerkar.

2. The text is structured as follows:

I.	*The Setting*	
[A]	Introduction, consisting of	
	(1) Hymn glorifying Unug's splendor	1–13
	(2) Godlike Enmerkar then ruled over Unug.	14–21
II.	*The Rulers' Contest*	
[B]	Aratta's challenge	
	(1) Inana is mine, and my feast is sumptuous.	22–39
	(2) The messenger's voyage to Unug	40–51
	(3) The message is delivered.	52–69
		(56–69 = 25–38)
[C]	Enmerkar's answer	
	(1) Ode to Enmerkar	70–76
	(2) Inana shares my bed!	77–90
		(78–81//27–30)
	(3) Inana truly favors me!	91–113
		(108–113//33–38)
[D]	The lord of Aratta admits defeat but will not submit.	
	(1) What can I still do?	114–127
	(2) Reproaches by the assembly of Aratta	128–132
	(3) Even so, I will not submit.	133–134
III.	*The Bewitching of Sumer*	
[E]	The Sorcerer	
	(1) Now there was this sorcerer...	135–138
	(2) The sorcerer's proposal to the chancellor	139–149
	(3) The chancellor's proposal to the Lord	150–162
		(153–162 = 140–149)
	(4) The proposal is accepted.	163–169
[F]	Black Magic	
	(1) The cows stop giving milk.	170–184
	(2) The goats stop giving milk.	185–197
		(= 172–184)
	(3) Hunger among the cattle	198–205
	(4) Despondency in the city	206–210
	(5) The shepherds plead to the sun god.	211–221
IV.	*The Magic Contest*	
[G]	The wise woman is sent.	222–227

[H] The Contest
(1) Five parallel quatrains 228–248
(2) The accusation 249–254
(3) The plea 255–263
(4) The verdict: black magic is a capital sin! 264–273

V. The Conclusion
[I] The lord of Aratta submits. 274–280

[J] Praise be to Nisaba! 281–283

3. The poem is well organized into three major episodes preceded by the setting and followed by the conclusion. The three major episodes are three different forms of contest, and the organizing principle does not consist of some overarching structural design, such as we find in other members of the cycle, but rather takes the form of a sometimes clever and imaginative use of kinds of repetition.

The basic structure starts with a straight challenge-and-response sequence that depends heavily on a series of close repetitions: 25–38 = 56–69; 27–30 = 58–61 = 78–81 (with reversal); 31–32 = 62–63 = 81–90 (with expansion); 33–38 = 64–69 = 108–113 (with counterargument). In this first bout Enmerkar is the victor. The bewitching of Sumer constitutes Aratta's second attempt. This is also highly repetitious in that the chancellor's proposal is identical to the sorcerer's proposal (153–162 = 140–149) and the *envoûtement*[2] scene is identical for the large and small cattle (172–184 = 185–197). Aratta, or the sorcerer, seems to have won. The final magic contest now pits the wise woman against the sorcerer; it is a fine example of what one might call "formulaic repetition": in the five quatrains (228–249) the first verses are identical, while in verses 2, 3, and 4 only the animals change.

In fact, these three confrontations, represented by three different types of repetition, are the kernel and structure of the poem, which can be represented simply as: (1) arguments at a distance (messenger!), won by Enmerkar; (2) witchcraft, won by Aratta; and (3) magic contest, won by the wise woman.

Apart from this elegant exercise in the different modes of repetition, there are a few more formal and/or stylistic observations to be made. First, the story moves on in a rather straight line and at a fast pace; in doing this it also shows many changes of location that are indicated only slightly: the two palaces and, one imagines, the bridal chambers therein; the court of Aratta; the byres of Ereš; the city of Unug; and the banks of the Euphrates. This series of different locations is not strictly coextensive with the development of the plot: thus sections [B] and [C] are placed in different but interchangeable locations; the court of Aratta straddles sections [D] and [E]; section [F] moves from Ereš to Unug. Second, the motif of the messenger, important in [B] and [C], seems to be taken over from ELA, which may explain the totally superfluous and indeed substantially unexplainable line 77. But from then on, the text takes a totally different direction, in which two (or even three, when including the chancellor) proxies carry the story. It is probably meaningful that these two proxies come from outside of the story, as it were: the sorcerer is a fugitive from Hamazu, and Sagburu has to be "sent for." Third, the first two sections are heavily dependent upon ELA in structure and expression (see lines 40–51, 53–55, and possibly also the somewhat damaged 70–76). But line 97 is an unmistakable reference to LB II lines 70–89, and lines 100–104 are more than reminiscent of Enmerkar's plea to Inana in LB II lines 308–318, where line 315 also refers back to the earlier episode. On the other hand, the passage lines 14–19 seems stylistically more akin to the sometimes "cosmic" introductions found, for example, in Enki and Ninhursaga,[3] Enlil and Ninlil,[4] or Gilgameš, Enkidu, and the Underworld[5]—but also found in the introduction to LB I. In other words, further study may well show that our poem is later than the other poems in the cycle.[6] Finally, the abundance of proper names, which serves no observable function, remains unexplained, although one may perhaps relate it to the list of different animal species mentioned in the magic contest[7]—and, of course, it is strange that the Arrattans have Sumerian names.

4. As to the contents it seems obvious that in this poem the confrontation between Unug and Aratta is expressed in terms of sexuality (Inana's favors) and food supply. The former occurs also in ELA, in a way, but here it is treated in a much more outspoken way and is combined somewhat with the theme of food supply (lines 33–38 = 64–69). The latter is prominent in the rest of the poem. The land's life force is threatened in the bewitching of Sumer because cows and goats withhold their milk. This is truly black magic. However, the contest is also on this topic: the animals created by Sagburu take all the sorcerer's animals *as their food.* It may not be immediately obvious, but this is the countermeasure to the black magic because it symbolically restores Sumer's feeding abilities. This is white magic, and the text is explicit that the sorcerer's sin was the taking away of Sumer's life force. This life force is to be restored by the immolation of the sorcerer himself.

This seems to imply that the burden of this poem is that Sumer is superior not only because its ruler has a better claim to Inana's favors but also because Sumer is devoted to maintain the vital force against the forces of evil. Therefore, Sumer is also morally superior to Aratta.

5. To date we possess thirty-six separate tablets/fragments belonging to this composition; joining has reduced this number to thirty-one. There is one fragment of unknown provenance, but all the others come from Nippur. There is no complete edition on one tablet; instead, the number of two-column tablets is about the same as that of the single-column tablets (imgidas). There are no evident exercise tablets or extracts smaller than an imgida of about thirty lines per side. Yet one of the better preserved two-column tablets stops suddenly in coloumn ii of the obverse, at line 54. The rest is anepigraphic. Further epigraphical study and autopsy of the tablets is needed to determine whether the two-column tablets and possibly the imgidas can be arranged into series.

6. After a short notice by Kramer and Jacobsen in 1953,[8] the text was edited in an exemplary way by Adele Berlin (Berlin 1979). The review by Hermann Behrens (1983–84) is important for the reconstruction of the text, that by Wolfgang Heimpel (1981) for a much-needed hand copy of a nearly perfect two-column tablet. For a modern translation, one may consult Vanstiphout 1998a (68–83).

Enmerkar and En-suhgir-ana
Composite Text

I. THE SETTING

A. Introduction

sig$_4$ kur-šuba-ta ed$_2$-a[9]
kul-aba$_4^{ki}$ iri^{ki} an ki-da mu$_2$-a
unug^{ki}-ga mu-bi ^{d}tir-an-na-gin$_7$
an-ne$_2$ us$_2$-sa-bi si-muš$_3$ gun$_3$-a
an-na gub-ba-bi ud-sakar gibil na-nam
me gal-[gal] nam-nun-na du$_3$-a
kur sikil-la ud dug$_3$-ga ki ğar-ra
iti$_6$-gin$_7$ kalam-ma ed$_2$-a
ud zalag-gin$_7$ kalam-ma si sa$_2$
ab$_2$-ur$_3$ ab$_2$-šar$_x$(NE)-gin$_7$ he-nun-ta ed$_2$-a
unug^{ki}-ga ka-tar-ra-bi kur-ra ba-teğ$_3$
me-lam$_2$-bi kug-me-a zid-da-am$_3$
aratta^{ki}-a tug$_2$-gin$_7$ ba-e-dul gada-gin$_7$ ba-e-bur$_2$

ud-ba ud en-na-am$_3$ ği$_6$ barag-ga-am$_3$ ^{d}utu lugal-am$_3$

sukkal en aratta^{ki}-ka sukkal an-sig$_7$-ga-ri-a mu-ni he$_2$-en-na-nam
sukkal en-me-er-kar$_2$ en kul-aba$_4^{ki}$-ke$_4$ nam-en-na-tum$_2$-ma mu-ni
en ri$_2$ e-ne nun ri$_2$ e-ne
en ği$_6$-ri$_2$ e-ne nun ği$_6$-ri$_2$ e-ne
en ği$_6$-ği$_6$-ri$_2$ e-ne nun ği$_6$-ği$_6$-ri$_2$ e-ne

lu$_2$ diğir-še$_3$ tu-ud e-ne
lu$_2$ diğir-še$_3$ pa ed$_2$ e-ne

II. THE RULERS' CONTEST

B. Aratta's Challenge

en unug^{ki}-ga en kul-aba$_4^{ki}$-ra ur$_5$-bi a-da-min$_3$ na-e-de$_3$

en aratta^{ki} en-suh-gir$_{11}$-an-na-ke$_4$
igi-bi igi unug^{ki}-še$_3$ kiğ$_2$-gi$_4$-a-ar inim mu-na-ni-ib$_2$-be$_2$
e-ne ğa$_2$-a-ra gu$_2$ ha-ma-an-ğa$_2$-ğa$_2$ ^{giš}šudun$_4$ ha-ma-ab-il$_2$-e
ud-da gu$_2$ ma-an-ğar gu$_2$ na-ma-an-ğar u$_3$ e-ne u$_3$ ğa$_2$-e
[e-ne] ^{d}inana-da e$_2$-ğar$_8$-a-ka hu-mu-da-an-til$_3$

Enmerkar and Ensuhgirana
Translation

I. THE SETTING

A. INTRODUCTION

O Brickwork rising up from the pristine mountain;[10]
O Kulab, city that reaches from heaven to earth;
O Unug, whose fame is like the rainbow[11]—
It reaches unto the sky with a dazzling sheen;
Like the new moon it stands against the sky.
It was built in princely fashion, gifted with all the great powers.
As the pristine[12] mountain it was founded on a day of bliss;
As the moonlight rising over the Land,[13]
As bright sunshine radiating over the Land,
As a cow with calf, a *pregnant* cow, it appears in opulence!
Unug's glory reaches unto the highlands,
And its awesome sheen, which is truly like that of refined silver,
Covers even Aratta like cloth, spreads over it like linen.

In those times—day was lord, night was prince, and the sun was king[14]—
The chancellor of the lord of Aratta was Chancellor Ansigaria by name;[15]
The chancellor of Enmerkar, the lord of Kulab, was called Namenatuma.
Now that one was lord, that one was prince![16]
He was lord, that one night; he was prince, that one night;
But that (other) one was lord those many nights; he was prince those many nights—
He was a man born to be god,
And he really looked a god!

II. THE RULERS' CONTEST

B. ARATTA'S CHALLENGE

It was with this lord of Unug and Kulab that Ensuhgirana had this contest.[17]
Ensuhgirana, the lord of Aratta,
Was the first to speak to a messenger about Unug:
"He must submit to me, he must bear my yoke!
"If he submits to me well and truly, then, for him and me this means:
"He may live with Inana in the Egara,

[ğa$_2$]-⸢e⸣ ^{d}inana-da e$_2$-za-gin$_3$ aratta^{ki}-ka hu-mu-da-an-til$_3$-e-en
^{ĝiš}nu$_2$ girin-a-ka hu-mu-un-de$_3$-nu$_2$
še-er-kan$_2$ dug$_4$ u$_3$ dug$_3$ ku-ku-de$_3$ hu-mu-de$_3$-nu$_2$-en
e-ne ^{d}inana-da ği$_6$-a ma-mu$_2$-da igi hu-mu-ni-in-du$_8$
ğa$_2$-e ^{d}inana-da ğir$_3$ babbar-ra-na inim mu-da-bal-e
e-ne kur-gi$_4$^{mušen} še he$_2$-bi$_2$-ib$_2$-gu$_7$-e
ğa$_2$-e kur-gi^{mušen} še ba-ra-bi$_2$-ib$_2$-gu$_7$-e
ğa$_2$-e kur-gi$_4$^{mušen} nunuz-bi ğir$_3$-lam-ma amar-[bi ĞAR la$_2$-e]
di$_4$-di$_4$-bi utul$_2$-mu-še$_3$ gal-gal šen mah-[mu-še$_3$]
kur-gi$_4$^{mušen} ki-a ba-ra-ab-tak$_4$-[a-bi]
ensi$_2$ kur-ra-ke$_4$ gu$_2$ mu-un-ğar-[re-eš-a] mu-da-an-gu$_7$-[u$_3$-ne]

en-me-er-kar$_2$-ra ur$_5$-gin$_7$ inim mu-na-ab-[be$_2$]

kiğ$_2$-gi$_4$-a du-ni šeg$_9$-bar-ra-am$_3$ im$_2$-mi-da-ni šur$_2$-du$_3$^{mušen}-am$_3$
ud-dam i$_3$-ed$_2$ an-u$_2$-sa$_{11}$-an-na-am$_3$ i$_3$-gi$_4$-gi$_4$
buru$_5$^{mušen} ud-zal-le-da-gin$_7$ gaba ki zag im-gub
buru$_5$^{mušen} ği$_6$-sa$_9$-gin$_7$ kur-šag$_4$-ge im-si
^{ĝiš}illar-gin$_7$ zag im-gub-gub-be$_2$

^{d}šakkan-gin$_7$ hur-sağ-ğa$_2$
dur$_3$^{ur3} uru$_{16}$ gal-gin$_7$ kušu i$_3$-tag-tag-ge
dur$_3$^{ur3} sal-la kaš$_4$-e kiğ$_2$-ğa$_2$ du-ru-uš bur$_2$
ur-mah a-šag$_4$-ga ud-zal-la mur-ma-ra mu-un-ša$_4$
ur-bar-ra sila$_4$ šu ti-a-gin$_7$ ul$_4$-ul-e im-ğin
ki tur-tur-bi ⸢mu⸣-un-ğin-na-a DUL$_3$-a mu-na-ab-si
ki gal-gal-⸢bi⸣ mu-un-ğin-na-a bulug-ga mu-na-ab-be$_2$

en-ra [ği$_6$-par$_4$] kug-ga-ni-še$_3$ im-ma-ši-in-ku$_4$-ku$_4$
52a[20] en-me-er-kar$_2$ <ki> kug-kug-ga-ni-še$_3$ im-ma-ši-in-ku$_4$-ku$_4$

za-e-še$_3$ lugal-mu mu-e-ši-in-gi$_4$-gi$_4$
en aratta^{ki} en-suh-gir$_{11}$-an-na-ke$_4$ mu-e-ši-in-gi$_4$-gi$_4$

Enmerkar

54a[21] lugal-zu dug$_4$-ga-ni nam-mu tah-a-ni nam-mu
54b en-suh-gir$_{11}$-an-na-ke$_4$ dug$_4$-<ga>-ni nam-mu tah-a-ni nam-mu

Messenger

54c lugal-mu a-na bi$_2$-in-dug$_4$ a-na bi-in-tah-am$_3$
54d en-suh-gir$_{11}$-an-na-ke$_4$ a-na bi$_2$-in-dug$_4$ a-na bi$_2$-in-tah-am$_3$
lugal-mu na-ab-be$_2$-a
e-ne ğa$_2$-a-ra gu$_2$ ha-ma-an-ğa$_2$-ğa$_2$ ^{ĝiš}šudun$_4$ ha-ma-ab-il$_2$-e
ud-da gu$_2$ ma-an-ğar gu$_2$ [na-ma-an-ğar u$_3$ e]-⸢ne⸣ u$_3$ ğa$_2$-e
e-ne ^{d}inana-da ⸢e$_2$-gar$_8$⸣-[a-ka] [hu-mu-da]-an-til$_3$

"But I shall live with Inana in the Ezagina of Aratta.
"He may lie with her on a flowery[18] bed,
"But I shall lie in sweet slumber with her on a bejeweled couch.[19]
"He may meet with Inana in his dreams at night,
"But I shall converse with Inana between her gleaming legs!
"He may fatten the geese with barley;
"I shall certainly fatten no geese with barley.
"No, I shall collect their eggs and goslings in a basket—
"The small ones for my pot, the large ones for my kettle—
"Whatever is left of the geese,
"The rulers of the highland that have submitted to me shall partake of that with me!"[22]
Thus he spoke to Enmerkar.

The messenger runs like a wild boar, flies like a falcon.
Leaving at daybreak, he returns at dusk;
Like the swarming birds at dawn, he *traverses* the open country;
Like the swarming birds at night, he penetrates into the heart of the highland.
As the throw-stick, he *runs at the side.*
Like Šakkan-of-the-hills,
Like a big strong donkey he gallops;
Like a slender donkey, eager to run, he races on.
He roars like the lion at dawn in the fields;
He speeds like the wolf that has caught a lamb.
The small places he passed by he filled with *reverence* for him;
The large places he passed by *he made speak to him respectfully.*

He entered into the presence of Lord Enmerkar in his holy Gipar,
He entered into the presence of Enmerkar in his most holy place and spoke: 52a
"To you my king has sent me;
"To you the lord of Aratta, Ensuhgirana, has sent me."

Enmerkar

"What is your king's word to me; what is his message to me? 54a
"What is Ensuhgirana's word to me; what is his message to me?"[23] 54b

Messenger

"This is my king's word; this is his message; 54c
"This is Ensuhgirana's word; this is his message: 54d
"Thus my king spoke:
"'He must submit to me; he must bear my yoke!
"'If he submits to me well and truly, then, for him and me this means:
"'He may live with Inana in the Egara,

ǧa$_2$-e ^{d}inana-da e$_2$-za-gin$_3$ [aratta^{ki}-ka hu-mu]-da-an-til$_3$-en
^{ǧiš}nu$_2$ girin-a-ka hu-mu-un-[de$_3$-nu$_2$]
še-er-kan$_2$ dug$_4$ u$_3$ dug$_3$ ku-ku-da [hu-mu-de$_3$-nu$_2$-en]
e-ne ^{d}inana-da ǧi$_6$-a ⸢ma-mu$_2$⸣-[da igi hu-mu-ni-in-du$_8$]
ǧa$_2$-e ^{d}inana-da ǧir$_3$ babbar-ra-na inim [mu-da-bal-e]
e-ne kur-gi$_4$^{mušen} še he$_2$-bi$_2$-[ib$_2$-gu$_7$-e]
ǧa$_2$-e kur-gi$_4$^{mušen} še ba-ra-bi$_2$-[ib$_2$-gu$_7$-e]
ǧa$_2$-e kur-gi$_4$^{mušen} nunuz-bi ǧir$_3$-lam-[ma amar-bi ǦAR la$_2$-e]
di$_4$-di$_4$-bi utul$_2$-mu-še$_3$ gal-gal šen mah-mu-še$_3$
kur-gi$_4$^{mušen} ki-a ba-ra-ab-tak$_4$-bi
⸢ensi$_2$ kur-ra gu$_2$⸣ [mu]-⸢un⸣-ǧar-re-eš-am$_3$ [mu-da]-gu$_7$-u$_3$-ne

C. Enmerkar's Answer

en unug^{ki}-ga [X] si$^?$-muš$_3$-bi X-da ^{ǧiš}zi-gan-bi-im
[. . .] ^{ǧiš}rab šu ri-bi
[. . .] ki us$_2$-sa-a-ba
sur$_2$-[du$_3$]^{mušen} an-na dal-e-da-bi gu mušen-na-bi-[im]
⸢sig$_4$⸣ [e$_2$] gal aratta^{ki}-ka sur-sur mah he$_2$-[. . .]-⸢im?⸣
[. . .] ⸢gal⸣-gal aratta^{ki}-⸢a nam⸣ [. . .] mah-bi-im
[. . .] ba$^?$-DU-a-aš [. . .]-ǧal$_2$

[im]-gin$_7$ šu bi$_2$-in-ra im-gin$_7$ igi i-ni-in-bar
[e-ne] ^{d}inana-da e$_2$ za-gin$_3$ aratta-ka hu-mu-da-an-til$_3$
ǧa$_2$-e [X] ⸢an⸣-ta ki-a gub-ba-ni hu-mu-da-an-til$_3$-en
še-er-kan$_2$-na dug$_4$ u$_3$ dug$_3$ ku-ku-da hu-mu-un-de$_3$-nu$_2$-en
ǧa$_2$-e ^{ǧiš}nu$_2$ gi-rin ^{d}inana-ka u$_2$ za-gin$_3$ barag-ga-a-ba
eǧir-bi-še$_3$ ug-am$_3$ saǧ-bi-še$_3$ piriǧ-am$_3$
ug-e piriǧ im-sar-re
piriǧ-e ug [im]-sar-re
ug-e piriǧ im-[sar]-re-da-bi
piriǧ-e ug im-[sar]-re-da-bi
ud nu-um-zal ǧi$_6$-[u$_3$-na] nu-ru-gu$_2$
ǧa$_2$-e ^{d}inana-da kaskal danna [X]-⸢am$_3$⸣ šu hu-mu-un-da-[niǧin]
^{d}utu suh kug-ǧa$_2$ igi nu-mu-un-[bar]
ǧi$_6$-par$_4$ kug-ǧa$_2$ ba-e-ši-in-[ku$_4$-ku$_4$]
^{d}en-lil$_2$-le aga zid ⸢ǧidru⸣ [. . .]
^{d}nin-urta dumu ^{d}en-lil$_2$-la$_2$-ke$_4$
ǧiš ^{kuš}ummu-da-gin$_7$ ur$_2$ ⸢mu-un-tal$_2$⸣-[tal$_2$]
^{d}a-ru-ru nin$_9$ ^{d}en-lil$_2$-la$_2$-ke$_4$
ubur zid-da-ni ma-an-la$_2$ ubur gub$_2$-bu-[ni ma-an-la$_2$]
eš$_3$ gal-še$_3$ ed$_3$-de$_3$-da-mu-ne

"'But I shall live with Inana in the Ezagina of Aratta.
"'He may lie with her on a flowery bed,
"'But I shall lie in sweet slumber with her on a bejeweled couch.
"'He may meet with Inana in his dreams at night,
"'But I shall converse with Inana between her gleaming legs!
"'He may fatten the geese with barley;
"'I shall certainly fatten no geese with barley;
"'No, I shall collect their eggs and goslings in a basket—
"'The small ones for my pot, the large ones for my kettle—
"'Whatever is left of the geese,
"'The rulers of the highland that have submitted to me shall partake of that with me!'"

C. Enmerkar's Answer

The lord of Unug ... he is their quant, he is their rudder;[24]
... he is the neck-stock that restrains them;
... to the place whereon it rests.
He is their falcon hovering in the skies; he is also their bird net.
The brickwork of the great temple of Aratta ...
... in Aratta ... great
... bring (?) ...

He patted clay into a clay-tablet; he examined it as a clay tablet:[25]
"He may live with Inana in the Ezagina of Aratta,
"But I live with her when she descends from heaven to earth!
"He may lie with her in sweet slumber on a bejeweled couch,
"But I lie in Inana's flowery bed strewn with glistening plants.
"At its back there is an ug-lion; at its front there is a piriğ-lion;
"The ug-lion chases the piriğ-lion;
"The piriğ-lion chases the ug-lion.
"The ug-lion is forever chasing the piriğ-lion,
"And the piriğ-lion is forever chasing the ug-lion.[26]
"And so day does not dawn, night does not pass.
"I *roam* with Inana for the whole journey of [...] leagues.
"Utu does not *set* eyes on my holy crown
"Once she has entered my holy Gipar![27]
"For Enlil *gave me* the true crown and scepter;
"Ninurta, Enlil's son,
"Held me on his lap[28] as the frame holds the water skin.
"Aruru, Enlil's sister,
"Laid me on her right breast, laid me on her left breast.
"When I go up to the great shrine,

nu-gig-e anzud^{mušen} amar-ra-gin$_7$ ⸢ur$_5$ mu⸣-[ša$_4$]
min$_3$-kam-ma-še$_3$ ed$_3$-de$_3$-da-mu-ne
uz amar-ra nu-me-en-na šeg$_{11}$ mu-un-[gi$_4$]
iri^{ki} tu-da-ni-ta NE im-ta-[. . .]
iri^{ki} du$_3$-gin$_7$ iri^{ki} na-me ba-ra-dim$_2$
^{d}inana unug^{ki}-ga he$_2$-en-til$_3$ aratta^{ki}-aš a-na-me-a-bi
sig$_4$ kul-aba$_4$^{ki}-ka he$_2$-en-til$_3$ kur me sikil-še$_3$ a-na-am$_3$ ab-ak-e

mu 5-am$_3$ mu 10-am$_3$ aratta^{ki}-aš ba-ra-ğin
ud aratta^{ki}-aš in-ga-an-du-a-ba
kug gal nin e$_2$-an-na-ke$_4$
ad-bi mu-un-da-gi$_4$-a-aš inim-bi mu-un-zu-a-aš aratta^{ki}-aš ba-ra-ğin
e-ne nu-tuku-da-am$_3$ kur-gi$_4$^{mušen} še ba-ra-bi$_2$-ib$_2$-gu$_7$-e
ğa$_2$-e kur-gi$_4$^{mušen} še he$_2$-bi$_2$-ib$_2$-gu$_7$-e
ğa$_2$-e kur-gi$_4$^{mušen} nunuz-bi ğir$_3$-lam-ma amar-bi ĞAR la$_2$-e
di$_4$-di$_4$-bi utul$_2$-mu-še$_3$ gal-gal šen mah-mu-še$_3$
kur-gi$_4$^{mušen} ki-a ba-ra-ab-tak$_4$-a-bi
ensi$_2$ ki-en-gi-ra gu$_2$ mu-un-ğar-re-eš-a mu-da-gu$_7$-e-ne

D. The Lord of Aratta Admits Defeat but Will Not Submit

kiğ$_2$-gi$_4$-a en-me-er-kar$_2$ en-suh-gir$_{11}$-an-na-ke$_4$
ği$_6$-par$_4$ kug ki kug-kug-ga-ni-še$_3$
ki kug-kug-ga ba-da-an-KU-a DAĞAL-bi ba-na-teğ$_3$
en-suh-gir$_{11}$-an-na-ke$_4$ a$_2$ ağ$_2$-ğa$_2$ gu$_3$ ba-an-de$_2$ inim im-kiğ$_2$-kiğ$_2$-e
išib lu$_2$-mah gudu$_4$ ğir$_3$-sig$_{19}$-ga ği$_6$-par$_4$-ra til$_2$-la
gu$_2$-X mu-ni-in-ğar šag$_4$ mu-da-ab-kuš$_2$-u$_3$
a-na ga-an-na-ab-be$_2$ a-na ga-an-na-ab-be$_2$
en unug^{ki}-ga en kul-aba$_4$^{ki}-ra a-na ga-an-na-ab-be$_2$
[gud]-da-ni gud-mu-da ⸢lirum?⸣ im-da-ab-zi
gud unug^{ki}-ga-ke$_4$ a$_2$ bi$_2$-ib-ğar
lu$_2$-ni lu$_2$-mu-da usu im-da-ab-ra$_2$
lu$_2$ unug^{ki}-ga-ke$_4$ a$_2$ bi$_2$-ib-ğar
ur-ra-ni ur-mu-da usu im-da-ab-ra
ur unug^{ki}-ga-ke$_4$ KA.NI ba-ab-ğar

unkin-ğar-ra si sa$_2$-na mu-un-na-ni-ib-gi$_4$-gi$_4$
za-e-me-en unug^{ki}-ga-še$_3$ dub-sağ-ta
niğ$_2$ gal-gal en-me-er-kar$_2$-ra kiğ$_2$-gi$_4$-a-aš mu-un-gi$_4$
en-me-er-kar$_2$ la-ba-du$_3$-e-en za-e-me-en ba-e-du$_3$-e-en
zi gi$_4$-ba šag$_4$-zu niğ$_2$ na-me na-an-tum$_3$ en-na ba-e-zu-zu

"The nu-gig cries out like Anzud to his chick;[29]
"And when I go there again,
"She coos like a young bird, though she is not.
"She *will not depart* from the city of her birth!
"Never was a city built so well as Unug!
"Inana lives in Unug; as for Aratta, what of it?
"She dwells in brick-built Kulab; the mount of the lustrous powers, what can it do?
"For five, ten years she will not go to Aratta!
"Because about her going to Aratta
"The great saintly mistress of the Eana
"Consulted with me; I know her decision: she will not go to Aratta!
"He who has nothing cannot fatten geese with barley,
"But I can surely fatten the geese with barley!
"Also, I will collect the eggs and goslings of the geese in a basket—
"The small ones for my pot, the large ones for my kettle—
"Of whatever is left of the geese,
"The rulers of Sumer that have submitted to me shall partake of that with me!"

D. The Lord of Aratta Admits Defeat but Will Not Submit

The messenger of Enmerkar reached Ensuhgirana,
In his holy Gipar, his most holy place,
The most holy place where he sat, and its *dais*.
Ensuhgirana asked for advice, searched for a reply.
The išib, lumah, gudu, and girsiga living in the Gipar,[30]
He summoned and consulted them.
"What shall I say to him? What shall I say to him?
"What shall I say to the lord of Unug, the lord of Kulab?
"His bull stood up to fight my bull,
"And the bull of Unug has won.
"His man wrestled with my man,
"And the man of Unug was stronger.
"His dog wrestled with my dog,
"And the dog of Unug *bested* him."[31]

The convened assembly answered him straightforwardly:
"You were the first to send to Unug
"Big words as a message for Enmerkar!
"You cannot *best* Enmerkar; you yourself will be *bested*!
"Give in! Your ambition will bring you nought; *when will you realize that?*"

En-suhgir-ana

iri-mu dul he$_2$-a ǧa$_2$-e šika-bi he$_2$-me-en
en unug^{ki}-ga en kul-aba$_4$^{ki}-ra gu$_2$ ba-ra-na-an-ǧa$_2$-ǧa$_2$

III. THE BEWITCHING OF SUMER

E. The Sorcerer

maš-maš dim$_2$-ma-ni dumu ha-ma-zu-ke$_4$

ur-ǧir$_3$-nun-na dim$_2$-ma-ni dumu ha-ma-zu-ke$_4$
ha-ma-zu hul-a-ta aratta^{ki}-aš bal-a
e$_2$-ǧi$_6$-par$_4$ nam-maš-maš-e da$^?$-ga$^?$-na na-mu-un-KU

sukkal an-sig$_7$-ga-ri-a gu$_3$ mu-un-na-de$_2$-e
lugal-mu ad-da gal-gal iri^{ki}-ke$_4$-ne
[libir-ra uš] ⸢ki⸣ ǧar-ra-ke$_4$-ne
[. . .]-X-ka a-na-aš-am$_3$ nu-um-ǧa$_2$-ǧa$_2$-ne ad nu-um-gi$_4$-gi$_4$-ne
[ǧa$_2$-e id$_2$] unug^{ki}-ga-ke$_4$ ga-am$_3$-ba-al
[itima] aratta^{ki}-ka gu$_2$ ga-mu-ni-ib$_2$-ǧar
[inim unug]^{ki}-ga-ke$_4$ KAxX um-mi-in-tag
[erin$_2$ gal-mu sig]-ta igi-nim-še$_3$ ab-ta kur ^{ǧiš}erin-še$_3$

igi-nim-[ta kur] šim ^{ǧiš}erin-na-še$_3$ gu$_2$ ga-mu-ni-ib-ǧar
unug^{ki}-ge niǧ$_2$-gur$_{11}$ ni$_2$-ba-ke$_4$ ^{ǧiš}ma$_2$ [he$_2$]-em-da-gid$_2$-de$_3$
^{ǧiš}ma$_2$ he$_2$-em-da-la$_2$-e e$_2$-za-gin$_3$ aratta^{ki}-še$_3$

sukkal an-sig$_7$-ga-ri-a iri$^?$-na mu-ni-zig$_3$ kiši$_4$-na mu-ni-šub
[X] lu$_2$ [. . .] an-sig$_7$-ga-ri-a na-mu-ni-⸢X-KA⸣-X
[. . .] X-e? nu-uš-ma-ab-X-[X]
lugal-mu ad-da gal-gal iri^{ki}-ke$_4$-[ne]
libir-ra uš ki ǧar-ra-ke$_4$-ne
⸢ki sukkal⸣ e$_2$-gal-la a-na-aš-am$_3$ [nu-um-ǧa$_2$-ǧa$_2$-ne] ad nu-um-[gi$_4$-gi$_4$-ne]
ǧa$_2$-e id$_2$ unug^{ki}-ga-ke$_4$ ga-am$_3$-ba-al
⸢itima⸣ aratta^{ki}-ka gu$_2$ ga-mu-ni-ib-ǧar
inim unug^{ki}-ga-ke$_4$ KAxX um-mi-in-tag
erin$_2$ gal-mu sig-ta igi-nim-še$_3$ ab-ta kur ^{ǧiš}erin-še$_3$

igi-nim-še$_3$ kur šim ^{ǧiš}erin-na-še$_3$ gu$_2$ ga-mu-ni-ib-ǧar
unug^{ki}-ga niǧ$_2$-ga ni$_2$-ba-ke$_4$ ^{ǧiš}ma$_2$ he$_2$-em-da-gid$_2$-de$_3$
^{ǧiš}ma$_2$ he$_2$-em-da-la$_2$-e e$_2$-za-gin$_3$ aratta^{ki}-še$_3$

En-suhgir-ana
"My city may become a mound of ruins, and I a potsherd in it,
"Yet never will I submit to the lord of Unug and Kulab!"

III. THE BEWITCHING OF SUMER

E. The Sorcerer

Now there was a sorcerer whose witchcraft was that of the Hamazites,[32]
Urgirnuna by name, whose witchcraft was that of the Hamazites:
Hamazu having been destroyed, he had crossed over to Aratta,
Where he now *practiced* his sorcery in the *inner chambers* of the Egipara.

He spoke to the chancellor Ansigaria:
"My Lord, why is it that the great elders of the city,
"The founding fathers of yore,
"No longer *respect the chancellor's rank,* no longer give sound advice?
"As for myself, I would make Unug dig canals;
"I would make it submit *at the shrine* of Aratta!
"Once the decision about Unug *has been taken,*
"I would make them all submit to my great armies, from south to north, from ocean to cedar mountain,
"From the north to the fragrant cedar mountain![33]
"Unug shall ferry its own produce by boat.
"The boats shall tie up at the Ezagina of Aratta!"

Chancellor Ansigaria rose up in his city; he ...
... Ansigaria
... should he not ...
"My Lord, why is it that the great elders of the city,
"The founding fathers of yore,
"No longer *respect the chancellor's rank,* no longer give sound advice?
"As for myself, I would make Unug dig canals;
"I would make it submit *at the shrine* of Aratta!
"Once the decision about Unug *has been taken,*
"I would make them all submit to my great armies, from south to north, from ocean to cedar mountain,
"From the north to the fragrant cedar mountain!
"Unug shall ferry its own produce by boat;
"The boats shall tie up at the Ezagina of Aratta!"

en-ra hul$_2$-la-gin$_7$ im-ma-na-ni-ib-ğar
5 ma-na kug-sig$_{17}$ mu-na-ab-šum$_2$-mu
5 ma-na kug-babbar mu-na-ab-šum$_2$-mu
u$_2$ nir-<ğal$_2$> gu$_7$ ba-bi mu-na-ab-be$_2$
a nir-<ğal$_2$> nağ ba-bi mu-na-ab-be$_2$
ud nam-ra-aš lu$_2$-bi ak-am$_3$
zi-zu niğ$_2$-ğa$_2$ a-la šu-zu he$_2$-ğal$_2$ mu-na-ab-be$_2$

F. Black Magic

maš-maš engar numun sağ-ğa$_2$-ke$_4$
ereš$_2$^{ki} iri^{ki} ^{d}nisaba-še$_3$ ğir$_3$ im-ma-ab-gub-be$_2$-en
⸢e$_2$-tur$_3$⸣-ra e$_2$ ab$_2$ dur$_2$-ru-na-aš ba-teğ$_3$
ab$_2$-[e] tur$_3$-ra sağ mu-da-ab-sig$_3$
ab$_2$-e inim bi$_2$-in-dug$_4$ lu$_2$-ulu$_3$-gin$_7$ inim mu-da-ab-bal-e

ab$_2$ i$_3$-zu a-ba-a i$_3$-gu$_7$-e ga-zu a-ba-a i$_3$-na$_8$-na$_8$
The cow
i$_3$-mu i$_3$-gu$_7$-e ^{d}nisaba-ke$_4$
[ga]-mu i$_3$-na$_8$-na$_8$ ^{d}nisaba-ke$_4$
[ga-ar$_3$-mu] suh$_{10}$ kug galam dug$_4$-ga
unu$_6$ gal [unu$_6$ ^{d}nisaba-ke$_4$ me-te-a-aš im-mi-ib-ğal$_2$]

⸢i$_3$-mu⸣ [tur$_3$ kug]-ta en-na-ga-mu-de$_6$-a-aš
ga-mu [amaš] kug-ta en-na-ga-mu-de$_6$-a-aš
u$_3$-sun$_2$ zid ^{d}nisaba dumu sağ ^{d}en-lil$_2$-la$_2$-ke$_4$ lu$_2$ nu-um-mi-in-zi-zi
The sorcerer
ab$_2$ i$_3$-zu si-muš$_3$-zu-še$_3$ ga-zu murgu-[zu-še$_3$]
ab$_2$ i$_3$-bi si-muš$_3$-bi-še$_3$ ba-ab-[BU] ga-bi murgu-bi-še$_3$ ba-ab-BU ğir$_3$ [. . .]

amaš kug amaš ^{d}nisaba-še$_3$ ba-[teğ$_3$]
⸢ud$_5$-de$_3$⸣ amaš-a sağ mu-da-ab-[sig$_3$]
ud$_5$-de$_3$ inim bi$_2$-in-dug$_4$ lu$_2$-[lu$_7$]-gin$_7$ inim mu-un-da-ab-bal-[e]

⸢ud$_5$⸣ i$_3$-zu a-ba-a i$_3$-gu$_7$-e ga-zu a-ba-a [i$_3$-na$_8$]-⸢na$_8$⸣
The goat
i$_3$-mu i$_3$-gu$_7$-e ^{d}nisaba-ke$_4$
ga-mu i$_3$-na$_8$-na$_8$ ^{d}nisaba-ke$_4$
ga-ar$_3$-mu suh$_{10}$ kug galam dug$_4$-ga
unu$_6$ gal unu$_6$ ^{d}nisaba-ke$_4$ me-te-a-aš im-mi-ib-ğal$_2$

This was so very pleasing to the lord
That he gave him five minas of gold
And five minas of silver.
He told him that his ration would be the finest food to eat
And the best beverages to drink.
"When those people will have been made into war booty,
"Your life will be (full of) possessions and enjoyment; your hand will touch prosperity!" he promised him.

F. Black Magic

The sorcerer, *having planted* the first seed,
Wended his way to Ereš, the city of Nisaba.
He arrived at the byre, the place where the cows live.
The cow in the byre *trembled* before him.
He made the cow speak so that it conversed with him as if it were human:
"O cow, who will eat your cream? Who will drink your milk?"

The cow

"Nisaba will eat my cream;
"Nisaba will drink my milk;
"And my cheese, the well-ripened shining crown,
"Will be properly served in the great dining hall, the dining hall of Nisaba.
"For unless my cream has been brought from this splendid byre,
"Unless my milk has been brought from this splendid pen,
"Faithful cow Nisaba, Enlil's oldest daughter, cannot institute the levy."[34]

The sorcerer

"Cow, your cream to your glistening horn, your milk to your back!"[35]
And so the cow's cream was pulled back into its glistening horn, and its milk *retreated* into its back.

He arrived at the splendid pen, the pen of Nisaba.
The goat in the pen trembled before him.
He made the goat speak, so that it conversed with him as if it were human:
"O goat, who will eat your cream? Who will drink your milk?"

The goat

"Nisaba will eat my cream;
"Nisaba will drink my milk;
"And my cheese, the well-ripened shining crown,
"Will be properly served in the great dining hall, the dining hall of Nisaba.

i$_3$-mu tur$_3$ kug-ta en-na-ga-mu-un-de$_6$-a-aš
ga-mu amaš [kug-ta] en-na-ga-mu-un-de$_6$-a-aš
u$_3$-sun$_2$ zid ^{d}nisaba dumu-sağ ^{d}en-lil$_2$-la$_2$-ke$_4$ lu$_2$ nu-um-mi-in-zi-zi

The sorcerer

ud$_5$ i$_3$-zu si-muš$_3$-zu-še$_3$ ga-zu murgu-zu-še$_3$
ud$_5$ i$_3$-bi si-muš$_3$-bi-še$_3$ ba-ab-BU ga-bi murgu-bi-še$_3$ ba-ab-ed$_2$

ud-bi-a tur$_3$ amaš-a e$_2$-si-ga ba-ab-du$_7$ niğ$_2$ ha-lam-ma ba-ab-ak
agan ab$_2$-ka ga nu-un-ğal$_2$ amar-e ud ⸢bi$_2$-in⸣-šu$_2$
amar tur-bi šag$_4$-su$_3$-ga mu-un-ğal$_2$ er$_2$ ⸢gig i$_3$-še$_8$-še$_8$⸣
agan ud$_5$-ka ga nu-un-[ğal$_2$ maš$_2$-e ud bi$_2$-in-šu$_2$]
maš$_2$ ud$_5$-da-bi šag$_4$ ka-tab-[ba ba-an-nu$_2$] zi-bi mi-ni-[. . .]
ab$_2$-e amar-bi-še$_3$ inim gig [bi-ib$_2$-be$_2$]
ud$_5$-de$_3$ maš$_2$-bi mu-na-ab-[. . .]
^{dug}šakir$_3$ kug-ga si-si-ig x [. . .] šag$_4$-su$_3$-ga mu-un-ğal$_2$ šag$_4$ ka-[tab . . . nu$_2$]
ud-bi-a tur$_3$ amaš-a e$_2$ si-ga ba-ab-dug$_4$ niğ$_2$-ha-lam-ma ba-ab-ak
unud-de$_3$ ešgiri šu-na bi$_2$-in-tak$_4$ igi-ni i$_3$-sig$_3$-ge
sipad-de$_3$ sibir zag-ga-na bi$_2$-in-la$_2$ er$_2$ gig i$_3$-še$_8$-še$_8$
kab-bar tur amaš tur$_3$-še$_3$ la-ba-X ğir$_3$ kur$_2$ ba-ra-an-dab$_5$

ga-il$_2$-bi ad-gal-še$_3$ nu-mu-ed$_3$ sila kur$_2$ ba-ra-an-dab$_5$

⸢unud⸣ sipad ^{d}nisaba-ke$_4$-ne
dumu tu-da ama dili-me-eš
tur$_3$ amaš-a a$_2$ ed$_2$-a-me-eš
1-kam-ma maš$_2$-gu-la mu-ni he$_2$-en-na-nam
2-kam-ma ur-edin-na mu-ni he$_2$-en-na-nam
2-na-ne-ne ka$_2$ mah igi ^{d}utu ed$_2$-a ki u$_6$-di kalam-ma
sahar-hub$_2$-sahar-hub$_2$-ba ba-an-dur$_2$-ru-ne-eš ^{d}utu an-ta i-im-gi$_4$-gi$_4$-ne
maš-maš-e lu$_2$ aratta^{ki}-ka e$_2$-tur$_3$-ra mu-un-kur$_9$
e$_2$-tur$_3$-ra gara$_2$ ba-an-kal amar tur la-ba-an-ri-ri

tur$_3$ amaš niğ$_2$-gig-bi bi$_2$-ak i$_3$ ga ba-e-ni-kal bi$_2$-in-la$_2$
[. . .] X-bi i$_3$-šub-šub niğ$_2$-ha-lam-ma ba-ab-ak

IV. THE MAGIC CONTEST

G. The Wise Woman Is Sent

[. . .] KA-bi ba-an-na-teğ$_3$
[. . .] ğal$_2$-la-am$_3$ igi mu-un-na-niğin$_2$

"For unless my cream has been brought from this splendid byre,
"Unless my milk has been brought from this splendid pen,
"Faithful cow Nisaba, Enlil's oldest daughter, cannot institute the levy."
The sorcerer
"Goat, your cream to your glistening horn, your milk to your back!"
And so the goat's cream was pulled back into its glistening horn, and its milk *retreated* into its back.

Thereupon pen and byre became a silent house, a ruin.[36]
There was no milk in the cow's udders; the calves' days darkened;
The young calf was hungry and mooed heart-rendingly.
There was no milk in the goat's udders; the kids' days darkened;
Both kid and goat lay down starving; their lives ...
Bitterly the cow spoke to its calf,
And the goat *commiserated* with its kid.
The holy churn remained empty; ... was hungry and lay starving.

Surely on that day pen and byre had become a silent house, a ruin.
The drover dropped his staff, his eyes vacant in shock;
The shepherd fastened his crook at his side, weeping bitterly;
The shepherd boy no longer frequented pen or byre; he went elsewhere;
The milkman no longer cried out loudly; he went elsewhere.

Now there were a cowherd and a shepherd of Nisaba;
Sons of one mother
And reared in pen and byre they were.
Mašgula was the name of the former,
Uredina of the latter.
At the great gate facing the rising sun, the marvel of the Land,
Both of them crouched in the dust and implored Utu in the sky:
"This sorcerer, a man from Aratta, broke into the pens.
"In the pens he caused a shortage of milk: even the calves do not get any.
"In pen and byre he brought misery: he made scarce cream and milk.
"He cast *their doom,* caused their devastation."

IV. THE MAGIC CONTEST

G. The Wise Woman Is Sent

... approached ...
... what was put *before her* (?) *she* (?) *inspected.*

[. . .] ereš$_2^{ki}$ [. . .]-X-an-gur
[gu$_2$] ⸢^{id2}⸣buranun-na id$_2$ NA$^?$ mah$^?$ KA ğal$_2$-la id$_2$ diğir-re-e-ne

[iri^{ki} nam]-tar-ra an ^{d}en-lil$_2$-la$_2$ [. . .] ğir$_3$ bi$_2$-in-gub
um-ma sağ-bur-ru šu ⸢mu-un-na-an⸣-[. . .]

H. The Contest

⸢2-na-ne-ne agargara id$_2$-da i-ni-in-šub⸣-[bu-uš]
⸢maš-maš-e suhur^{ku6} gal a-ta⸣ im-ta-an-[ed$_2$]
um-ma sağ-bur-ru [hu-ri$_2$]-in^{mušen} a-ta im-ta-an-[ed$_2$]
hu-ri$_2$-in^{mušen}-e suhur^{ku6} gal in-kar hur-sağ-še$_3$ ba-[an-kur$_9$]
2-kam-ma-aš agargara id$_2$-da i-ni-in-šub-bu-uš
maš-maš-e u$_8$ sila$_4$-bi a-ta im-ta-an-[ed$_2$]
um-ma sağ-bur-ru ur-bar-ra a-ta im-ta-an-[ed$_2$]
ur-bar-ra ⸢u$_8$ sila$_4$!-bi⸣ in-kar edin dağal-še$_3$ ba-an-ur$_3$
3-kam-ma-aš agargara id$_2$-da i-ni-in-šub-bu-uš
maš-maš-e ab$_2$ amar-bi a-ta im-ta-an-ed$_2$
um-ma sağ-bur-ru ur-mah-e a-ta im-ta-an-ed$_2$
ur-mah-e ab$_2$ amar-bi in-kar ğiš-gi-še$_3$ ba-an-kur$_9$
4-kam-ma-aš agargara id$_2$-da i-ni-in-šub-bu-uš
maš-maš-e šeg$_9$ šeg$_9$-bar-e a-ta im-ta-an-ed$_2$
um-ma sağ-bur-ru nemur hur-sağ-ğa$_2$ a-ta im-ta-an-ed$_2$
nemur-e šeg$_9$ šeg$_9$-bar-e in-kar hur-sağ-še$_3$ ba-an-kur$_9$

5-kam-ma-aš agargara id$_2$-da i-ni-in-šub-bu-uš
maš-maš-e amar maš-da$_3$ a-ta im-ta-an-ed$_2$
um-ma sağ-bur-ru ur-šub$_5$ ur-nim-e a-ta im-ta-an-ed$_2$
ur-šub$_5$ ur-nim-ma amar maš-da$_3$ in-kar ^{ğiš}tir-tir-še$_3$ ba-an-kur$_9$

maš-maš-e igi-ni ba-ku$_{10}$-ku$_{10}$ dim$_2$-ma-ni ba-suh$_3$

um-ma sağ-bur-ru gu$_3$ mu-na-de$_2$-e
maš-maš nam-maš-maš-zu he$_2$-ğal$_2$ dim$_2$-ma-zu me-a
a-na-gin$_7$-nam ereš$_2^{ki}$ iri ^{d}nisaba-še$_3$
iri^{ki} nam tar-ra an ^{d}en-lil$_2$-la$_2$
iri^{ki} ul iri ki ağ$_2$ ^{d}nin-lil$_2$-la$_2$
nam-maš-maš ak-de$_3$ a-gin$_7$ im-da-ğin-ne-en

⸢maš⸣-maš-e mu-un-na-ni-ib-gi$_4$-gi$_4$
nu-zu-a-mu-ne i-im-ğin-ne-en
nam-gur$_4$-ra-zu i$_3$-zu nam-ba-an-sis-e-de$_3$-en
šu kir$_4$-na i-ni-in-ğal$_2$ šud$_3$ mu-un-na-an-ra$_2$-aš

... to Ereš *she* (?) went,
(Which lies) on the bank of the Euphrates, the mighty river, the river of the gods.
She went to the city whose fate was fixed by An and Enlil;
Wise Woman Sagburu ... her hand upon him.

H. The Contest

Both threw fish spawn[37] into the river.
The sorcerer drew out a big carp, but
Wise Woman Sagburu drew out an eagle.
The eagle caught the big carp and fled to the mountains.
Again they threw fish spawn into the river.
The sorcerer drew out a ewe with lamb, but
Wise Woman Sagburu drew out a wolf.
The wolf caught the ewe with lamb and dragged them to the open plain.
A third time they threw fish spawn into the river.
The sorcerer drew out a cow with calf, but
Wise Woman Sagburu drew out a lion.
The lion caught the cow with calf and took them to the reed-marsh.
A fourth time they threw fish spawn into the river.
The sorcerer drew out an ibex and a wild sheep, but
Wise Woman Sagburu drew out a mountain lion.
The mountain lion caught the ibex and the wild sheep and dragged them to the mountains.
A fifth time they threw fish spawn into the river.
The sorcerer drew out a young gazelle, but
Wise Woman Sagburu drew out a tiger and a NIM-lion.
The tiger and the NIM-lion caught the young gazelle and dragged it to the woods.
The sorcerer's face darkened, and his mind was in turmoil.

Then Wise Woman Sagburu spoke to him:
"O sorcerer, for all your magic lore, do you not understand anything?
"How could you go to Ereš, the city of Nisaba,
"The city whose fate was fixed by An and Enlil,
"The primeval city, the city well loved by Ninlil,
"In order to work your evil magic? How did you dare?"

The sorcerer replied:
"I went there without knowing what I did;
"Now I acknowledge your authority—please do not be angry!"
He did obeisance; he pleaded with her:

šu ba-mu-u$_8$ nin-mu šu ba-mu-u$_8$
silim-ma-bi iri^{ki}-mu-še$_3$ ga-ğin
aratta^{ki} kur me sikil-la-še$_3$ zi-mu ga-ba-ši-de$_6$

nam-mah-zu kur-kur-ra ga-bi$_2$-ib-zu
aratta^{ki} kur me sikil-la-ka ka-tar-zu ga-si-il

um-ma sağ-bur-ru mu-un-na-ni-ib-gi$_4$-gi$_4$
tur$_3$ amaš-a niğ$_2$-gig-ga bi$_2$-ak i$_3$ ga ba-e-ni-kal
^{giš}banšur an-bar$_7$ ^{giš}banšur kiğ$_2$-[nim kiğ$_2$]-sig mu-e-su$_3$
kiğ$_2$-sig unu$_6$ gal-la i$_3$ ga ba-e-ku$_5$ niğ$_2$-gig-bi X-DU
nam-tag-zu i$_3$ ga [. . . igi] nu-mu-e-tum$_3$
^{d}nanna lugal ⸢X amaš-a⸣? MU X ga ba-e-šum$_2$-mu
nir-da i$_3$-ğa$_2$-ğa$_2$ ⸢zi nu-mu⸣-ra-ab-šum$_2$-mu
um-ma sağ-bur-ru maš-maš-e unken-ni inim-ma-ni mu-ni-in-sig$_3$
šaga-a-ni gu$_2$ ^{id2}buranun-na-[ka] i-ni-in-šub
zi nam-til$_3$-la ba-da-an-kar iri^{ki}-ni ereš$_2$^{ki}-še$_3$ ba-e-gur

V. THE CONCLUSION

I. The Lord of Aratta Submits

en-suh-gir$_{11}$-an-na-ke$_4$ inim-bi ğiš ba-an-tuku-a-ta
en-me-er-kar$_2$-ra lu$_2$ mu-un-ši-in-gi$_4$-gi$_4$
za-e-me-en en ki ağ$_2$ ^{d}inana-me-en dili-zu-ne mah-me-en
^{d}inana-ke$_4$ ur$_2$ kug-ga-ni-še$_3$ zid-de$_3$-eš ⸢mu-un-pad$_3$-de$_3$-en ki ağ$_2$-ğa$_2$⸣-ni-me-en
sig-ta igi-nim-še$_3$ en gal-bi za-e-me-en ğa$_2$-e us$_2$-sa-zu-me-en
a ri-a-ta gaba-ri-zu nu-me-en šeš-gal za-e-me-en

ğa$_2$-e nu-mu-da-sa$_2$-e-en ud da-ri$_2$-še$_3$

J. Praise Be to Nisaba

en-me-er-kar$_2$ en-suh-gir$_{11}$-an-na a-da-min$_3$ dug$_4$-ga
en-me-er-kar$_2$ en-suh-gir$_{11}$-an-na diri-ga-a-ba
^{d}nisaba zag-mi$_2$

"Let me go, oh sister, let me go!
"Let me return safely to my city!
"Let me go back unharmed to Aratta, the mountain of the inviolate powers!
"I will proclaim your greatness in all countries;
"I will sing your praise in Aratta, the mountain of the inviolate powers!"

Wise Woman Sagburu replied to him:
"In pen and byre you brought misery; you made scarce cream and milk.
"You abolished lunch, breakfast, and dinner meals.
"You cut off cream and milk from the supper in the great hall; misery. . .
"Your sin of withholding cream and milk cannot be overlooked!
"King Nanna granted everlasting milk . . . in the byre;
"Therefore your sin is a capital offense: I cannot grant you life!"
Wise Woman Sagburu confirmed her statutory verdict on the sorcerer;
She threw down her victim on the bank of the Euphrates,
Took away his vital force[38] and returned this to her city Ereš.

V. THE CONCLUSION

I. The Lord of Aratta Submits

When Ensuhgirana had heard this
He sent to Enmerkar:
"You are indeed the beloved of Inana; you alone are the greatest;
"Inana has truly chosen you for her holy loins; you are her lover;

"From the west to the east you are the great lord, and I humbly follow.
"From your conception onward I was never your equal; you are senior;
"I can never match you!"

J. Praise Be to Nisaba

In the contest between Enmerkar and Ensuhgirana,
Because Enmerkar was greater than Ensuhgirana,
Praise be to Nisaba!

Notes

[1] At the end of Enmerkar and the lord of Aratta there also appears a wise woman (lines 588–594), but there she seems to be Inana in disguise.

[2] An *envoûtement* is a spell that works by the force of the spoken word alone.

[3] See Attinger 1984.

[4] See Behrens 1978.

[5] See provisionally ETCSL: www-etcsl.orient.ox.ac.uk/section1/b1824.htm.

[6] Other types of text may also have played a role: lines 198–210 might easily be found in any of the city laments.

[7] Proper names and names of animals belonged to the scribal fodder of an earlier stage in schooling.

[8] Kramer and Jacobsen 1953.

[9] One manuscript notes on the edge of the tablet gi$_4$-ba (= *incipit*) sig$_4$ muš$_3$ za-gin$_3$-t[a e$_3$-a].

[10] One manuscript reads the opening line as "O Brickwork rising up from the shimmering plain" (see note 9 above). This alternative reading might have been an appropriate opening line in its own right: the huge tell still rises abruptly and imposingly above the surrounding plain that, though heavily silted, shimmers in the summer and even autumn heat. On the other hand, the "pristine mountain" seems somewhat awkward here, although it is taken up again in line 7.

[11] An allusion to Inana; the rainbow is one of her symbols or properties.

[12] The Sumerian term used here (sikil) is difficult to translate. It seems to combine the meanings "pristine, unblemished, inviolate, holy," and it is therefore hard, if not misleading, to try to translate it consistently.

[13] The notion of "Land" is central to Mesopotamian thought; it stands for the country, state, nation, and even "civilized region" of what they understood as Sumer. Furthermore, it is expressed consistently with a single Sumerian term, kalam.

[14] Expressions comparable to lines 14 and 18–19 occur elsewhere as an indication of a time long past. Note that the sun (i.e., the god Utu) is named as king and that Enmerkar is regularly called "son of the sun." This notion is amplified in lines 17–21.

[15] "Chancellor," though an anachronism, seems more apt as a translation of the Sumerian term sukkal than the orientalizing "vizier" from Arabic Wāzir. We have no idea of the reason for the explicit identification—by name—of the two opposing officials. Their presence and their identification have little or no significance in the development of the story.

[16] Lines 17–21 are not perfectly clear, partly due to their formulaic character. The translation assumes that Ensuhgirana is meant in lines 17–18 and Enmerkar in lines 19–21. But other variations on the play with "that one … that one"—where we would probably say "this one … that one"—are perfectly possible. The "nights" refer to the subsequent passage about lovemaking.

[17] The term used here, adaman(dug$_4$-ga), literally means "verbal contest, quarrel, dispute." It is the technical term for the academic poetical debates that formed an important part of the training in Sumerian rhetoric (even eloquence?).

[18] The term used here for the bed ($^{\check{g}i\check{s}}$nu$_2$ girin-a) is well known from sacred marriage texts. It is sometimes translated neutrally as "splendid," but

"flowery" or "blossoming" seems to be much nearer the mark, as seems clear from the opposition between lines 29 and 30. It can be defended that it is also a transparent metaphor for Inana's vulva.

[19] Lines 29–30, repeated as lines 60–61, are an extremely subtle couplet. Ostensibly, the opposition is between the primitive couch Enmerkar can offer and a richly adorned bed offered by Ensuhgirana. Yet in the corresponding passage 80–86, it is the "primitive couch" whose adornment is described in detail—and with a highly significant twist.

[20] This line is in only one manuscript.

[21] Not all manuscripts have these four lines.

[22] The passage 33–38, repeated as 64–69 and corresponding to 108–113, is still imperfectly understood. The motif may be akin to the killing of the goose that lays golden eggs, in that the lord of Aratta improvidently proposes a potlatch-like exuberance, while Enmerkar is so careful—and rich—that he can raise *and* consume geese and goslings.

[23] This couplet, a stock phrase introducing the speech reported by a messenger, also occurs elsewhere in the cycle.

[24] "Their" refers to the people of Unug.

[25] This line is totally out of place here. The motif of the tablet has no meaning or function at all in this text. Still, the line appears in three manuscripts! Is it an intrusion borrowed from the famous invention of writing in Enmerkar and the Lord of Aratta? If so, it might be a clue to a perceived "order" in which the pieces of the cycle have to be read.

[26] See above, notes 16–17. The "flowery bed strewn with glistening plants" turns out to be a hardly impenetrable metaphor or image of Inana's vulva, while the lions (male and female?) in their unending chase stand for—or are—the lovers in their unending love-play, as confirmed by the following line.

[27] The night of lovemaking will not end!

[28] This is, of course, literally "cradling."

[29] A reference to the first episode in The Return of Lugalbanda. But also again a hardly hidden expression of Inana's cries of desire and delight when Enmerkar enters the great shrine, which here may also stand for her sexual parts.

[30] The išib, lumah, and gudu are kinds of priests; the girsiga are temple or palace attendants.

[31] Refers to the passage in Enmerkar and the Lord of Aratta where the fight between the two dogs represents the final challenge. The parallel between lu_2, which undoubtedly means "man" in lines 124–125, and ur in lines 126–127 may indicate that ur has to be understood as "champion" after all.

[32] Hamazi/u is a city lying to the northeast of Babylonia, east of Kirkuk.

[33] The geography seems to be based on a triangle: from the southern plains (sig) to the Zagros highlands (igi-nim), from the Persian Gulf (ab) to the Lebanon (cedar mountain), from igi-nim to the Lebanon. By implication this encloses the known world.

[34] Nisaba as goddess of writing is also and by that token the goddess of administration and bureaucracy. When she starves, civilization will starve. This is a stark expression of their realization of the fact that writing ultimately must serve the administration of civilized life.

[35] The "back (side)" seems adequate, since it can stand for belly or hindquarter. The horns (si-muš) are more difficult. Perhaps the idea is that the milk is sent back into the cow's/goat's body as far as it can go and away from udder and subsequently milk pail.

[36] Lines like this abound in the genre of the city laments, where the cities and the whole of Sumer are consistently presented as a byre that has been abandoned by its personnel and livestock. In fact, the whole passage might well appear in a lament—but in this instance it is to be taken literally.

[37] Fish spawn, Sumerian agargara (lit. "disseminated semen"), is used by both magicians to create a series of animals. The animals created by Sagburu are consistently bigger and stronger than those created by the sorcerer. But the real emphasis of the magical contest is that the animals created by Sagburu use the others as food. The principle of providing food, which had been put to a stop by the sorcerer's first activity, is here shown to be stronger than its opposite. In other words, white magic has conquered black magic. Note also that the text shows here a clever bilingual pun or, perhaps better, a play on signs. The cuneiform sign for the *Sumerian* word agargara can be read more simply and much more generally as NUN; the *Akkadian,* and almost generally Semitic, word for "fish" is *nūnu.*

[38] Since he had threatened the life force of Ereš/Sumer.

II

Enmerkar and the Lord of Aratta

Introduction

Most Sumerologists will agree that this relatively long composition (about 640 lines) is probably the finest piece of poetic storytelling ever produced by the Old Babylonian authors. The general theme of the cycle, namely, the rivalry between Unug/Sumer and Aratta, is presented here at first sight as a mere contest in cleverness. Yet there are several layers of meaning defining both the central narrative strategy and the obvious symbolism.

1. The story seems deceptively simple. Enmerkar, king of Unug, wants to embellish his city and the whole of Sumer with precious metals and stones, goods that are not to be found in Sumer but only in the fabulously wealthy city Aratta, which lies behind the mountains. Since trade does not as yet exist, he asks the goddess Inana what he should do: Inana is the goddess of Aratta as well. She favors Enmerkar and advises him to send a messenger with a challenge to Aratta, requisitioning what he wants and enforcing his claim by stating that she favors him. He does so, but the (unnamed) lord of Aratta refuses, claiming that Inana is his goddess as well and that anyway his mountain city is an impregnable fastness. Still, he is willing to enter into a contest with Enmerkar in order to see whose side Inana is really on. This results in a counterchallenge that takes the form of an unsolvable riddle: if Enmerkar succeeds in carting grain to Aratta in open nets instead of bags, he might reconsider. Enmerkar finds a solution: he uses sprouting barley to close the interstices of the nets so that no grain is spilled. Sending off the grain, he repeats his challenge. This time the lord of Aratta asks him to bring him a scepter made of no existing material. Enmerkar solves this riddle as well: he prepares a gluelike plastic substance that he pours into a hollow reed; after this mass has hardened,

which takes a long time, he breaks away the reed mould and sends off the scepter with a renewed challenge. Finally, the lord of Aratta requests a dog of no known color to fight his own dog. Enmerkar again finds a solution: he weaves a cloth of no known color. When this is sent off to Aratta the messenger complains that the message has become too long and difficult for him to remember and reproduce. Thereupon Enmerkar invents writing—which throws the lord of Aratta in despair. At this point Iškur, the god of storm and rain, intervenes, and the famine and drought that was scourging Aratta at the time is over. The fight between the two dogs now appears as part of a festival. Inana reappears, confirms her predilection for Enmerkar, but also tells him to institute peaceful trade with Aratta from now on.

2. Arranged according to the several episodes and subparagraphs, the story looks somewhat like this:

I.	*The Argument*	
[A]	General introduction, subdivided into:	
	(1) Short hymn to Unug	1–5
	(2) Unug's wealth/absence of trade	6–27
	(3) Inana favors Unug.	28–32
[B]	Reason for and origin of the conflict: Enmerkar's plea and Inana's answer	
	(1) Introduction to Enmerkar's plea	33–37
	(2) Enmerkar's plea: have Aratta deliver its riches!	38–64
	(3) Introduction to Inana's reply	65–68
	(4) Inana's reply: Send a messenger!	69–79
	(5) Inana's reply: Aratta shall submit!	80–95 (= 49–64)
	(6) Inana's reply: Praise to you, Enmerkar!	96–104
II.	*The Contest*	
[C]	Enmerkar's first challenge	
	(1) Marching orders to the messenger	105–113 (106–112 = 71–78)
	(2) Enmerkar's threat	114–133
	(3) The Spell of Nudimmud	134–155
[D]	First voyage: Unug to Aratta	
	(1) Go now, messenger!	156–159
	(2) The voyage	160–174 (164–169 = 73–78)

[E]	Delivering the first challenge	
	(1) Opening formulae	175–178
	(2) My king is supreme!	179–186
	(3) Enmerkar's threat	187–207 (= 115–135)
	(4) I shall carry back your (submissive) answer!	208–217
[F]	Aratta's reply; first counterchallenge	
	(1) Aratta shall not submit!	218–226
	(2) Messenger: Inana has taken Unug's part!	227–235
	(3) Aratta and Unug shall have a contest!	236–261
	(4) Beware of Aratta's forces!	262–277
	(5) Counterchallenge: deliver grain in nets!	278–293
[G]	Second voyage: Aratta to Unug	294–298
[H]	Solution and second challenge	
	(1) Enmerkar's reaction	299–307
	(2) Ritual (and prayer?)	308–316
	(3) Nisaba's solution: soaking the wheat	317–336
	(4) Second challenge: a scepter to match mine!	337–346
[I]	Third voyage: Unug to Aratta	347–351
[J]	Delivering the second challenge	
	(1) Arrival in Aratta	352–375
	(2) Opening formulae	376–380
	(3) Hand over a scepter like mine!	381–388 (= 340–345)
[K]	Aratta's reply: second counterchallenge	
	(1) Aratta's anxiety	389–396
	(2) Counterchallenge: an impossible scepter	397–411
[L]	Fourth voyage: Aratta to Unug	412–416
[M]	Enmerkar's solution: a manmade substance	417–434
[N]	Fifth voyage: Unug to Aratta	435–437
[O]	Third counterchallenge	
	(1) Aratta's despondence	438–453
	(2) Counterchallenge: a dog of no known color	454–461

[P]	Sixth voyage: Aratta to Unug	462–467
[Q]	Final challenge	
	(1) Solution: a cloth of no known color	468–476
	(2) Final challenge	477–496
		(486–489 = 115–117)
	(3) Enmerkar invents writing.	497–506
[R]	Seventh voyage: Unug to Aratta	507–510
[S]	Aratta's reaction	
	(1) Opening formulae	511–517
	(2) Repetition of the challenge; tablet	518–535
	(3) Aratta's reaction: he cannot read.	536–541
III.	*The Resolution*	
[T]	The final confrontation	
	(1) Iškur sends rain; wheat begins to grow in Aratta.	542–555
	(2) Inana has saved Aratta!	556–568
	(3) Now let the champions fight!	569–580. . .?[1]
[U]	The argument resolved	
	(1) Inana pleases Dumuzid.	584–587
	(2) Inana orders Enmerkar to institute trade.	588–625
	(3) Inana's final counsel	626–636[2]

3. This representation is thought to show the strong sense of structure, balance, and composition pervading this poem. An analysis of the structural features cannot be undertaken here, but many of them are obvious at first reading. The poem can be neatly divided into three parts, of which the first and the last are roughly equal in size. The *argument* (lines 1–104) as a unit is balanced by the *resolution* (lines 542–636+). What is more, these are the only sections in which Inana has a major part. The *resolution* does indeed resolve the argument in that now trade is invented, and thus Enmerkar is enabled to fulfill his ambitions. The *contest* (lines 105–541) takes up most of the poem and is itself divided into twice three parts consisting of an initial challenge followed by three counterchallenges—or riddles—and their solutions. This works out as a series of seven voyages that, as the texts says, have to cross seven mountain ranges. On the other hand, this game of numbers and parallel situations is handled with consummate skill. Word-for-word repetitions do occur, but they are mostly highly functional in that they generally emphasize basic elements of the opening argument or Enmerkar's original threat

(see, e.g,. 49–64//80–95; 71–78//106–112; 115–135//187–207//486–489). In a literary environment that abounds in repetitions, it is striking that here precisely those narrative situations that would easily lead to automatic repetition—that is, the messenger's seven voyages—are differentiated, even somewhat artificially.[3] The text also shows a penchant for cross-reference that goes beyond the expected instances of fulfillment—or not—of earlier expectations. The most important instance of this technique is also very subtle. A major part of Enmerkar's first challenge is the famous spell of Nudimmud, which is seemingly not very much to the point in its immediate context. Indeed, when the messenger delivers this first challenge, the spell is not repeated as such; it is merely noted that it has to be spoken. Many of us now agree that the burden of this spell is that in an ideal world of peace and bliss, which Enmerkar is striving for, only Sumerian will be spoken.[4] It often escapes attention that the episode of Enmerkar's last challenge—in fact, merely a stronger assertion of his original challenge—contains a neat parallel of sorts. Enmerkar's invention of writing seems somewhat out of place here: the message is far shorter than the first one. But on the other hand, the invention of writing—explicitly cuneiform writing—complements the notion of Sumerian as the international language, as was already put in the spell of Nudimmud. Within the cultural ambience of the group of poems edited here, the e d u b a , it was clear to everyone that knowing and using Sumerian was equivalent to knowing how to write, and vice versa. This subtle cross-reference thus becomes yet another structural element holding the story together.

4. One of the most intriguing features of this text is partly formal and partly substantial. At first glance it seems that the rivalry for sanctioned superiority, which lies at the base of all the Aratta poems, is resolved here by the simple expedient of a well-known folktale motif: that of the riddle to which no solution seems possible. These "riddles" have a tendency to appear in threes. On a purely formal level, this does seem to be the case here, although I hasten to add that I know of no other examples from Sumerian literature. Yet the riddles themselves, and even more so their solutions, show three other levels of significance.

First, there is the matter of the materials required. In the first case, the gold and precious stones are ultimately exchanged for Unug's wealth in grain. This is indeed what both parties want: Enmerkar needs the luxury goods; Aratta, in the throes of a famine, needs food. In the second instance, the proposed exchange of scepters does not actually take place, but Enmerkar succeeds in manufacturing the required item. Third, the episode of the dogs can hardly be called an exchange, but again Enmerkar succeeds against the expectations of Aratta. Thus, the truly relevant substances are found only in the first exchange, which is taken up again at the end of the story.

Second, there is the symbolic meaning of the required objects. For Enmerkar the precious goods are necessary because of his responsibility for his city, which he wants to embellish as it should be. For Aratta grain is absolutely crucial at this point in time, and thus it also belongs to the responsibility of the lord of Aratta.[5] The scepter episode, on the other hand, is an overt allusion to the thorny matter of overlordship. The fight between the dogs[6] is probably a somewhat proleptic indication of the festivities accompanying the peaceful solution of the conflict.

There is also the manner in which Enmerkar solves the riddles. His first solution is a trick, but the point is that he is so conversant with the technology of wheat production that he can come up with this solution. The second instance is again a feat of technology: the very first manmade substance in history. And the third solution comes, somewhat unfairly one may think, from textile technology. So within one story we have not only references to the three main export products of Sumer—namely, wheat, manufactures, and textile—but also and perhaps mainly to the technological superiority of Sumer over the mere owners of raw though precious materials.

Thus one can see that the reason for Enmerkar's victory in this battle of wits lies not only in Enmerkar's superior intelligence and cleverness but also in the substance of the solutions he brings to the seemingly impossible tasks. All three have to do with technology and with the three most important export articles Sumer can produce.

Finally, to cap it all, this superiority that becomes evident as the story unfolds is further enhanced by the fourth and perhaps most important feat of technology. This consists of the introduction of Sumerian and cuneiform as the necessary means of administration, bookkeeping, and, finally, trade, the lack of which stands at the origin of the conflict. The overriding importance is clearly exemplified by the ingenious trick of presenting this motif in two parts—the Spell of Nudimmud and the Invention of Writing—which elegantly encompass the doubly threefold series of impossible tasks and their solution. Thus large-scale trade is seen to depend on writing, which simply implies Sumerian. And indeed, the very first cuneiform documents, without doubt written in Sumerian, are what we now call administrative and economic in nature. The scribes who are responsible for this text not only coined a term concordant with "cuneiform" (see line 540). They also hinted at the indubitable fact that writing was invented for economic, not intellectual, reasons.

5. The composite text presented here is based upon all the twenty-seven tablets and fragments known at the present time.[7] The material comes

predominantly from Nippur: twenty-three pieces out of twenty-seven. The Nippur material certainly shows two complete editions. One is a beautiful and well-preserved large tablet with six columns of about fifty lines per side, and another, of which we have only the right half, had sixty to sixty-five lines per column and five columns per side. There are at least nine partial editions on two-column tablets. Further study must decide whether these are parts of "complete editions" on sequences of two or three tablets, but it is striking that the first half or first third of the poem predominates on these tablets. There are seven good examples of imgidas (i.e., one column extracts); the rest of the fragments must remain undecided for the moment. Two largish one-column extracts were found in Ur; one imgida comes from Kish, and finally there is a fragment of a two-column tablet of unknown provenance[8] in Berlin.

6. The poem was first published in its (then) entirety in Kramer 1952, which was a remarkable achievement for its time. The reworking by Jestin (1957) is still useful in places. Cohen (1973), an unpublished dissertation, added much to the material, the reading, and the interpretation. Relevant recent translations are Jacobsen 1987 and Vanstiphout 1998 (84–112).

Enmerkar and the Lord of Aratta
Composite Text

I. THE ARGUMENT

A. General Introduction

iri gud huš AN.TEŠ$_2$ ni$_2$ gal gur$_3$-ru
[kul]-⸢ab$_4$⸣^{ki} bad$_3$ [. . .]
gaba ud-da ki nam tar-[re-da]
unug^{ki} kur-gal šag$_4$ [. . .]
kiğ$_2$-sig unu$_2$ gal an-⸢na⸣ [. . .]

ud ri-a nam ba-[tar-ra-ba]
unug^{ki} kul-ab$_4^{ki}$ e$_2$-⸢an⸣-[na] [. . .]
sağ il$_2$-la nun gal-e-ne ⸢mi⸣-[ni-. . .]
he$_2$-ğal$_2$ a eštub ğal$_2$
šeg$_x$(IM.A) še gu-nu ğal$_2$
unug^{ki} kul-ab$_4^{ki}$-a ib-da-an-tab
kur dilmun^{ki} [(. . .)] X in-nu
e$_2$-an-na unug^{ki}-e kul-ab$_4^{ki}$-a-ka ki us$_2$-sa-a
ği$_6$-par$_4$ kug ^{d}inana-ke$_4$
sig$_4$ kul-ab$_4^{ki}$-ke$_4$ kug ki-in-dar-ra-gin$_7$ pa ed$_2$ ak-am$_3$
[. . .] X X X nu-il$_2$ bala nu-ak-e
[. . . nu]-il$_2$ nam-ga-raš nu-ak-e
[kug-sig$_{17}$ kug]-babbar urud nagga ^{na4}lagab za-gin$_3$-na
[na$_4$ hur-sağ-ğa$_2$] ⸢kur⸣-bi-ta teš$_2$-bi nu-mu-un-ed$_3$-de$_3$
[. . .] ⸢ezen⸣-ma a nu-un-tu$_5^!$
[. . .] nu-mu-un-dur$_2$-ru
[. . .] ud bi$_2$-in-[zal]
[. . .]
[. . .]
[. . . gun$_3$]-gun$_3$
[. . .] ki kug X [. . . ^{na4}za]-gin$_3$ duru$_5$-am$_3$
⸢šag$_4$⸣-[bi] ^{ğiš}mes babbar-gin$_7$ gurun il$_2$-la sig$_7$-ga-am$_3$

^{d}inana-ra en aratta^{ki}-ke$_4$
sağ men kug-sig$_{17}$-ga mu-na-ni-in-ğal$_2$
en kul-ab$_4^{ki}$-a-gin$_7$ nu-mu-na-sag$_9$
aratta^{ki} eš$_3$ e$_2$-an-na ği$_6$-par$_4$ ki kug-gin$_7$

kug ^{d}inana-ra sig$_4$ kul-ab$_4^{ki}$-gin$_7$ nu-mu-un-na-du$_3$

Enmerkar and the Lord of Aratta
Translation

I. THE ARGUMENT

A. General Introduction

O city, fierce bull radiating force and awe,
[O Kulab], *rampart* [of the Land],
Breastwork of[9] the storm, where the destinies are ever fixed,
O Unug, great mountain in the heart of. . . ,
There the evening meal of An's abode [*is ever set.*]

In days of yore, when the destinies were fixed,
The Great Princes[10] granted Unug-Kulab's Eana
Head-lifting pride.
Opulence, carp floods[11]
And rains that bring forth dappled wheat
Abounded in Unug-Kulab.
The land Dilmun[12] did not yet exist,
When the Eana of Unug-Kulab was already well-founded,
And the Gipar of Holy Inana
And Kulab, the Brickwork, glinted like silver in the lode.
[. . .] was not yet *imported;* there was no trading;
[. . .] was not *exported;* there was no commerce.
[Gold], silver, copper, tin, blocks of lapis lazuli,
[The mountain ores,] were not yet brought down from the highlands.
[. . .] there was no bathing for the festivals;
[. . .] were not sitting
[. . .] time passed
[. . .]
[. . .]
[. . .] was brightly colored;
[. . .] the holy place was [*replete with*] polished lapis lazuli;
Its interior was beautiful like the silvery MES-tree in fruit.

For Inana did the lord of Aratta
Don his golden crown and diadem,
But he did not please her as well as did the lord of Kulab,
For nothing even resembling the shrine Eana, or the Gipar, the holy place,[13]
Did Aratta ever build for Holy Inana, unlike brickwork Kulab!

B. Reason for and Origin of the Conflict: Enmerkar's Plea and Inana's Answer

ud-ba en šag$_4$-ge pad$_3$-da ^{d}inana-ke$_4$
kur šuba-ta šag$_4$ kug-ge pad$_3$-da ^{d}inana-ke$_4$
en-me-er-kar$_2$ dumu ^{d}utu-ke$_4$
nin$_9$-a-ni nin kurku$_2$ dug$_3$-ga
kug ^{d}inana-ra u$_3$-gul mu-un-na-ğa$_2$-ğa$_2$

nin$_9$-mu aratta^{ki} unug^{ki}-še$_3$
kug-sig$_{17}$ kug-babbar ha-ma-an-galam-e
^{na4}za-gin$_3$ duru$_5$ lagab-ta [. . .]
sud-ra$_2$-ağ$_2$ ^{na4}za-gin$_3$ ⸢duru$_5$⸣ [. . .] X
unug^{ki}-ga kur kug [. . .] X X du$_3$
e$_2$ an-ta [ed$_3$-da ki]-gub-ba-za
[aratta^{ki} eš$_3$] e$_2$-an-na he$_2$-en-du$_3$
[ği$_6$]-par$_4$ kug-ga [dur$_2$] ğar-ra-za
šag$_4$-bi aratta^{ki} ha-ma-an-galam-e
ğa$_2$-e šag$_4$-ba amar za-gin$_3$-na gu$_2^{?}$ ga-mu-ni-[. . .]-la$_2$
aratta^{ki} ⸢unug⸣-[ki-še$_3$] ğiš ha-ma-[ğa$_2$-ğa$_2$]
nam-lu$_2$-u$_{18}$-lu aratta^{ki}-[ke$_4$]
na$_4$ hur-sağ-ğa$_2$ ⸢kur⸣-[bi] ha-ma-ab-ed$_3$
eš$_3$ gal ha-ma-du$_3$-e unu$_2$ gal ha-ma-ğa$_2$-ğa$_2$
unu$_2$ gal ⸢unu$_2$⸣ [diğir-re-e-ne-ke$_4$ pa] ed$_2$ [ha]-ma-ab-ak-e

me-mu kul-ab$_4^{ki}$-[a] si ha-ma-ni-ib-sa$_2$-e
abzu kur kug-gin$_7$ ha-ma-ab-mu$_2$-mu$_2$
eridug^{ki} hur-sağ-gin$_7$ ha-ma-ab-sikil-e
eš$_3$ abzu kug ki-in-dar-ra-gin$_7$ pa ed$_2$ ha-ma-ab-ak-e

ğa$_2$-e abzu-ta zag-mi$_2$ dug$_4$-ga-mu-ne
eridug^{ki}-ta me de$_6$-a-mu-ne
nam-en-na men eš$_3$ bar-gin$_7$ sig$_7$-ga-mu-ne

unug^{ki} kul-ab$_4^{ki}$-a sağ men kug ğal$_2$-la-mu-ne
[PA.A] eš$_3$ gal-la-ke$_4$ ği$_6$-par$_4$-ra hu-mu-un-tum$_2$-mu
[PA.A] ği$_6$-par$_4$-ra-ke$_4$ eš$_3$ gal-la hu-mu-un-tum$_2$-mu
[nam]- ⸢lu$_2$⸣-ulu$_3$ u$_6$ dug$_3$-ge-eš hu-mu-un-e
[^{d}]⸢utu⸣ igi hul$_2$-la he$_2$-em-ši-bar-bar-re

[ud-bi]-a giri$_{17}$-zal an kug-ga nin kur-ra igi ğal$_2$

in-nin$_9$ ^{d}ama-ušumgal-an-na šim-zid-da-ni

B. Reason for and Origin of the Conflict: Enmerkar's Plea and Inana's Answer

In those days did the lord, whom Inana chose in her heart,
Whom Inana from her shining mountain chose in her holy heart,
Enmerkar, son of the Sun,
Address a plea to his sister, the Lady who grants wishes;
He addressed a loud plea to Holy Inana:

"My sister, let Aratta for Unug
"Artfully work gold and silver for my sake!
"[Let them cut for my sake] polished lapis lazuli from its block;
"[Let them *work* for my sake] the translucent smooth lapis lazuli;
"[Let them] build [for my sake] the holy mountain in Unug!
"A temple [descended] from heaven—your place of worship,
"The shrine Eana—let [Aratta] build that!
"The holy Gipar, your dwelling,
"Let Aratta artfully adorn its inner chamber for my sake
"So that I, the beaming youth, may embrace you therein!
"Let Aratta submit to Unug!
"Let the people of Aratta
"Bring down for me the stones of their hills and mountains
"And build for me the great shrine, erect for me the great abode!
"For my sake, let them make illustrious the great abode, the abode of the gods!
"Let thus my power[14] become evident in Kulab;
"Let the Abzu flourish like the holy mountain,
"Let Eridug scintillate like the hill ranges,
"For my sake, let them make shrine Abzu illustrious like silver in the lode!
"When I then sing in praise from the Abzu,
"When I then bring back the power from Eridug,
"When I am then dressed with the crown of lordship like a *pure* shrine,
"When I then don the holy crown of Unug-Kulab,
"May then the [*mace-bearers*?][15] of the great shrine escort me to the Gipar,
"And may the [*mace-bearers*?] of the Gipar escort me to the great shrine.
"The people will applaud and admire me,
"And the Sun will behold me with benevolence!"
Thereupon the splendor in the sacred sky, the Lady who watches over the highland,
The divine Lady who embellishes herself for Ama-ušumgalana,[16]

^{d}inana nin kur-kur-ra-ke$_4$
en-me-er-kar$_2$ dumu ^{d}utu-ra gu$_3$ mu-na-de$_2$-e

en-me-er-kar$_2$ ğa$_2$-nu na ga-e-ri na-ri-mu he$_2$-e-dab$_5$
inim ga-ra-ab-dug$_4$ ğizzal he$_2$-ši-ak
kiğ$_2$-gi$_4$-a inim zu zag-še tuku erin$_2$-ta u$_3$-ba-e-re-pad$_3$

inim gal ^{d}inana gal zu inim-ma-ke$_4$ me-a hu-mu-na-ab-tumu$_3$
hur-sağ zubi-še$_3$ he$_2$-bi$_2$-in-ed$_3$-de$_3$
hur-sağ zubi-ta he$_2$-em-ma-da-ra-ed$_3$-de$_3$
šušin^{ki}-e kur an-ša$_4$-an^{ki}-a-še$_3$
peš$_2$ tur-gin$_7$ kiri$_3$ šu hu-mu-na-ab-ğal$_2$
hur-sağ gal-gal ni$_2$-ba lu-a
sahar-ra hu-mu-na-da-gur$_4$-gur$_4$-e
aratta^{ki} unug^{ki}-še$_3$ gu$_2$ ğiš <ha>-ma-ğa$_2$-ğa$_2$

nam-lu$_2$-ulu$_3$ aratta^{ki}-ke$_4$
na$_4$ hur-sağ-ğa$_2$ kur-bi um-ta-ab-ed$_3$
eš$_3$ gal ha-ra-du$_3$-e unu$_2$ gal ha-ra-ğa$_2$-ğa$_2$
unu$_2$ gal unu$_2$ diğir-re-e-ne-ke$_4$ pa ed$_2$ ha-ra-ab-ak-e

me-zu kul-ab$_4$^{ki}-a si ha-ra-ni-ib$_2$-sa$_2$-e
abzu kur kug-gin$_7$ ha-ra-ab-mu$_2$-mu$_2$
eridug^{ki} hur-sağ-gin$_7$ ha-ra-ab-sikil-e
eš$_3$ abzu kug ki-<in>-dar-ra-gin$_7$ pa ed$_2$ ha-ra-ab-ak-e

za-e abzu-ta zag-mi$_2$ dug$_4$-ga-zu-ne
eridug^{ki}-ta me de$_6$-a-[zu-ne]
nam-en men-na eš$_3$ bar-[gin$_7$ sig$_7$-ga]-zu-ne

unug^{ki}-e kul-ab$_4$^{ki}-a sağ ⸢men⸣ [kug ğal$_2$-la]-zu-ne
PA.A eš$_3$ gal-la-ke$_4$ ği$_6$-par$_4$-ra hu-mu-e-tum$_2$-mu
[PA.A] ği$_6$-par$_4$-ra-ke$_4$ eš$_3$ gal-la hu-mu-e-tum$_2$-mu
[nam-lu$_2$-ulu$_3$] u$_6$ dug$_3$-ge-eš he$_2$-mu-e-e
^{d}utu igi hul$_2$-la he$_2$-mu-e-ši-bar-bar-re

[nam]-lu$_2$-ulu$_3$ aratta^{ki}-ke$_4$
[X] NE ud šu$_2$-uš-ta um-[ta]-ab-il$_2$-ke$_4$-eš
[X] NE ud te-en-e um-ma-[teğ$_3$]-e-ta
ki ^{d}dumu-zid-da u$_8$ maš$_2$ sila$_4^{?}$-ni lu-a
a kalag-ga a-šag$_4$ ^{d}dumu-zid-da-ka
udu kur-ra-gin$_7$ dug$_3$ ha-ra-ni-ib-ğar
gaba kug-ğa$_2$-a ud-gin$_7$ ed$_2$-i$_3$

Inana, mistress of all the lands,
Thus spoke to Enmerkar, son of the Sun:

"Come Enmerkar, I shall advise you—let my advice be heeded!—
"I shall speak a word—let it be heard!
"Having chosen among the troops a messenger, clever of speech and hardy,
"Where and to whom shall he carry the grave word of word-wise Inana?
"He shall carry it up into the Zubi range;
"He shall carry it down from the Zubi range.
"Šušin and the land of Anšan
"Will salute her[17] humbly, like small mice.
"In the great mountain ranges the teeming multitudes
"Will grovel in the dust before her.
"Aratta shall submit to Unug!

"When the people of Aratta
"Have brought down the stones of their hills and mountains
"And built for you the great shrine, erected for you the great abode,
"For your sake, let them make illustrious the great abode, the abode of the gods!
"Let thus your power become evident in Kulab;
"Let the Abzu flourish for you like the holy mountain,
"Let Eridug scintillate for you like the hill ranges,
"For your sake, let them make shrine Abzu illustrious like silver in the lode!
"When you then sing in praise from the Abzu,
"When you then bring back the power from Eridug,
"When you are then dressed with the crown of lordship like a *pure* shrine,
"When you then don the holy crown of Unug-Kulab,
"May then the *mace-bearers*? of the great shrine escort you to the Gipar,
"And may the *mace-bearers*? of the Gipar escort you to the great shrine.
"The people will applaud and admire you,
"And the Sun will behold you with benevolence!"

"The people of Aratta
"Having carried [*their burdens*?] all day,
"[. . .] when the cool of the evening has come,
"At the place of Dumuzid, where teem the ewes and kids and lambs,
"Yea, in the Akalag meadows, those of Dumuzid,
"They will come flocking to you like so many mountain sheep!
"Now, rise like the Sun over my holy bosom,

zi-pa-ağ$_2$-ğa$_2$ niğ$_2$-muš$_3$-bi he$_2$-me-en
za-ra en-me-er-kar$_2$ dumu ^{d}utu zag-mi$_2$

II. THE CONTEST

C. Enmerkar's First Challenge

en-e inim kug ^{d}inana-ka-še$_3$ sağ-KEŠ$_2$ ba-ši-in-ak
kiğ$_2$-gi$_4$-a inim zu zag-še [tuku erin$_2$-ta] ba-ra-an-pad$_3$

inim gal ^{d}inana gal zu inim-ma-ke$_4$ me-a mu-na-ab-tum$_3$
hur-sağ zubi-ka he$_2$-bi$_2$-in-ed$_3$-de$_3$-en
hur-sağ zubi-ta he$_2$-em-ma-da-ra-an-ed$_3$-de$_3$-en
šušin^{ki}-e [kur] [an]-ša$_4$-an^{ki}-a-ke$_4$
peš$_2$ tur-gin$_7$ kiri$_3$ šu hu-mu-na-ab-ğal$_2$
hur-sağ gal-gal ni$_2$-ba lu-a
sahar-ra hu-mu-na-da-gur$_4$-gur$_4$-e

kiğ$_2$-gi$_4$-a en aratta^{ki}-ra u$_3$-na-dug$_4$ u$_3$-na-de$_3$-tah
iri-bi ir$_7$-sağ^{mušen}-gin$_7$ ğiš-bi-ta na-an-na-ra-ab-dal-en

mušen-gin$_7$ gud$_3$ us$_2$-sa-bi-a nam-bi$_2$-ib-dal-en
ganba ğal$_2$-la-gin$_7$ na-an-si-ig-en
iri gul-gul-lu-gin$_7$ sahar nam-bi$_2$-ib-ha-za-en
aratta^{ki} a$_2$-dam ^{d}en-ki-ke$_4$ nam ba-an-kud
⸢ki bi$_2$⸣-in-gul-la-gin$_7$ ki nam-ga-bi$_2$-ib-gul-en
eğir-bi ^{d}inana ba-ši-in-zig$_3$
gu$_3$ im-[mi-in-ra šeg$_{11}$ im]-mi-in-gi$_4$
kuš$_7$ bi$_2$-[in-su-a-gin$_7$] kuš$_7$ nam-ga-bi$_2$-ib-su-su
kug-sig$_{17}$ [u$_3$-tud-da]-ba ^{kuš}LU.UB$_2$+LU.UB$_2$-šir a-ba-ni-in-ak
kug me-a sahar-ba zag u$_3$-ba-ni-in-us$_2$
kug sağ-PA-[še$_3$] u$_3$-mu-un-dim$_2$-dim$_2$
anše kur-kur-ra-ke$_4$ barag um-mi-in-la$_2$-la$_2$
ğa$_2$-e-še$_3$-am$_3$ ^{d}en-lil$_2$ ban$_3$-da ki-en-gi-ra-ke$_4$
en ^{d}nu-dim$_2$-mud šag$_4$ kug-ge pad$_3$-da
kur me sikil-la-ke$_4$ ha-ma-du$_3$-e
^{ğiš}taskarin-gin$_7$ hi-li ha-ma-ab-ak-e
^{d}utu e$_2$-nun-ta ed$_2$-a-gin$_7$ si-muš$_2$ ha-ma-ab-gun$_3$-gun$_3$

zag-du$_8$-zag-du$_8$-bi uri$_3$ ha-ma-mul-e

e$_2$-nun- e$_2$-nun-ba šir$_3$ kug nam-šub tuku-a-ba

"For you are the jewel on my chest!
"Praise to you, O Enmerkar, son of the Sun!"

II. THE CONTEST

C. Enmerkar's First Challenge

The lord gave heed to the word of Inana;
He chose [among the troops] a messenger, clever of speech and hardy;
[*Enmerkar spoke*] to his messenger [. . .]:
"Where and to whom shall you carry the grave word of word-wise Inana?
"You shall carry it up into the Zubi range;
"You shall carry it down from the Zubi range.
"Šušin and the land of Anšan
"Will salute her humbly, like small mice.
"In the great mountain ranges the teeming multitudes
"Will grovel in the dust before her.

"Messenger, speak to the lord of Aratta, and say to him:
"Beware lest I make (the people of Aratta) flee from their city like a dove from its tree,
"Lest I make them fly away like a bird from its permanent nest,
"Lest I put a price on them as on mere merchandise,
"Lest I make Aratta gather dust as does a devastated city,
"Lest, like as when Enki has cursed a settlement
"And utterly destroyed it, I too destroy Aratta,
"Lest like the sweeping devastation, in whose wake Inana rose
"Shrieking and yelling aloud,
"I too make a sweeping devastation there!
"Therefore,[18] Aratta, having packed gold nuggets in leather sacks,
"And packed them tight with *gold dust,*
"And wrapped the precious metals in bales,
"And loaded mountain asses with the crates,
"Must build for me, the young Enlil of Sumer,
"Chosen by Nudimmud in his sacred heart,
"A mountain of lustrous powers!
"Let them make it sumptuous with boxwood!
"Let them make its horns shine like the Sun coming forth from its chamber!
"Let them make its doorposts sparkle brightly!'

"In its (Aratta's) chambers you must also chant to him this holy song, this spell:

nam-šub ^{d}nu-dim$_2$-mud-da-kam e-ne-ra dug$_4$-mu-na-ab
ud-ba muš nu-ğal$_2$-am$_3$ ğiri$_2$ nu-ğal$_2$-am$_3$
kir$_4$ nu-ğal$_2$-am$_3$ ur-mah nu-ğal$_2$-am$_3$
ur-gir$_{15}$ ur-bar-ra nu-ğal$_2$-am$_3$
ni$_2$ teğ$_3$-ğa$_2$ su zi-zi-i nu-ğal$_2$-am$_3$
lu$_2$-ulu$_3$^{lu} gaba šu ğar nu-tuku
ud-ba kur šubur^{ki} ha-ma-zi^{ki}
eme ha-mun ki-en-gi kur gal me nam-nun-na-ka

ki-uri kur me-te ğal$_2$-la
kur mar-tu u$_2$-sal-la nu$_2$-a
an-ki niğin$_2$-na un sağ sig$_{10}$-ga
^{d}en-lil$_2$-ra eme 1-am$_3$ he$_2$-en-na-da-ab-dug$_4$
ud-ba a-da en a-da nun a-da lugal-la

^{d}en-ki a-da en a-da nun a-da lugal-la
a-da en-e a-da nun-e a-da lugal-la
^{d}en-ki en he$_2$-ğal$_2$-la en dug$_4$-ga zid-da
en ğeštug$_2$-ga igi ğal$_2$ kalam-ma-ke$_4$
mas-su diğir-re-e-ne-ke$_4$
ğeštug$_2$-ge pad$_3$-da en eridug^{ki}-ga-ke$_4$
ka-ba eme i$_3$-kur$_2$ en-na mi-ni-in-ğar-ra
eme nam-lu$_2$-ulu$_3$ 1 i$_3$-me-[am$_2$]

D. First Voyage: Unug to Aratta

2-kam-ma-še$_3$ en-e kiğ$_2$-gi$_4$-a kur-še$_3$ du-ur$_2$
aratta^{ki}-aš inim mu-na-ab-tah-e
kiğ$_2$-gi$_4$-a gi$_6$-u$_3$-na-ka im 1-gin$_7$ šeg$_3$-ğa$_2$
an-bar$_7$-gan$_2$-ka im-du$_8$-gin$_7$ zig$_3$-ga

kiğ$_2$-gi$_4$-a inim lugal-la-na-ke$_4$ sağ-KEŠ$_2$ ba-ši-in-ak
gi$_6$-u$_3$-na-ka mul-am$_3$ im-ğin
an-bar$_7$-gan$_2$-ka ^{d}utu an-na-ta mu-un-de$_3$-ğin
inim gal ^{d}inana gi zu$_2$-lum-ma DU me-a mu-na-ab-tumu$_3$

hur-sağ zubi-še$_3$ bi$_2$-in-ed$_3$-de$_3$
hur-sağ zubi-ta im-ma-da-ra-ab-ed$_3$-de$_3$
šušin^{ki}-e kur an-ša$_4$-an^{ki}-a-še$_3$
peš$_2$ tur-⌜gin$_7$⌝ kiri$_3$ šu mu-na-ab-ğal$_2$
hur-sağ gal-gal ni$_2$-ba lu-a
sahar-ra mu-na-da-gur$_4$-gur$_4$
hur-sağ 5 hur-sağ 6 hur-sağ 7-e im-me-re-bal-bal

"It is the spell of Nudimmud![19]
"One day there will be no snake, no scorpion,
"There will be no hyena, nor lion,
"There will be neither (wild) dog nor wolf,
"And thus there will be neither fear nor trembling,
"For man will then have no enemy.
"On that day the lands of Šubur and Hamazi,
"As well as twin-tongued Sumer—great mound of the power of lordship—
"Together with Akkad—the mound that has all that is befitting—
"And even the land Martu, resting in green pastures,
"Yea, the whole world of well-ruled people,[20]
"Will be able to speak to Enlil in one language!
"For on that day, for the debates[21] between lords and princes and kings
"Shall Enki, for the debates between lords and princes and kings,
"For the debates between lords and princes and kings,
"Shall Enki, Lord of abundance, Lord of steadfast decisions,
"Lord of wisdom and knowledge in the Land,
"Expert of the gods,
"Chosen for wisdom, Lord of Eridug,
"Change the tongues in their mouth, as many as he once placed there,
"And the speech of mankind shall be truly one!' "

D. First Voyage: Unug to Aratta

Furthermore, the lord gave these instructions to the messenger
Who was to go to the highlands, to Aratta:
"Messenger, at night, run swiftly as the south wind;
"At daybreak, rise like the dew!"

The messenger heeded the words of his king.
At night he journeyed by starlight;
By day he traveled with the sun in the sky.
Whither and to whom should he carry the grave word of word-wise Inana?
He carried it up into the Zubi range;
He carried it down from the Zubi range.
Šušin and the land of Anšan
Saluted her humbly, like small mice.
In the great mountain ranges the teeming multitudes
Groveled in the dust before her.
Five, six, seven mountain ranges he crossed,[22]

[igi mu-un]- ⸢il$_2$⸣ aratta^{ki}-aš ba-teğ$_3$
[kisal] ⸢aratta⸣^{ki}-ka ğiri$_3$ hul$_2$-la mi-ni-in-gub
nam-nir-ğal$_2$ lugal-a-na mu-un-zu
bur$_2$-ra-bi inim šag$_4$-ga-na bi$_2$-ib$_2$-be$_2$

E. Delivering the First Challenge

kiğ$_2$-gi$_4$-a en aratta^{ki}-ra mu-na-ab-bal-e
a-a-zu lugal-mu mu-e-ši-in-gi$_4$-in-nam
en unug^{ki}-ga en kul-ab$_4$^{ki}-a-ke$_4$ mu-e-ši-in-gi$_4$-nam

Lord of Aratta

lugal-za dug$_4$-ga-ni nam-mu tah-a-ni nam-mu

Messenger

lugal-mu a-na bi$_2$-in-dug$_4$ a-na bi$_2$-in-tah-am$_3$
lugal-mu u$_3$-tud-da-ni-ta nam-en-na tum$_2$-ma
en unug^{ki}-ga muš sağ-kal ki-en-gi-ra til$_3$-la kur zid$_2$-gin$_7$ ma$_5$-ma$_5$

tarah-maš kur bad$_3$-da a$_2$ nun ğal$_2$
šilam-za maš nağa kug-ga umbin sud$_2$-sud$_2$-e
ab$_2$ zid-da kur šag$_4$-ga tud-da
en-me-er-kar$_2$ dumu ^{d}utu-ke$_4$ mu-e-ši-in-gi$_4$-nam
lugal-mu na-ab-be$_2$-a

iri-ni ir$_7$-sağ^{mušen}-gin$_7$ ğiš-bi-ta na-na$^{?}$-⸢ra-ab⸣-dag-e

mušen-gin$_7$ gud$_3$ us$_2$-sa-bi-a nam-bi$_2$-ib$_2$-hu-luh-e
ganba ğal$_2$-la-gin$_7$ na-an-si-ge-en
iri gul-gul-la-gin$_7$ sahar na-an-bi$_2$-[ib-ha-za]-en
aratta^{ki} a$_2$-dam ^{d}en-ki-ke$_4$ nam ba-an-kud
ki bi$_2$-in-gul-la-gin$_7$ ki nam-ga-bi$_2$-ib-gul-en
eğir-bi ^{d}inana ba-ši-in-zig$_3$
gu$_3$ im-mi-in-ra šeg$_{11}$ im-mi-in-gi$_4$
kuš$_7$ bi$_2$-in-su-a-gin$_7$ kuš$_7$ na-an-ga-bi$_2$-ib-su-su-un
kug-sig$_{17}$ u$_3$-tud-da-ba ^{kuš}LU.UB+LU.UB$_2$-šir a-ba-ni-in-ak
kug me-a sahar-ba zag u$_3$-ba-ni-in- us$_2$
kug sağ-PA-še$_3$ u$_3$-mu-un-dim$_2$-dim$_2$
anše kur-kur-ra-ke$_4$ barag um-mi-in-la$_2$-la$_2$
ğa$_2$-e-še$_3$-am$_3$ ^{d}en-lil$_2$ ban$_3$-da ki-en-gi-ra-ke$_4$
en ^{d}nu-dim$_2$-mud-e šag$_4$ kug-ge pad$_3$-da
kur me sikil-la-ke$_4$ ha-ma-du$_3$-e
^{ğiš}taskarin-gin$_7$ hi-li ha-ma-ab-ak
^{d}utu e$_2$-nun-ta ed$_2$-a-gin$_7$ si-muš$_2$ ha-ma-ab-gun$_3$-gun$_3$

And when he lifted his eyes, he had arrived in Aratta.
Overjoyed he stepped into the courtyard of Aratta
And proclaimed the glory of his king.
Openly he spoke the words (that he had remembered) in his heart.[23]

E. Delivering the First Challenge

The messenger spoke thus to the lord of Aratta:
"Your father, my king, has sent me to you;
"The lord of Unug and Kulab has sent me to you!"

Lord of Aratta

"What is it to me what your king spoke, what he said?"

Messenger

"This is what my king spoke, what he said:
"My king was destined for overlordship since his birth;
"He is lord of Unug, the sagkal-snake living in Sumer yet grinding the highland to flour;
"He is the stag of the highlands, with great antlers;
"He is the buffalo, the deer trampling with its hooves the holy soapwort;
"He is the one the true cow bore in the heart of the highlands.
"He is Enmerkar, son of the Sun, and has sent me to you.
"This is what my king has spoken:

"'Beware lest I make (the people/Aratta) flee from their city like a dove from its tree,
"'Lest I make them fly away like a bird from its permanent nest,
"'Lest I put a price on them as on mere merchandise,
"'Lest I make Aratta gather dust as does a devastated city,
"'Lest, like when Enki has cursed a settlement
"'And utterly destroyed it, I too destroy Aratta,
"'Lest like the sweeping devastation, in whose wake Inana rose
"'Shrieking and yelling aloud,
"'I too make a sweeping devastation there!
"'Therefore, Aratta, having packed gold nuggets in leather sacks,
"'And packed them tight with *gold dust,*
"'And wrapped the precious metals in bales,
"'And loaded mountain asses with the crates,
"'Must build for me, the young Enlil of Sumer,
"'Chosen by Nudimmud in his sacred heart,
"'A mountain of lustrous powers!
"'Let them make it sumptuous with boxwood!
"'Let them make its horns shine like the Sun coming forth from its chamber!

zag-du$_8$-zag-du$_8$-ba uri$_3$ ha-ma-mul-e
e$_2$-nun-e$_2$-nun-ba šir$_3$ kug nam-šub tuku-a-ba
[nam-šub] ^{d}nu-dim$_2$-mud-ke$_4$ ğa$_2$-ra dug$_4$-⸢mu⸣-[na-ab]

a-na ma-ab-be$_2$-en-na-bi u$_3$-mu-[e-dug$_4$]
a ru-a su$_6$ ^{na4}za-gin$_3$ [KEŠ$_2$]-da-[ar]
ab$_2$ kal-la-ga-ni kur me sikil-la-ka [tud-da-ar]
sahar aratta^{ki}-ka a$_2$ ed$_2$-[a-ar]
ubur ab$_2$ zid-da ga gu$_7$-[a-ar]
kul-ab$_4$^{ki} kur me gal-gal-la-ka nam-nun-na tum$_2$-ma
en-me-er-kar$_2$ dumu ^{d}utu-ra
inim-bi eš$_3$ e$_2$-an-na-ka inim dug$_3$ ga-na-ab-dug$_4$
ği$_6$-par$_4$ ^{giš}mes gibil-gin$_7$ gurun il$_2$-la-na
lugal-mu en kul-ab$_4$^{ki}-ra šu-a ga-mu-na-ab-gi$_4$

F. Aratta's Reply; First Counterchallenge

ur$_5$-gin$_7$ hu-mu-na-ab-be$_2$-a-ka
kiğ$_2$-gi$_4$-a lugal-zu en kul-ab$_4$^{ki}-a-ra u$_3$-na-dug$_4$ u$_3$-na-de$_3$-tah
ğa$_2$-e-me-en en šu sikil-la tum$_2$-ma
^{giš}rab mah an-na nin an-ki-ke$_4$

in-nin$_9$ me šar$_2$-ra kug ^{d}inana-ke$_4$
aratta^{ki} kur me sikil-la-še$_3$ hu-mu-un-de$_6$-en
kur-ra ^{giš}ig gal-gin$_7$ igi-ba bi$_2$-in-tab-en
aratta^{ki} unug^{ki}-še$_3$ gu$_2$ a-gin$_7$ i$_3$-ğa$_2$-ğa$_2$
aratta^{ki} unug^{ki} še$_3$ gu$_2$ ğa$_2$-ğa$_2$ nu-ğal$_2$ e-ne-ra dug$_4$-mu-na-ab

ur$_5$-gin$_7$ hu-mu-na-ab-be$_2$-a-ka
kiğ$_2$-gi$_4$-a en aratta^{ki}-ra mu-na-ni-ib-gi$_4$-gi$_4$
nin gal an-na me huš-a u$_5$-a
hur-sağ kur šuba-ka dur$_2$ ğar-ra
barag kur šuba-ka še-er-ka-an dug$_4$-ga
en lugal-mu šubur-a-ni-im
diğir nin e$_2$-an-na-ka mu-un-di-ni-ib-kur$_9$-re-eš
en aratta^{ki} gu$_2$ ki-še$_3$ ba-ni-in-ğal$_2$
sig$_4$ kul-ab$_4$^{ki}-a-ka ur$_5$-gin$_7$ hu-mu-na-ab-be$_2$

ud-bi-a en-e šag$_4$ mu-un-sig$_3$ zi mu-un-ir-ir
gaba-ri nu-mu-da-ğal$_2$ gaba-ri i$_3$-kin-kin
ğiri$_3$ ni$_2$-te-a-na-ka igi lib-ba bi$_2$-in-du$_8$-ru gaba-ri i$_3$-pad$_3$-de$_3$
gaba-ri in-pad$_3$ gu$_3$ im-ta-an-ed$_2$
kiğ$_2$-gi$_4$-a inim-ma gaba-ri-bi

"'Let them make its doorposts sparkle brightly!'
"'In its chambers, the holy song, the spell,
"'Chant to him for me the spell of Nudimmud!'[24]

"Now, when you will have replied to me whatever you want,
"To the scion of the one with the gleaming beard,
"To him whom his mighty cow bore on the hill of the lustrous power,
"To him who grew up on the soil of Aratta,[25]
"To him who was suckled by the teat of the true cow,
"To him, suited for office in Kulab, mountain of the great powers,
"To Enmerkar, son of the Sun,
"I will speak that word as glad tidings in the shrine Eana.
"In his Gipar, bearing fruit like a young MES-tree,
"I shall repeat it to my king, the lord of Kulab."

F. ARATTA'S REPLY; FIRST COUNTERCHALLENGE

When he had spoken in this vein <the lord of Aratta replied:>
"Messenger, address your king, the lord of Kulab, and say to him:
"'It is I, being the lord proper for the lustrations,
"'I, whom the great neck-stock of heaven, the Queen of Heaven and Earth,
"'The goddess of the myriad powers, Holy Inana
"'Brought to Aratta, the mountain of the inviolate powers;
"'I whom she made block the entrance to the highlands as a great door!
"'Why then should Aratta submit to Unug?
"'There can be no submission of Aratta to Unug! Tell him that!'"[26]

When he had spoken in this vein
The messenger replied to the lord of Aratta:
"This great Queen of Heaven who drives the fearsome powers,
"Who dwells on the peaks of the bright mountains,
"Who thus embellishes the bright mountain dais[27]—
"It was my lord and king, her servant,
"Who had her installed as the divine Queen of the Eana!
"'O lord, Aratta shall bow in deep submission!'
"This she has promised in brick-built Kulab!"

Thereupon the lord's mood became dark and troubled.
He had no rejoinder; he kept searching for a rejoinder,
Staring at his feet with sad eyes, seeking a rejoinder.
Finally he found a rejoinder and cried out.
The rejoinder to the message

gud-gin$_7$ gu$_3$-nun mu-un-di-ni-ib-be$_2$
kiĝ$_2$-⸢gi$_4$-a⸣ lugal-zu en kul-ab$_4^{ki}$-a-ra u$_3$-na-dug$_4$ u$_3$-na-de$_3$-tah
hur-saĝ gal ^{ĝiš}mes an-da mu$_2$-a
ur$_2$-bi-še$_3$ sa-par$_4$-am$_3$ pa-bi ĝiš-bur$_2$-am$_3$
buru$_5$ umbin-bi anzud^{mušen} hu-ri$_2$-in^{mušen}-na
KEŠ$_2$-da [^{d}]inana-⸢ka⸣ šar$_2$ dug$_4$-ge gilim-ma
umbin hu-ri$_2$-in^{mušen}-bi u$_3$-mun kur$_2$-ra kur šuba-da ed$_3$-da
aratta^{ki} er$_2$ [še$_8$-še$_8$ . . .]
a bal-bal-am$_3$ zid$_2$ dub-dub-ba-am$_3$
kur-ra siskur a-ra-zu-a kiri$_3$ šu ĝal$_2$-la-am$_3$
lu$_2$ 5 nu-me-a lu$_2$ 10 nu-me-a
unug^{ki} zig$_3$-ga hur-saĝ zubi-še$_3$ saĝ a-gin$_7$ i$_3$-ĝa$_2$-ĝa$_2$
lugal-zu ^{ĝiš}tukul-ĝa$_2$ saĝ ha-ba-an-šum$_2$
ĝa$_2$-e a-da-min$_3$-na saĝ ⸢ga-ba⸣-an-šum$_2$
a-da-min$_3$ nu-um-zu teš$_2$ [nu]-⸢um⸣-gu$_7$
gud-de$_3$ ⸢gud⸣ a$_2^{!}$-ĝal$_2$-bi [nu-um]-zu
[a-da]-⸢min$_3$⸣ um-zu teš$_2$ um-[gu$_7$]
[gud]-⸢de$_3$⸣ gud a$_2^{!}$-ĝal$_2$-bi um-⸢zu⸣
[e]-⸢ne⸣ a-da-min$_3$ mi-ni-in-tak$_4$-tak$_4$-an
[. . .]-⸢gin$_7$⸣ niĝ$_2$ lu$_2$ nu-sig$_{10}$-ge
[e]-ne in-ga-mu-ni-in-tak$_4$-tak$_4$-an

[2-kam]-ma-še$_3$ kiĝ$_2$-gi$_4$-a inim mu-ra-be$_2$-en
[. . .] de$_2$-a ša-ra-ab-galam-e-en DU-a he$_2$-mu-e-ši-dib
[e$_2$]-an-na piriĝ šu-ba nu$_2$-a
šag$_4$-bi-ta gud gu$_3$ nun di-dam
ĝi$_6$-par$_4$ ^{ĝiš}mes gibil-gin$_7$ gurun il$_2$-la-na
lugal-zu en kul-ab$_4^{ki}$-a-ra šu-a gi$_4$-mu-na-ab
hur-saĝ ur-saĝ sukud si-ga-am$_3$
an-usan-na ^{d}utu e$_2$-bi-še$_3$ du-gin$_7$
igi-bi-ta uš$_2$ la$_2$-la$_2$-e-gin$_7$
^{d}nanna si-un$_3$-na mah-a-gin$_7$
saĝ-ki-bi me-lam$_2$ ĝal$_2$-la-gin$_7$
ĝiš-gin$_7$ kur-kur-ra gilim-ba-gin$_7$
saĝ muš$_3$ aratta^{ki}-ke$_4$
^{d}lama sag$_9$-ga kur me sikil-la-še$_3$
ud-da aratta^{ki} aga kug an-na-gin$_7$ si mu-na-an-sa$_2$
ĝa$_2$-e ud-ba nam-mah-mu ga-an-zu
še barag-ga nam-mu-un-si-si-ig-ge mar-e nam-me-e
še-bi kur-kur-ra nam-il$_2$-e
erin$_2$-na mu-un-kud nam-mu-un-ĝa$_2$-ĝa$_2$
še sa-al-kad$_5$-e u$_3$-mu-ni-in-si-si
anše barag la$_2$-e um-mi-in-la$_2$

He bellowed it loudly like a bull to the messenger:
"Messenger, to your king, lord of Kulab, speak and say:
"This great mountain range is a MES-tree grown high into the skies;
"Its roots are a net, its branches a snare;
"It is a bird whose talons are like those of the Anzud-eagle!
"This barrier of Inana is perfectly impenetrable;
"Its eagle talons make the bright mountains run with enemy blood.
"In Aratta there may be weeping [*and hunger* . . .],
"But water is being poured, flour is being sprinkled;[28]
"In the highlands sacrifices and prayers are reverently offered.
"With only five or ten men,[29]
"How could the levy of Unug march against the Zubi mountain?
"Your king may be eager to confront me with arms,
"But I am eager for another kind of contest.
"He who does not understand this contest *shall not prevail,*[30]
"Just like a bull that does not know the strength of the other bull;
"But he who understands this contest *shall prevail,*
"Just like a bull that perceives the strength of the other bull.
"Dare he refuse this contest
"Like [. . .], something no one can match?
"Dare he refuse this contest?'

"Another thing I will tell you, O messenger;
"[I will] *spell it out* in careful terms . . . so that you can grasp it.[31]
"In the Eana, to the lion crouching there on its paws,
"To the bull bellowing there,
"In his Gipar, bearing fruit like a young MES-tree,
"To your king, the lord of Kulab, repeat this:
"'This mountain range is a warrior, tall and fierce:
"'Like Utu wending his way home in the evening,
"'It is as if blood is dripping from his face.
"'Like Nanna, majestic in the high heaven,
"'It is as if his brow carries a terrible sheen![32]
"'It is like an impenetrable wood in the mountains.
"'Since she of the *crown* of Aratta,[33]
"'The benevolent guardian of the mountain of the inviolate powers,
"'Will warrant Aratta the holy crown of heaven,
"'I shall surely proclaim my preeminence!
"'Now, he may not pour grain into bags, nor into carts;
"'He may not have that grain portaged over the mountains;
"'He may not *have it collected by work parties.*[34]
"'If he were able to pour grain into nets
"'And load these nets on pack-asses

anše bala-e da-bi-a a-ba-an-sig$_{10}$
tukum-bi kisal aratta^{ki}-ka gur$_7$-še$_3$ mu-dub-be$_2$
i$_3$-ge-en am$_3$-dub-be$_2$ gur$_7$-a hi-li-bi

kur-kur-ra izi ĝar-ra-bi a$_2$-dam me-te-bi
bad$_3$ 7-e še-er-ka-an dug$_4$-ga
nin ur-saĝ me$_3$-a tum$_2$-ma
^{d}inana ur-saĝ me$_3$ sahar-ra-ke$_4$ saĝ ešemen ^{d}inana di-dam

i$_3$-ge-en aratta^{ki} ur adda sar-gin$_7$ šu-ta im-ta-ri
ĝa$_2$-e ud-ba ša-ba-na-gam-e-de$_3$-en
e-ne nam-mah-a-ni ši-im-ma-an-zu-zu-un
iri-gin$_7$ nam-tur-ĝa$_2$ gu$_2$ ši-im-ma-ĝa$_2$-ĝa$_2$-an e-ne-ra dug$_4$-mu-na-ab

G. Second Voyage: Aratta to Unug

ur$_5$-gin$_7$ hu-mu-na-ab-be$_2$-a-ka
kiĝ$_2$-gi$_4$-a en aratta^{ki}-ke$_4$
ka-ni-gin$_7$ inim ka-na ba-an-sig$_{10}$
sun$_2$-gin$_7$ haš$_2$-a-na mu-un-gur
nim sahar-ra-gin$_7$ tir ud zal-le-na mu-un-ĝin

H. Solution and Second Challenge

sig$_4$ kul-ab$_4$^{ki}-a-ka ĝiri$_3$ hul$_2$-la mu-ni-in-gub
kisal mah-e kisal gu$_2$-en-na-ka kiĝ$_2$-gi$_4$-a i-ib$_2$-bur$_2$

lugal-a-ni-ir en kul-aba$_4$⸢^{ki}⸣-[ra]
ka-ni-gin$_7$ šu mu-na-an-gi$_4$
gud-gin$_7$ gu$_3$ mu-na-an-sig$_{10}$
gud ri-ri-gin$_7$ ĝeštug$_2$ mu-na-an-[ĝa$_2$-ĝa$_2$]
lugal-e zag zid-da-ni NE im-mi-in-⸢tuš⸣
zag gub$_3$-bu-ni im-ma-ni-in-gi$_4$
i$_3$-ge-en aratta^{ki} ĝalga šum$_2$-ma im-ma-zu im-me

ud im-zal ^{d}utu im-ta-ed$_2$-a-ra
^{d}utu kalam-ma-ka saĝ bi$_2$-ib-il$_2$
lugal-e ^{id2}idigna ^{id2}buranun-bi-da im-ma-da-an-tab
^{id2}buranun-na ^{id2}idigna-da im-ma-da-an-tab
bur gal-gal an-ne$_2$ ba-su$_8$-su$_8$-ug
bur tur-tur sila$_4$ u$_2$-šim dur$_2$-gin$_7$ zag-bi-a im-ma-an-us$_2$

"'With remounts at their side,
"'And if he were able to pile it up in the courtyard of Aratta—
"'Truly, if he were able to pile it up in this manner, then the joy of the grain-pile,
"'The torch of the mountains, the emblem of the settlements,
"'The ornament of the seven walls,
"'The heroic mistress fit for battle,
"'Inana, the heroine of the battleground who makes the troop dance her dance,[35]
"'Will then truly have cast out Aratta as a carrion-eating dog!
"'Only then shall I kneel before him,
"'Since only then will he have proven his preeminence,
"'And, like the city, only then shall I concede my inferiority!' Tell him that!"

G. Second Voyage: Aratta to Unug

When he had spoken to him in this vein,
The lord of Aratta made the messenger
Repeat the message as he himself had spoken it.[36]
The messenger turned, as the wild cow does on its haunches;
Like the sandfly he sped forward in the cool of the morning.

H. Solution and Second Challenge

Joyfully he stepped into Kulab, the Brickwork.
The messenger sped to the great courtyard, the courtyard of the throne-room.
To his king, the lord of Kulab,
He repeated (the message) *word for word*.
He bellowed like a bull,
And Enmerkar listened to him like the ox-driver.
The king bade him sit at his right side ...
And turned his left side to him.
"Does Aratta truly understand this proposal it made?" he said.

When day broke, to the rising Sun,
The Sun of the Land[37] raised his head.
The king joined Tigris with Euphrates
And Euphrates with Tigris.[38]
Large jars were put out in the open,
And small vases were placed against their sides, like lambs lying in the grass;

bur i-gi$_8$ an-na da-bi-a ba-su$_8$-ug
lugal-e eš-da kug-sig$_{17}$-ga-ke$_4$
en-me-er-kar$_2$ dumu ^{d}utu-ke$_4$ dug$_3$ mu-un-ba$_9$-ba$_9$-re$_7$
ud-bi-a dub i-gi$_8$ IM me-a gi-gag unkin-na

alan kug-sig$_{17}$-ga ud dug$_3$-ga tud-da
^{d}nanibgal sig$_7$-ga KAxLI sikil mu$_2^{?}$-da
^{d}nisaba nin ğeštug$_2$ dağal-la-ke$_4$
e$_2$ ĞEŠTUG$_2$.^{d}NISABA kug-ga-ni ğal$_2$ mu-na-an-tak$_4$
e$_2$-gal an-na-ka kur$_9$-ra-ni ğeštug$_2$ mu-un-ğa$_2$-ğa$_2$
en-e e$_2$-nun mah-a-ni ğal$_2$ ba-an-tak$_4$
^{ğiš}li$_2$-id-ga mah-a-ni ki ⸢ba⸣-[an]-us$_2$
lugal-e še-ta še libir-ra-ni šu ba-ra-an-⸢bal⸣
munu$_4$ ki-šar$_2$-ra a ba-ni-in-[si]
nundum-bi ^{u2}hirin$^{hu-ri2-in}$ AN [X]-su$_3$-ge
sa-al-kad$_5$-e igi im-mi-in-tur-tur
še gur$_7$ ka i-ni-in-si zu$_2$ buru$_5^{mušen}$-e bi$_2$-in-tah

anše barag la$_2$-e um-mi-in-la$_2$
anše bala-e da-bi-a ba-an-sig$_{10}$
lugal en ğeštug$_2$ dağal-la-ke$_4$
en unug^{ki}-ga en kul-ab$_4^{ki}$-ke$_4$
har-ra-an aratta^{ki}-ke$_4$ si bi$_2$-in-sa$_2$
nam-lu$_2$-ulu$_3$ kiši$_6$ ki-in-dar-ra-gin$_7$
aratta^{ki}-aš ni$_2$-ba mu-un-sub$_2$-be$_2$-eš

en-e kiğ$_2$-gi$_4$-a kur-še$_3$ du-ur$_2$
aratta^{ki}-aš inim mu-na-ab-tah-e
kiğ$_2$-gi$_4$-a en aratta^{ki}-ra u$_3$-na-dug$_4$ u$_3$-na-de$_3$-tah
ğidru-ğa$_2$ ur$_2$-bi me nam-nun-na-ka
pa-bi kul-ab$_4^{ki}$-a an-dul$_3$-eš i$_3$-ak
pa mul-mul-la-bi eš$_3$ e$_2$-an-na-ke$_4$
kug ^{d}inana-ke$_4$ ni$_2$ im-ši-ib-te-en-te
ğidru um-ta-an-kid$_7$ hu-mu-un-da-ğal$_2$
^{na4}gug ğiš dili ^{na4}za-gin$_3$ ğiš dili-gin$_7$ šu-ni-a hu-mu-un-ğal$_2$

en aratta^{ki}-ke$_4$ igi-mu-še$_3$ hu-mu-un-tum$_2$ e-ne-ra dug$_4$-mu-na-ab

I. Third Voyage: Unug to Aratta

ur$_5$-gin$_7$ hu-mu-na-ab-be$_2$-a-ka
kiğ$_2$-gi$_4$-a aratta^{ki}-aš du-ni
sahar kaskal-la ğiri$_3$-ni mu-un-si

Shining jars were stood in the open next to them.
The king himself placed the golden ešda-vessels;
Enmerkar himself, the son of the Sun, placed them wide apart.
Thereupon the *shining* tablet of clay, the sharpened reed of the assembly,[39]
The golden statue fashioned on a blissful day,
Fair Nanibgal, grown up to lustrous luxuriance,
Nisaba, the Lady of broad understanding,[40]
Opened for him her holy house of wisdom.
Entering the heavenly palace, he paid attention;
The lord opened up his lofty storehouse
And fixed his lidga-measure in the earth.
The king separated the old grain from the (other) grain;
Greenmalt he soaked all through;
Its *sprouts* ... grew long like the hirin-plant,
And so he reduced the meshes of the nets.
He filled the nets with grain for the piles, and added some for the locust's tooth;
He loaded it on pack-asses,
And placed remounts at their side.
The king, the lord of broad understanding,
The lord of Unug, the lord of Kulab,
Set them on the road to Aratta.
The people, (numerous) like ants from their crevices,
He made go to Aratta by themselves.

To the messenger who was to go to the highlands,
To Aratta, the lord added these instructions:
"Messenger, speak to the lord of Aratta and say:
"My scepter's base is the power of overlordship;
"Its crown provides a protective shadow for Kulab;
"Under its starlike branches in the shrine Eana
"Holy Inana finds her cool refreshment.
"If he *can cut a scepter from it,* let him hold it in his hand;[41]
"Let him hold it in his hand like a string of carnelian and lapis lazuli beads;
"Let the lord of Aratta bring that to me! Tell him that!"

I. Third Voyage: Unug to Aratta

After Enmerkar had spoken to him in this vein,
The messenger, on his way to Aratta,
Plunged his feet in the dust of the road.

na$_4$ tur-tur hur-sağ-ğa$_2$-ke$_4$ suh$_3$-sah$_4$ mu-un-da-ab-za
ušumgal edin-na-ba kiğ$_2$-ğa$_2$-gin$_7$ gaba-ri nu-mu-ni-in-tuku

J. Delivering the Second Challenge

kiğ$_2$-gi$_4$-a aratta^{ki}-aš um-ma-teğ$_3$-a-ra
nam-lu$_2$-ulu$_3$ aratta^{ki}-ke$_4$
anše barag la$_2$-e u$_6$ di-de$_3$ im-ma-su$_8$-su$_8$-ge-eš
kiğ$_2$-gi$_4$-a kisal aratta^{ki}-ka
še gur$_7$ ka bi$_2$-in-si zu$_2$ buru$_5$^{mušen}-e bi$_2$-in-tah

šeg$_x$ (IM.A) an-na ud ğal$_2$-la-gin$_7$
aratta^{ki} he$_2$-ğal$_2$-la i$_3$-du$_3$
diğir dur$_2$-bi-a ba-da-ab-gi$_4$-a-⸢gin$_7$⸣
aratta^{ki} ša$_3$-ğar-ra-ni am$_3$-la$_2$-[la$_2$]
nam-lu$_2$-ulu$_3$ aratta^{ki}-[ke$_4$]
munu$_4$ a si-ga-na a-šag$_4$ mu-ni-[ib-X]
⸢eğir ⸣-ba ra$_2$-gaba ša$_3$-tam [. . .]
[X] ki a tak$_4$-ba [. . .]
X [X] X [. . .]
dumu-[dumu] aratta^{ki} ⸢ğeštug$_2$⸣ [. . .]
aratta^{ki}-aš inim mu-un-bur$_2$
ur$_5$-da aratta^{ki}-a šu-⸢ta⸣ [. . .]
en unug^{ki}-ga-ra šu-ni i-im-[. . .]

Citizens of Aratta?

me-en-de$_3$ su$_3$-ga lul-la-⸢bi⸣-[še$_3$]
en kul-ab$_4$^{ki}-a-ra ^{na4}gug ⸢lul⸣-[la-me-a] ga-mu-na-dur$_2$-ru-ne-en-de$_3$-en
ab-ba-ab-ba inim zu-ne
šu teš$_2$-a bi$_2$-ib-ri-⸢eš⸣ zag e$_2$-gar$_8$-e bi$_2$-ib-us$_2$[-eš]
en-ra e$_2$-sikil-bi hu-mu-un-ğa$_2$-ğa$_2$-[e-ne]

[(X) X] ⸢kin⸣ ğidru -ni DU.DU šag$_4$ e$_2$-⸢gal⸣-[la . . .]
[bur$_2$-ra-bi inim šag$_4$-ga]-na bi$_2$-[ib-be$_2$]
[a-a-zu lugal- mu] mu-e-ši-⸢in⸣-[gi$_4$-in-nam]
[en-me-er]-⸢kar$_2$⸣ dumu ^{d}utu-[ke$_4$] mu-e-ši-in-gi$_4$-in-nam

Lord of Aratta

lugal-zu dug$_4$-ga-ni nam-mu tah-[a]-ni [nam]-mu

Messenger

lugal- mu a-na ⸢bi$_2$-in⸣-dug$_4$ a-na [bi$_2$-in-tah]-⸢am$_3$⸣
ğidru-ğa$_2$ ur$_2$-bi me ⸢nam⸣-nun-⸢na-ka⸣
pa-bi kul-ab$_4$^{ki}-a ⸢an-dul$_3$⸣-eš i$_3$-ak
pa mul-mul-[la-bi] eš$_3$ e$_2$-an-na-⸢ke$_4$⸣
kug ^{d}inana-ke$_4$ ni$_2$ im-ši-ib-te-en-te

He made the pebbles rattle down the hills;
As if he were a dragon prowling the desert, there was no stopping him.

J. DELIVERING THE SECOND CHALLENGE

When the messenger had reached Aratta,
The people of Aratta
Came running to wonder at the pack-asses.
In the courtyard of Aratta
The messenger piled up the heaps of wheat, adding some for the tooth of the locust.
As if caused by rain and sun from heaven,[42]
Aratta was now full of wealth.
As gods returning to their dwellings[43]
Aratta's hunger was stilled.
The people of Aratta
[*Covered*] the fields with his water-soaked greenmalt.
After that, couriers and merchants [. . .]
[. . .] . . . [. . .]
. . . [. . .]
The citizens of Aratta *paid attention* [. . .]
He revealed the matter to Aratta.
Thus, in Aratta, from his hand [. . .]
To the lord of Unug[44] he [. . .] his hand.

Citizens of Aratta?

"As for us, in our sharpest hunger,
In our dire famine, let us prostrate ourselves to the lord of Kulab!"
The word-wise elders
Were wringing their hands, leaning against the wall.
To the lord they proferred their *treasure chests*.[45]

[. . .] . . . his scepter . . . in the midst of the palace [. . .]
[Openly] he spoke [the words he had learnt by heart]:
"[Your father, my king], sent me to you;
"Enmerkar, son of the Sun, sent me to you!"

Lord of Aratta

"What is it to me what your king spoke, what he said?"

Messenger

"This is what my king spoke, what he said:
"'My scepter's base is the power of overlordship;
"'Its crown provides a protective shadow for Kulab;
"'Under its starlike branches in the shrine Eana
"'Holy Inana finds her cool refreshment.

ğidru um-ta-an-kid$_7$ hu-mu-⸢un-da⸣-ğal$_2$
^{na4}gug ğiš dili ^{na4}za-gin$_3$ ğiš dili-gin$_7$ šu-ni-a hu-mu-un-ğal$_2$

en aratta^{ki}-ke$_4$ igi-mu-še$_3$ hu-mu-un-tum$_2$ ğa$_2$-a-ra ha-ma-an- dug$_4$

K. Aratta's Reply: Second Counterchallenge

ur$_5$-gin$_7$ hu-mu-na-ab-be$_2$-a-ka
nam-bi-še$_3$ itima$^!$-a KA ba-an-kur$_9$ šag$_4$ ka-tab-ba ba-an-nu$_2$

ud im-zal inim im-šar$_2$-šar$_2$
inim ka-še$_3$ nu-ğar-ra im-me
inim-ma še anše gu$_7$-a-gin$_7$ ğir$_3$ mi-ni-ib-niğin-e
i$_3$-ne-še$_3$ lu$_2$ lu$_2$-u$_3$-ra a-na na-an-dug$_4$
lu$_2$ lu$_2$-ra AŠ a-na na-an-tah
lu$_2$ lu$_2$-ra in-na-ab-be$_2$-a ur$_5$ he$_2$-en-na-nam-ma-am$_3$

kiğ$_2$-gi$_4$-a lugal-zu en kul-ab$_4$^{ki}-ra [u$_3$]-na-a-dug$_4$ u$_3$-na-de$_3$-tah
ğidru ğiš nam-me mu ğiš na-an-še$_{21}$-še$_{21}$
X [X] šu -na um-ma-ni-in-ğar igi um-ši-bar-bar
^{ğiš}ildag$_2$ nam-me ^{ğiš}šim-gig nam-me
^{ğiš}erin nam-me ^{ğiš}šu-ur$_2$-me nam-me
^{ğiš}ha-šu-ur$_2$ [nam-me ^{ğiš}nimbar] ⸢nam⸣-me
^{ğiš}esi nam-me [^{ğiš}za-ba-lum nam-me]
^{ğiš}asal-lam ^{ğiš}gigir-ra nam-me
^{ğiš}kid-da ^{ğiš}kuš-usan$_3$-na nam-me
kug-sig$_{17}$ nam-me urud nam-me
kug me-a zid kug-babbar nam-me
^{na4}gug nam-me ^{na4}za-gin$_3$ nam-me
ğidru um-ta-an-kid$_7$ hu-mu-un-da-ğal$_2$
^{na4}gug ğiš dili ^{na4}za-gin$_3$ ğiš dili-gin$_7$ šu-ni-a hu-mu-un-ğal$_2$

en kul-ab$_4$^{ki}-a-ke$_4$ igi-mu še$_3$ hu-mu-un-tum$_2$ e-ne-ra dug$_4$-mu-na-ab

L. Fourth Voyage: Aratta to Unug

ur$_5$-gin$_7$ hu-mu-na-ab-be$_2$-a-ka
kiğ$_2$-gi$_4$-a dur$_2$^{ur3} si gigir ku$_5$-ra$_2$-gin$_7$ ka si-il-la mu-un-ğin

anše edin-na par$_2$-rim$_4$-ma kaš$_4$ di-gin$_7$ kušu i$_3$-tag-tag-ge
ka-ni im-a bi$_2$-ib-zi-zi-zi
udu suluhu udu ⸢šur$_2$⸣-ba du$_7$-du$_7$-gin$_7$ dug$_3$ us$_2$ 1 mu-un-dab$_5$

"'If he *can cut a scepter from it,* let him hold it in his hand;[46]
"'Let him hold it in his hand like a string of carnelian and lapis lazuli beads;
"'Let the lord of Aratta bring that to me!' Tell him that!"

K. Aratta's Reply: Second Counterchallenge

This having been said,
(The lord of Aratta), because of this, entered his cella and lay there fasting.
When day broke he was *raving;*
He spoke *gibberish;*
He was stumbling around in words like a feeding donkey in wheat.[47]
Now, what could the one say to the other?
What could the one say in addition to the other?
What the one said to the other, it was thus:

"Messenger, speak to your king and tell him:
"A scepter, not of wood, nor with the name of wood[48]
"When ... it is taken in hand and inspected,
"Not ildag-wood, nor šimgig-wood,
"Nor cedar, nor cypress,
"Nor hašur, nor palm,
"Nor hardwood, nor zabalum,
"Nor poplar as in a chariot,
"Nor worked reed as in whip handles,
"Nor gold, nor copper,
"Nor genuine refined silver, nor silver,
"Nor carnelian, nor lapis lazuli—
"If he can cut a scepter from such a substance, let him show it;
"Let him hold it in his hand like a string of carnelian and lapis lazuli beads;
"Let the lord of Kulab bring that to me! Tell him that!"

L. Fourth Voyage: Aratta to Unug

When he had spoken in this vein
The messenger rushed off braying like a colt cut loose from the chariot's harness;
He raced like an onager running on dried-out soil,
Filling his mouth with wind;
He made a straight track, like the long-tufted sheep furiously butting (other) sheep.

M. Enmerkar's Solution: A Manmade Substance

sig$_4$ kul-ab$_4^{ki}$-a-ka ğir$_3$ hul$_2$ mi-ni-in-gub
lugal-a-ni en kul-ab$_4^{ki}$-a-ra
inim-inim-ma mu-na-ra-si-si
en-me-er-kar$_2$-ra ^{d}en-ki-ke$_4$ ğeštug$_2$ mu-na-⸢an⸣-šum$_2$
en-e agrig mah-a-[ni] a$_2$ ba-da-⸢an⸣-ağ$_2$
e$_2$-ni? [. . .]
lugal-e ⸢munsub⸣ [. . .] šu ba-ra-an-ti
mu-un-dul-gin$_7$ ⸢šu⸣ bi$_2$-[in-gur-gur] igi bi$_2$-⸢in⸣-ğa$_2$!-ğa$_2$!
^{na4}na KA.KA šim-gin$_7$ ⸢zu$_2$⸣ [ba-ni]-⸢in⸣-ra
gi su-lim-ma-ka i$_3$-gin$_7$ mu-ni-in-de$_2$
ud-ta ğissu-še$_3$ am$_3$-ed$_2$-e
ğissu-ta ud-še$_3$ am$_3$-ed$_2$-e
mu 5-am$_3$ mu 10-am$_3$ ba-zal-[la]-ri
gi su-lim-ma giğ$_4$-gin$_7$ bi$_2$-in-gaz
en-e igi hul$_2$-la im-ši-in-bar
i$_3$-li i$_3$-li kur šuba-a-ka sig$_3$-ga i-ni-in-de$_2$
en-e kiğ$_2$-gi$_4$-a kur-še$_3$ du-ur$_2$
ğidru šu-na mu-un-na-ğa$_2$-ğa$_2$

N. Fifth Voyage: Unug to Aratta

kiğ$_2$-gi$_4$-a aratta^{ki}-aš du-a-ni
u$_5^{mušen}$-gin$_7$ hur-sağ-ğa$_2$ nim-gin$_7$ sahar ⸢niğin⸣-a

HI.SUHUR^{ku6}-gin$_7$ kur ur$_3$-ur$_3$-ru-[da]-ni aratta^{ki}-aš ⸢ba⸣-teğ$_3$

O. Third Counterchallenge

kisal aratta^{ki}-ka ğiri$_3$ hul$_2$-la mi-ni-in-gub
ğidru TE SI NA mu-un-gub
šu kiğ$_2$ si bi$_2$-in-sa$_2$ a kiğ$_2$ ⸢bi$_2$-ib⸣-ak-e
en aratta^{ki}-ke$_4$ ğidru-ta igi tab-ba
itima-ka ki-tuš kug-ga-ni-a ni$_2$ im-kar$_2$-kar$_2$-ka
en-e ša$_3$-tam-a-ni-ir gu$_3$ mu-na-de$_2$-e
aratta^{ki} u$_8$ ⸢sag$_2$⸣-[gin$_7$] he$_2$-em kaskal-bi [kur] ⸢ki⸣-bal he$_2$-em

mah aratta^{ki} kug ^{d}inana-ke$_4$
en kul-ab$_4^{ki}$-ra mu-na-an-šum$_2$-ma-ta
lu$_2$ kiğ$_2$-gi$_4$-a mu-un-gi$_4$-a-ni
^{d}utu ed$_2$-de$_3$ inim dugud pa ed$_2$-de$_3$
a-da-al kug ^{d}inana-ke$_4$ igi me-ši-kar$_2$-kar$_2$

M. Enmerkar's Solution: A Manmade Substance

Joyfully he stepped into Kulab, the Brickwork.
To his king, the lord of Kulab,
He repeated the message word for word.
Enki now granted insight to Enmerkar.[49]
The lord gave orders to his chief steward.
[In] his house [. . .]
The king took a *hairy hide* [. . .]
As if wrapping (*something in it*), he *rolled it up* and looked at it.
With a pestle he pounded it like a herb
And poured (the mass) into a *gleaming* reed.
From the sunlight he brought it into the shadow,
And from the shadow he brought it into the sunlight.
Five, maybe ten years[50] passed,
And then he split the gleaming reed with an axe.
The lord looked at it with pleasure
And poured on *its mass* fine oil, oil from the bright mountains.
In the hands of the messenger who was to travel to the mountains
The lord then placed the scepter.

N. Fifth Voyage: Unug to Aratta

The messenger's race to Aratta
Was like the U-bird('s flight) over the hills, like a fly('s dashing) over the dust.
He darted over the highland like a swimming carp and reached Aratta.

O. Third Counterchallenge

Joyfully he stepped into the courtyard of Aratta
And put the scepter in his . . .
He polished the scepter and washed it.
The lord of Aratta *was blinded* by the scepter;
In his cella, his sacred room, undone by fear
The lord cried out to his šatam-official:
"Verily, Aratta is like *scattered* ewes: its road is now that of the rebel lands![51]
"Holy Inana now has given over
"Mighty Aratta to the lord of Kulab,
"Since upon this man, who sent his messenger
"To make the grave message as clear as sunlight,
"Holy Inana now seems to be looking with favor!

aratta^{ki}-a lul-e me-a he$_2$-en-de$_3$-dib-e
al me-da-aš šu al-zil$_2$-zil$_2$-i-a
me-en-de$_3$ su$_3$-ga lul-la-bi-še$_3$
en kul-ab$_4$^{ki}-ra ^{na4}gug lul-la-me-a mu-na-dur$_2$-ru-ne-en-de$_3$-en

en aratta^{ki}-ke$_4$ kiğ$_2$-gi$_4$-a-ar
inim-ma dub mah-gin$_7$ šu mu-na-an-sig$_{10}$
kiğ$_2$-gi$_4$-a lugal-zu en kul-ab$_4$^{ki}-a-ra u$_3$-na-dug$_4$ u$_3$-na-de$_3$-tah
ur na-an-gig$_2$-ge ur na-an-babbar-re
ur na-an-si$_4$-e ur na-an-dara$_4$-e
ur na-an-sig$_7$-sig$_7$-ge ur na-an-gun$_3$-gun$_3$^{gu2} ur hu-mu-ra-ab-šum$_2$-mu

ur-mu ur-ra-ni a-da-min$_3$ he$_2$-em-da-e
a$_2$-ğal$_2$ he$_2$-zu e-ne-ra dug$_4$-mu-na-ab

P. Sixth Voyage: Aratta to Unug

ur$_5$-gin$_7$ hu-mu-na-ab-be$_2$-a-ka
kiğ$_2$-gi$_4$-a u$_2$-lum-a-lam mu-un-ğin
sig$_4$ kul-ab$_4$^{ki}-ke$_4$ eğir sig$_{10}$-ga-gin$_7$ inim ⸢mu⸣-un-gi$_4$
ud$_5$$^{!}$-gin$_7$ ka gaba kur-ra-ka igi mi-ni-ib-il$_2$-il$_2$-i
mir$^{!}$ mah ul$_4$-ul$_4$-ta zig$_3$-ga-gin$_7$ e$_2$ me MIN$_3$ mu-un-ta-la$_2$-la$_2$
[X X X X]-ka sağ mi-ni-in-il$_2$

Q. Final Challenge

[...] aratta^{ki} -a-ke$_4$ [...]
ki-tuš-a-ni-ta a mah [ed$_2$-a-gin$_7$ mu-un-na-ab]-be$_2$
kiğ$_2$-gi$_4$-a en ⸢aratta⸣^{ki}-ra u$_3$-na-dug$_4$ u$_3$-na-de$_3$-tah
tug$_2$ na-an-gig$_2$-ge tug$_2$ na-an-babbar-re
tug$_2$ na-an-si$_4$-e tug$_2$ na-an-dara$_4$-e
tug$_2$ na-an-sig$_7$-sig$_7$-ge tug$_2$ na-an-gun$_3$-gun$_3$^{gu2} tug$_2$ ga-mu-na-ab-šum$_2$-<<mu>>
ur-mu gu$_2$-da ğal$_2$ ^{d}en-lil$_2$- la$_2$ ur šu ga-mu-na-tak$_4$
ur-mu ur-ra-ni a-da-min$_3$ he$_2$-em-di-e
a$_2$-ğal$_2$ he$_2$-zu-zu e-ne-ra dug$_4$-mu-na-ab
2-kam-ma-še$_3$ u$_3$-na-dug$_4$ u$_3$-na-de$_3$-tah
en$_3$-tukum-še$_3$ lul-da LI-a he$_2$-ni-ib-dib-e
iri-na udu-gin$_7$ igi-ni hu-mu-un-su$_8$-ub
e-ne sipad-bi-gin$_7$ eğir-bi he$_2$-em-us$_2$-e
du-a-ni kur kug ^{na4}za-gin$_3$-na
gi niğ$_2$-dub-ba-gin$_7$ gu$_2$ hu-mu-na-ab-ğar
kug-sig$_{17}$ kug-babbar sud-ra$_2$-ağ$_2$-bi

"This misery of Aratta, where shall it lead us?
"For how long shall the yoke-rope have to be our *lot*?
"Must we, because of this dire famine,
"crawl before the lord of Kulab in our stark hunger?"

The lord of Aratta then entrusted to the messenger
A message, important like a tablet.[52]
"Messenger, speak to your king, lord of Kulab, and say:
"A dog that is not black, a dog that is not white,
"A dog that is not brown, a dog that is not red,
"A dog that is not yellow, a dog that is not pied—such a dog he must give you!
"My dog will wrangle with his dog,
"So that the stronger one be known! Tell him that!"[53]

P. Sixth Voyage: Aratta to Unug

(The lord) having spoken to him in this vein,
The messenger set off *in all haste.*
Brickwork Kulab *answered like a* ....
Like a goat on the mountain slopes he lifted his eyes;
like a huge MIR snake coming out of the fields he...;
In ... he lifted his head.

Q. Final Challenge

[*The lord of*] of Aratta[54]...;
From his throne he spoke to him [like a raging torrent:]
"Messenger, when you speak to the lord of Aratta, say this:
"A cloth that is not black, a cloth that is not white,
"A cloth that is not brown, a cloth that is not red,
"A cloth that is not yellow, a cloth that is not pied—such a cloth I will give him!
"My dog is embraced by Enlil; this dog I will send to him.
"My dog will wrangle with his dog
"So that the stronger one be known. Tell him that!
"Second, when you speak to him, say also this:
"He must now stop prevaricating[55] and come to *a decision.*
"Those of his city shall walk before him like sheep,
"And he, like a shepherd, shall follow them.
"At his coming, the holy mound of lapis lazuli
"Shall humble itself before him like a crushed reed.
"They shall amass shining gold and silver

^{d}inana nin e$_2$-an-na-ra
kisal aratta[^{ki}]- ⸢ka⸣ gur$_7$-še$_3$ hu-mu-un-dub-dub-bu
3-kam-ma-[še$_3$] u$_3$-na-dug$_4$ u$_3$-na-de$_3$-tah
iri-ni ir$_7$-sağ^{mušen}-gin$_7$ ğiš-bi-ta na-an-tar-ta-ta-an

[. . .]-⸢gin$_7$⸣ na-an-dub$_2$-be$_2$-en
[ganba ğal$_2$-la]-⸢gin$_7$⸣ na-an-si-ig-en
[. . .] lil$_2$-e nam-mi-ni-in-dib-be$_2$-en
du-a-ni na$_4$ hur-sağ-ğa$_2$ šu u$_3$-mu-ni-in-ti
eš$_3$ gal eridug^{ki} abzu e$_2$-nun ha-ma-du$_3$-e
a-sal-bar-bi im-šu$_2$-ra-ke$_4$ šu ⸢ha⸣-[ma-ni]-ib-tag-ge
ğissu-bi kalam-[ma ha-ma]-ni-ib-la$_2$-la$_2$-e
inim dug$_4$-ga-ni [. . .]-šar$_2^{?}$-a-ka
ğiškim-a-ni [e-ne-ra] dug$_4$-mu-na-ab

ud-ba en$^{?}$ [. . .]-⸢ka⸣-am$_3$
[. . .] barag-ga dur$_2$ ğar-ra numun nun-na-ke$_4$-ne
[X X] diš-a mu$_2$-a
dug$_4$-ga-ni [mah]-am$_3$ šag$_4$-bi su-su-a-am$_3$
kiğ$_2$-gi$_4$-a ka-ni dugud šu nu-mu-un-da-an-gi$_4$-gi$_4$
bar kiğ$_2$-gi$_4$-a ka-ni dugud šu nu-mu-un-da-an-gi$_4$-gi$_4$-da-ka

en kul-ab$_4^{ki}$-a-ke$_4$ im-e šu bi$_2$-in-ra inim dub-gin$_7$ ⸢bi$_2$-in⸣-gub

ud-bi-ta inim im-ma gub-bu nu-ub-ta-ğal$_2$-la
i$_3$-ne-še$_3$ ^{d}utu ud ne-a ur$_5$ he$_2$-en-na-nam-ma-am$_3$
en kul-ab$_4^{ki}$-a-ke$_4$ ⸢inim⸣ [dub-gin$_7$] ⸢bi$_2$⸣-in-gub ur$_5$ ⸢he$_2$⸣-[en-na]-nam-ma

R. Seventh Voyage: Unug to Aratta

kiğ$_2$-gi$_4$-a mušen-gin$_7$ a$_2$ dub$_2$ i$_3$-ak-e
ur-bar-ra maš$_2$-e us$_2$-sa-gin$_7$ guru$_5$-uš i$_3$-bur$_2$-bur$_2$-re
hur-sağ 5 hur-sağ 6 hur-sağ 7-e im-me-re-bal-bal
igi mu-un-il$_2$ aratta^{ki}-aš ba-teğ$_3$

S. Aratta's Reaction

kisal aratta^{ki}-ka ğiri$_3$ hul$_2$-la mi-ni-in-gub
nam-nir-ğal$_2$ lugal-a-na mu-un-zu
bur$_2$-ra-bi inim šag$_4$-ga-na bi$_2$-ib$_2$-be$_2$
kiğ$_2$-gi$_4$-a en aratta^{ki}-ra mu-na-ab-bal-e
a-a-zu lugal-⸢mu⸣ mu-e-ši-in-gi$_4$-in-nam
en unug^{ki}-⸢ga en⸣ kul-ab$_4^{ki}$-a-ke$_4$ mu-[e-ši]-in-gi$_4$-in-nam

"For Inana of the Eana
"In the courtyard of Aratta in great piles.
"Third, when you speak to him, say also this:
"Beware lest I make (the people/Aratta) flee from their city like a dove from its tree,
"Lest I make them fly away like [a bird from its permanent nest],
"Lest I put a price on them [as on mere merchandise],
"[Lest I *make*] the wind *carry them away*!
"At his coming, when he holds the precious stones of the hills,
"He must build for me the shrines of Eridug, Abzu, and Enun;
"He must adorn for me its architrave with a *slip of clay;*
"He must make it spread its shadow over the Land for me!
"When he speaks …
"Tell him this as a sign for him!"

Thereupon the lord …
… on the throne dais, on the throne, the noble seed of princes,
… grown all alone.
His speech was very grand, its meaning very deep;
The messenger's mouth was too *heavy;* he could not repeat it.
Because the messenger's mouth was too *heavy,* and he could not repeat it,
The lord of Kulab patted some clay and put the words on it as on a tablet.
Before that day, there had been no putting words on clay;
But now, when the sun rose on that day—so it was:
The lord of Kulab had put words as on a tablet—so it was!

R. Seventh Voyage: Unug to Aratta

The messenger was like a bird flapping its wings.
Raging like a wolf chasing a kid
He crossed five, six, seven mountain ranges.
Lifting his head, he had reached Aratta.

S. Aratta's Reaction

Joyfully he stepped into the courtyard of Aratta
And proclaimed the preeminence of his king.
He spoke out what was in his heart
And transmitted it to the lord of Aratta:
"Your father, my king, has sent me;
"The lord of Unug and Kulab has sent me."

Lord of Aratta

lugal-zu ⸢dug$_4$⸣-[ga-ni] nam-mu tah-a-ni nam-mu

Messenger

lugal-mu [a-na bi$_2$]-⸢in⸣-dug$_4$ a-na bi$_2$-in-tah-am$_3$
lugal-mu [^{giš}mes] gal dumu ^{d}en-lil$_2$-la$_2$-ke$_4$
ğiš-bi [an-ki]-da mu$_2$-a
⸢pa⸣-[bi an]-ne$_2$ us$_2$-sa-am$_3$
[ur$_2$-bi ki-a] gub-ba-bi
nam-en nam-lugal-la pa ed$_2$ ak-a
en-me-er-kar$_2$ dumu ^{d}utu-ke$_4$ im ma-an-šum$_2$
en aratta^{ki} ke$_4$ im igi u$_3$-ni-bar šag$_4$ inim-ma u$_3$-bi$_2$-zu

a-na ma-ab-be$_2$-en-na-bi u$_3$-mu-e-dug$_4$
a ru-a su$_6$ ^{na4}za-gin$_3$ KEŠ$_2$-da-ar
ab$_2$ kal-la-ga-ni kur me sikil-la-ka tud-da-ar
sahar unug^{ki}-ka[*sic*][56] a$_2$ ed$_2$-a-ar
ubur ab$_2$ zid-da-ka ga gu$_7$-a-ar
kul-ab$_4$^{ki} kur me gal-gal-la-ka nam-en-na tum$_2$-ma-ar
en-me-er-kar$_2$ dumu ^{d}utu-ra
inim-bi eš$_3$ e$_2$-an-na-ka inim dug$_3$ ga-mu-na-ab-dug$_4$
ği$_6$-par$_4$ ^{giš}mes gibil-gin$_7$-gin$_7$ gurun il$_2$-la-na
lugal-mu en kul-ab$_4$^{ki}-ra šu-a ga-mu-na-ab-gi$_4$

ur$_5$-gin$_7$ hu-mu-na-ab-be$_2$-a-ka
en aratta^{ki}-ke$_4$ kiğ$_2$-gi$_4$-a-ar
^{im}ŠU.RIN.NA-ni šu ba-ši-in-ti
en aratta^{ki}-ke$_4$ im-ma igi i-ni-in-bar
inim dug$_4$-ga gag-am$_3$ sağ-ki mi-re$_2$-da-am$_3$
en aratta^{ki}-ke$_4$ imŠU.RIN.NA-ni igi im-bar-bar-re

III. THE RESOLUTION

T. The Final Confrontation

ud-ba en men nam-en-na tum$_2$-ma dumu ^{d}en-lil$_2$-la$_2$-ke$_4$
^{d}iškur an-ki-a gu$_3$ nun-bi di-dam
ud du$_7$-du$_7$ ug gal-la ki-[X X]-ka nam-mi-ni-in-gub
kur-kur [. . .] ⸢mu-un⸣-tuk$_4$-tuk$_4$-e
hur-sağ [. . . mu]- ⸢un⸣-da-peš$_{11}$-peš$_{11}$-e
ni$_2$ [me]-lam$_2$$^{?}$ [X X] gaba-na ğal$_2$-la-bi
hur-sağ giri$_{17}$-zal-la gu$_3$ mi-ni-in-il$_2$
aratta^{ki} bar ud-bi šag$_4$ hur-sağ-ğa$_2$-ka
gig ni$_2$-bi mu$_2$-a gu$_2$ ni$_2$-bi an-ga-mu$_2$-a

Lord of Aratta
"What is it to me what your king spoke, what he said?"
Messenger
"This is what my king spoke, what he said:
"My King is a tall MES-tree, the son of Enlil.
"This tree has grown so tall that it links heaven and earth;
"Its crown reaches heaven;
"Its roots are set fast in the earth.
"He who has manifested lordship and kingship,
"Enmerkar, son of the Sun, gave me this tablet.
"O lord of Aratta, when you have read this tablet, learned the gist of the message,
"When you will have replied to me whatever you want,
"To the scion of the one with the gleaming beard,
"To him whom the mighty cow bore on the hill of the lustrous power,
"To him who grew up on the soil of Aratta,
"To him who was suckled by the teat of the true cow,
"To him, suited for office in Kulab, mountain of the great powers,
"To Enmerkar, son of the Sun,
"I will speak that word as glad tidings in the shrine Eana.
"In his Gipar, bearing fruit like a young MES-tree,
"I shall repeat it to my king, the lord of Kulab."

This having been said,
The lord of Arratta took from the messenger
The tablet (and held it) next to a brazier.
The lord of Aratta inspected the tablet.
The spoken words were mere wedges[57]—his brow darkened.
The lord of Aratta kept looking at the tablet (in the light of) the brazier.

III. THE RESOLUTION

T. The Final Confrontation

At that moment the lord worthy of the holy crown, the son of Enlil
Iškur thundered in heaven and on earth.
A storm he caused, raging like a great lion.
He made the highlands quake,
He shook the hillsides.
The awesome radiance ... of his breast ...
He made the highland,
Aratta's parched flank in the midst of the mountains, raise its voice in joy.
Wheat began growing of its own accord, and so did chickpeas;

gig ni$_2$-bi mu$_2$-a gur$_7$ [X (X)]-ka
en aratta^{ki}-ra mu-na-ni-in-⸢ku$_4$⸣-[ku$_4$]
kisal aratta^{ki}-a-ka igi-ni-še$_3$ i-im-dub$^?$
en aratta^{ki}-ke$_4$ gig-e igi bi$_2$-in-du$_8$
kiğ$_2$-gi$_4$-a igi sig$_3$-sig$_3$-a-ni mu-un-ši-ib-UR$_2$xTAK$_4$.UR$_2$xTAK$_4$-e

en aratta^{ki}-ke$_4$ kiğ$_2$-gi$_4$-a-ar gu$_3$ mu-un-na-de$_2$-e
mah-bi ^{d}inana nin kur-kur-ra-ke$_4$
iri-ni aratta^{ki} šu li-bi$_2$-in-dag unug^{ki}-e la-ba-an-KA
e$_2$-za-gin$_3$-na-ka-ni šu li-bi$_2$-in-dag eš$_3$ e$_2$-an-na-ka la-ba-an-dug$_4$
kur me sikil-la-ka šu li-bi$_2$-in-dag sig$_4$ kul-ab$_4$^{ki}-a-ke$_4$ la-ba-an-dug$_4$

^{ğiš}nu$_2$ še-er-kan$_2$ dug$_4$ šu li-bi$_2$-in-dag ^{ğiš}nu$_2$ gi-rin-na la-ba-an-dug$_4$
en-ra šu sikil-la-ka-ni šu li-bi$_2$-in-dag en unug^{ki}-ga en kul-ab$_4$^{ki}-a-ra la-ba-an-dug$_4$
aratta^{ki} zid-da gub$_3$-bu-ba
^{d}inana nin kur-kur-ra-ke$_4$
a mah ed$_2$-a-gin$_7$ mu-un-na-niğin
lu$_2$-bi-ne lu$_2$ lu$_2$-ta dar-a
lu$_2$ ^{d}dumu-zid-de$_3$ lu$_2$-ta ed$_2$-a-me-eš
inim kug ^{d}inana ki-bi-še$_3$ ğar-ğar-me-eš
ur igi-ğal$_2$-la ⸢DA⸣.A.SAR ^{d}dumu-zid-da he$_2$-ši-im-niğin
⸢ul$_4$ ğa$_2$-nam-ma⸣ dumu ur$_4$-[. . .]
[igi] a-ma-ru-ka gub-ba-me-eš
eğir a-ma-ru ba-ur$_3$-ra-ta
^{d}inana nin kur-kur-ra-ke$_4$
nam-gal ki-ağ$_2$ ^{d}dumu-zid-da-ke$_4$
a nam-til$_3$-la-ka mu-un-ne-sud-sud
gu$_2$ kalam-ma-ka ğiš mu-un-ne-en-ğal$_2$

ur igi-ğal$_2$-la du-a-ni
^{tug2}sağšu gun$_3$-a ugu-na i-im-šu$_2$
tug$_2$ piriğ-piriğ-⸢ga$_2$⸣ zag mu-ni-in-KEŠ$_2$
[X] il$_2$-⸢la⸣ X šu? mi-ni-in-du$_8$-[X]- ⸢am$_3$⸣
[. . .]-te-na mi-ni-in-dug$_4$
[. . .] nin [. . .]⸢ba⸣-an-PA^{di}
[. . .]-a-ni

U. The Argument Resolved

[. . .]^{d}inana
en$_3$-du-ni ^{d}ama-ušumgal-an-na nitalam-a-na ba-dug$_3$
ud-bi-ta ğeštug$_2$ kug ⸢ğeštug$_2$⸣ [kug] ^{d}dumu-zid-da-ke$_4$

The wheat grown of its own accord, into the granary of ...
They brought for the lord of Aratta,
And before him they heaped it up in the courtyard of Aratta.
The lord of Aratta looked at the wheat;
The messenger looked *amazed,* he ...

The lord of Aratta cried to the messenger:
"In her majesty has Inana, Lady of all the countries,
"Not yet abandoned Aratta to surrender it to Unug!
"Nor did she abandon her Ezagina to surrender it to the Eana;
"Nor did she abandon the mountain of the shining powers to surrender it to Kulab, the Brickwork;
"Nor did she abandon her sweet bed to surrender it to the flowery bed;[58]
"Nor did she abandon the purity of her lord to surrender it to the lord of Unug and Kulab!
"(On the contrary), the right and left flanks of Aratta—
"Inana, Lady of all the countries,
"Protects them when the mighty flood is rising!
"Its people are distinct from other people;
"They are a nation Dumuzid selected among the other nations,
"One that firmly establishes the holy word of Inana!
"So let now the Wise Dog and the ... of Dumuzid lock on to each other.
"Quick, come, [my] young ...!"
"They were steadfast before the flood.
"After the flood had swept over,
"Inana, Lady of all the countries,
"Out of her great love for Dumuzid,
"Sprinkled the water of life over them,
"And subjected the Land to them!"[59]

The Wise Dog, when he came,
Had covered his head with a pied head cloth
And wrapped his body in a lion skin
...
...
...
...

U. The Argument Resolved

Inana ...
Her song pleased Ama-ušumgalana, her husband,
And since that day, for the holy ear, the ear of Dumuzid,

šu mu-ni-in-du$_7$ šir$_3$ mu-⸢ni⸣-[in]-dug$_4$ inim mu-ni-in-zu

um-ma kur me sikil-še$_3$ du-a-ni

ki-sikil ud-da-na til-la-gin$_7$ im-ma-na-ta-ed$_2$
šim-zid-da igi-na mu-un-gun$_3$
[tug$_2$] babbar-ra zag mu-ni-in-KEŠ$_2$
[aga] zid-da iti$_6$-gin$_7$ mu-un-ed$_2$
[X] X X sağ si ba-ni-in-sa$_2$
[nitalam]-a-ni en-me-er-kar$_2$ barag-ge$_4$ mu-un-da-ab-si
[. . .] um-mi-in-zi-zi
[ga-nam] im-da-lu-lu aratta^{ki}-aš u$_8$-da sila$_4$-bi
[ga-nam im]-da-lu-lu aratta^{ki}-aš ud$_5$-da maš$_2$-bi
[ga-nam im]-da-lu-lu aratta^{ki}-aš ab$_2$-da amar-bi
[ga-nam] ⸢im⸣-da-lu-lu aratta^{ki}-aš eme$_5$ dur$_3$^{ur2} im$_2$ gig$_2$-ga-<bi>
aratta^{ki}-a na-an-da-be$_2$-a
[gur$_7$-še$_3$] he$_2$-em-dub-dub gu$_2$ he$_2$-em-ğar-ğar
[he$_2$]-⸢ğal$_2$⸣ za-a he$_2$-ğal$_2$-zu
[. . .] en aratta^{ki}-ra u$_3$-mu-ni-in-ak
[. . .]X X X-ra he$_2$-en-[X (X)]
[. . .] mu-un-di-ni-ib-X-e
[. . .] mu-un-ta-ed$_2$
[. . .] si mu-un-na-ab-sa$_2$

Three lines missing.

[. . .] me-te-aš [. . .]-ğal$_2$
[. . .]X SI i-lu šag$_4$-[ga . . .] X
[. . .]-ni-a he$_2$-ğal$_2$-zu nagga [. . .]
[. . .]^{d}en-lil$_2$-le sağ-eš mu-ri-in-rig$_7$ [X]-⸢la⸣-la-ğa$_2$ he$_2$-zu-zu
[. . .]kar$_2$ a-a-ni nu-lam-lam a nu-un-de$_2$
^{d}en-[lil$_2$] [lugal] ⸢kur⸣-kur-ra-ke$_4$ hu-mu-un-kar$_2^{?}$-re ni$_2$-ba
eš$_2$-gar$_3$ ⸢im⸣-ma-an-du$_3$-a-gin$_7$
nam-lu$_2$-u$_{18}$-[lu] aratta^{ki}-a-ke$_4$
kug-sig$_{17}$ kug ^{na4}[za]-gin$_3$ bala ak-de$_3$ eš$_2$-gar$_3$ X (X) X
lu$_2$ gurun kug-sig$_{17}$ gurun ğiš gub-bu-de$_3$
^{ği}peš$_3$ ğeštin-ba niğ$_2$-ta ub$_4$-ba-gin$_7$ gur$_7$ gal-še$_3$ [u$_3$]-mu-un-dub

^{na4}za-gin$_3$ duru$_5$ ur$_2$-ba mu-un-bur$_2$-re-ne
^{gi}ušub pa-ba mu-un-ta-bal-e-ne
^{d}inana nin e$_2$-an-na-ra
kisal e$_2$-an-na^{ki}-ka gur$_7$-še$_3$ mu-un-dub-bu-ne

She perfects it, singing the song and teaching the words.[60]

The Wise Woman,[61] when she came to the mountain of the shining Powers,
Went up to him like a maiden whose period is at an end;
She painted her eyes with kohl,
She donned a dazzling white robe,
She made the true crown sparkle like moonlight,
She arranged [*her tresses*?] on her head;
She sat her [spouse] Enmerkar on the throne with her (and spoke):
"When you have raised ...
"[Verily,] for Aratta ewes and their lambs shall multiply;
"[Verily,] for Aratta goats and their kids shall multiply;
"[Verily, for Aratta] cows and their calves shall multiply;
"[Verily, for Aratta] donkey mares and their swift foals shall multiply!
"Since in Aratta they will now agree,
"They will heap up ... in piles
"The abundance that is truly yours.
"When you have instituted [*trade*] with the lord of Aratta,
"He will [...]
"He did [...]
"He came forth [...]
"He set right [...]
"[...]
"[...]
"[...]
"[...] what is fitting [...]
"[...] the ilu-song of the heart [...]
"[...] your abundance in his [...] is *tin* [...]
"[...] Enlil has granted you; my [luxuriousness] be known!
"[...] his father was not fertile, produced no semen.[62]
"Enlil, King of all countries,
"Has now established this execution of the tasks:
"The people of Aratta
"Have as their task the trading of gold and lapis lazuli
"And the fashioning of golden fruits and fruity bushes
"Laden with figs and grapes...; they shall heap up these fruits in great piles;
"They shall dig out flawless lapis lazuli in lumps;
"They shall remove the crowns of the sweet reeds,
"And for Inana, Lady of the Eana,
"They shall heap them up in piles in the courtyard of the Eana.

lugal-mu ğa$_2$-nu na ga-e-ri na-ri-mu he$_2$-e-dab$_5$
inim ga-ra-ab-dug$_4$ ğizzal he$_2$-e-ak
lu$_2$ x ⸢BI$^?$ e⸣ kur-kur-ra un-e u$_3$-⸢un⸣-pad$_3$
[nam-lu$_2$]-⸢ulu$_3$⸣ aratta^{ki}-[ke$_4$]
[X]-me-še$_3$ i-im-da he$_2$-em-me-ne
ğa$_2$-e gu$_2$-e-ta du-a-mu-ne
⸢nam-lugal⸣-mu nin mul-mul-e ma-an-šum$_2$
^{d}ğeštin-an-na [...]

iri-ba lil$_2$ [...]
ezen nu-mu-[...]
ud-šu$_2$-uš nam-[...]
About six lines missing

"Now, my king, I shall advise you: heed my counsel;
"I shall speak a word: listen!
"Having chosen a man from a foreign country,
"The people of Aratta
"Shall say: '[. . .]'
"When I go from here [*to there*?],
"My kingship the starry Lady gave me,
"Geštinana [. . .]"

In that city [. . .]
Festivals were not [. . .]
Daily [. . .]
About six lines missing

Notes

[1] There is a lacuna of about five lines at this point.

[2] Five or six lines are missing.

[3] See Vanstiphout 1992c.

[4] See Vanstiphout 1994.

[5] There is a Sumerian proverb that illustrates the prime importance of grain: "Whosoever possesses gold, or silver, or cattle, or sheep / shall wait at the gate of him who possesses grain." This proverb is used as the argument for the conclusive verdict—in favor of grain—at the end of the Disputation between Ewe and Grain (Alster and Vanstiphout 1987: 30–31 and 39).

[6] The text is not yet absolutely clear at this point.

[7] For an indication of the sigla, provenance, and publication (if any) of the tablets, see the Oxford web site: www-etcsl.orient.ox.ac.uk/section1/b1823.htm.

[8] In all probability this fragment comes from Nippur.

[9] Or perhaps better "against."

[10] An epithet for the great gods.

[11] "Carp flood" is a traditional poetic term for agricultural abundance.

[12] Dilmun, the present island Bahrain, is used here as a symbol for foreign trade, the major topic of this poem.

[13] The Gipar is to be taken as Inana's private room, or bower, in the Eana.

[14] "Power" translates the untranslatable Sumerian term ME, whose meaning is somewhat akin to "quintessence." In the present context, it seems to denote something like *charisma* or *karma* or *baraka*—an attribute reserved for gods and kings.

[15] Highly uncertain. The Sumerian term is PA.A, and PA can be read as ğidru "staff, scepter." From the context, a meaning like palanquin seems also possible.

[16] Another name for Inana's spouse Dumuzid.

[17] Inana, whose word the messenger is carrying.

[18] I.e., "to avoid this, this is what Aratta must do."

[19] The interpretation of the Spell of Nudimmud is still in dispute. An alternative reading, which puts it in the past, not in the (immediate) future, is not impossible.

Grammar and philology could bear such a reading. Yet the style of the episode and certainly its meaning and function in the story argue strongly for my interpretation. Putting it in the past cannot be of any use in the development of the narrative. Reference to the future—as one expects from a spell—can and does, since it makes a very neat and sophisticated pendant to Enmerkar's invention of cuneiform, which accompanies the last challenge.

[20] "The whole world of well-ruled people" refers to the imagined or ideological state of Ur III Sumer, described in its different provinces, to wit Šubur and Hamazi (north and east), Sumer and Akkad (center), and Martu (west).

[21] The Sumerian word for debate, adaman duga, is also the term for formal school disputations. It also occurs as a qualification in the last lines of Enmerkar and Ensuhgirana. This has led some scholars to classify both that poem and Enmerkar and the Lord of Aratta as disputations. I do not think that there are sufficient grounds for this.

[22] The threefold series of challenges and replies going to and fro between Unug and Aratta works out naturally at a total of seven journeys, since the series starts at Unug but ends in Aratta and is not merely a sequence of challenge-and-response: the responses carry their own challenges. The messenger also has to travel over seven mountain ranges. This is a fine instance of the very sophisticated interpretation or reuse of a common folktale technique.

[23] The messenger has had to learn the message by heart. At the occasion of the ultimate message from Enmerkar this will cause a problem. Enmerkar will find a highly appropriate solution.

[24] Presumably the messenger now recites the spell of Nudimmud, but somewhat unexpectedly the spell itself is not repeated.

[25] Unclear. Why should Enmerkar have been born on the soil of Aratta?

[26] Note that the lord of Aratta's answer does not reply to the challenge as such, nor does the spell of Nudimmud seem to have had any effect.

[27] The mountains are here represented as a throne, which is "embellished" by Inana when she sits on it.

[28] Traditional "sacrifices" accompanying an entreaty or appeal to the gods.

[29] This traditional way of expressing a small number or a short time always puts the smaller number before the larger one, somewhat against our expectation.

[30] That is, the lord of Aratta is willing to join battle only in a new kind of contest: a contest of cleverness. In doing so, he is laying down the rules (the negative conditions in lines 279–280). If his antagonist is unable to fulfill these conditions—"or cannot fathom the meaning of the contest"—he will lose, just like a fighting bull that does not reckon with the strength of its opponent.

[31] The second time the oral means of communication is highlighted.

[32] Both similes are about the aspect of the mountains' bare flanks reflecting the blood-red light of the westering sun and the pale sheen of the moon.

[33] I.e., Inana.

[34] I.e., he may not collect the wheat en route from Unug to Aratta.

[35] Battle is called "the dance of Inana."

[36] Here and in line 302 we find again an insistence on the spoken word as the only means of communication.

[37] Enmerkar, who elsewhere is called "son of the Sun."

[38] This is, of course, a stupendous operation. Is Enmerkar collecting a vast amount of water? If so, to what purpose? The passage remains unclear and physically impossible: it is very hard to connect the Euphrates to the Tigris when based in Uruk.

[39] For the first time the notion of a tablet is introduced. This will finally lead up to the solution of the communication problem much later on. Here the tablet only figures as a rather involved epithet of Nisaba, goddess of both wheat and writing. The reader is warned.

[40] Nisaba is identical to Nanibgal.

[41] The meaning is not altogether clear. Does it mean: "if he can make a scepter like this"? The broader meaning, however, is clear: if the Lord of Aratta should surrender his scepter—however he came by it—to Enmerkar, he would thereby accept Enmerkar's superiority! It is quite possible that Enmerkar's "scepter" is in fact the holy MES-tree of Unug. Enmerkar then seems to offer a small piece of the tree to the lord of Aratta so that he may share in its authority under the superior rule of Unug. The lord of Aratta counters this by agreeing to accepts Unug's overlordship only if an impossible scepter is given to him.

[42] I.e., by the normal succession of the seasons, implying sowing and reaping.

[43] After having been feasted?

[44] Thus the text. A mistake for Aratta? Owing to the state of preservation (broken passage; only one manuscript), the matter cannot as yet be decided.

[45] Perhaps an indication of the outcome of the whole story, which is the institution of trade. Do the elders offer their treasure hoards in return for Enmerkar's unexpected supply of wheat?

[46] See above, note 39.

[47] A fine simile, making clever use of the fact that grain has just arrived in Aratta.

[48] The section ĞIŠ (wood) of the great lexical list ur_5-ra *hubullu* contains a number of entries beginning with the ĞIŠ sign but that designate objects that are strictly speaking not made out of wood. It is probable that the meaning here is that a clever use of the lexical lists as a solution to the riddle is not allowed.

[49] Enki appears here in his customary role as the helper of heroes—and in this case as the god of technique as well as understanding.

[50] It is uncertain but not impossible that a period of ten years is really intended. The Sumerian word mu can also mean "time(s)." The process apparently involves braying and macerating hides and pouring the bone-glue into a hollow reed to let it set and harden. This may have taken considerable time, but ten years seems excessive. Still, this is undoubtedly the first instance of a manmade substance in human history.

[51] The image is that of a city vanquished and destroyed by barbarians. Its populace is then taken away to the foreign countries.

[52] As the text unfolds, the references to Enmerkar's great invention become clearer and clearer.

[53] There is much literature about these lines but little doubt that ur here does indeed mean "dog." An almost identical passage occurs in the animal section of the lexical list ur_5-ra *hubullu*.

[54] This is certainly a mistake for Unug.

[55] The text has a term that implies subterfuge.

[56] Scribal mistake. Must be aratta^{ki}-ka.

[57] This reading has been challenged on the grounds that Sumerian gag "nail, wedge" is not the technical term for cuneiform signs or their elements. But that is just the point. How is the lord of Aratta supposed to have known this?

[58] An allusion to the opening challenge of the poem Enmerkar and Ensuhgirana.

[59] The "them" is very ambiguous, as is much of this passage.

[60] Could this be a reference to the poem itself? The colophon is missing, so we do not know to which divine patron it was dedicated.

[61] Although the term used here (um-ma) means "mother" or "old woman," the reference is in all probability to Inana herself. The function of a mother/old woman as a wise woman is well nigh universal.

[62] The passage remains frustratingly unclear. Does line 615 refer to the lord of Aratta (being, of course, the father in question)? In that case, is then the "man from a foreign country" Enmerkar, who is now elected by the people of Aratta as their own "man" ("the man from X" can mean "the king of X")?

III

The Lugalbanda Poems

Introduction

There can be but little doubt that the two poems that have Lugalbanda as their hero belong together. Neither of them is a complete story without the other. In the broadest outline the complete story runs somewhat like this.

I. Lugalbanda in the Wilderness

Enmerkar of Unug wants to conquer Aratta. During the march, Lugalbanda (his son?[1]) falls mortally ill and is abandoned in a cave in the mountains. He prays to the great luminaries, who save his life. Being all alone, he reinvents fire, cooking, and baking. He captures a wild bull and a wild goat. Acting on a portentous dream, he sacrifices these animals to the great fods. A band of spirits[2] arrives. The hero masters them with the help of Utu. There seems to follow a battle between the forces of light and the forces of darkness. The former seem to win this battle.

II. The Return of Lugalbanda

Lugalbanda is now stranded in the highlands. He decides to go and look for the Anzud bird, who rules over that region. He feasts Anzud's chick so well that it is stuffed with food and probably asleep when its parents return from foraging; therefore, it does not answer their call. The frightened parents are very happy when Lugalbanda appears and tells them what has happened. Anzud rewards him with the gift of superhuman speed. He returns to his companions, who are laying siege to Aratta. To force a decision, Enmerkar sends Lugalbanda back to Unug in order to ask for Inana's advice. In a single day Lugalbanda reaches Unug, and Inana gives her advice. Aratta seemingly submits peacefully.

The main arguments—or evidence—for regarding these two poems as a single story may be summarized as follows.[3]

First, there is the general framework. The campaign that Enmerkar undertakes against Aratta stops being the main story line at about line 132 of the first part (Lugalbanda in the Wilderness), when Lugalbanda's brothers abandon him in the mountains, and only resurfaces seamlessly, and as miraculously as Lugalbanda himself, at line 220 of the second part (The Return of Lugalbanda). In addition, it is made clear that campaign would have remained inconclusive at best but for the reappearance of Lugalbanda. On another level one may also point to the fact that Enmerkar seems to be the main hero at the outset of the first part but that he plays a role again only after Lugalbanda has come back and that from that point onward Enmerkar and Lugalbanda share the position of protagonist. It is important to note that indeed Lugalbanda will enforce Unug's victory—but that he does so in the service of Enmerkar. His major contribution consists in being an incredibly effective messenger, but the message he is to carry is Enmerkar's. Thus it is easily seen that the larger part of Lugalbanda's adventures or, perhaps better, tribulations in the two poems *together* form the middle part of a larger single story, which begins with LB I line 1 and only ends with LB II line 417.

There is also a consideration of formal matter. Lugalbanda in the Wilderness starts with an introductory passage of almost twenty lines taking us back to the days long past, when Unug was ruled by the glorious King Enmerkar. The Return of Lugalbanda starts without any introduction, simply stating that Lugalbanda is lost in the highlands. While it is regrettable that we still lack the final verses of Lugalbanda in the Wilderness, the text that we have—still poorly understood, alas—gives no indication that we are drawing to a conclusive ending. In other words, the first part seems to have no ending, and the second part has no beginning. While it is true that there are some texts that start *in medias res,* they are very rare, and in the whole of the epic corpus we know of only one example.[4]

Third, there is the matter of contents. As stated above, the final part of Lugalbanda in the Wilderness is still poorly understood, but what goes on between line 133 and certainly 394 describes not merely Lugalbanda's survival; it describes also how he acquires the special protection of the gods and therewith his special status, which may be compared to that of a savior saint.[5] This sanctity in the sense of divine election and protection, coupled with immunity to even supernatural dangers (the demonic forces at the end of LB I; Anzud) straddles both parts and finally leads to the acquisition of superhuman—but secret—powers. These in turn are necessary for the unfolding of the plot and the resolution of the difficulties Enmerkar—in the "outer plot"—is experiencing. In other words, everything hangs together, but only if we see the poems as a narrative unit.

In the fourth instance, it is striking that both poems make heavy use of a specific stylistic device. There are four passages in part I[6] that, significant as they may be, are mere descriptions interrupting the flow of narration, and they occur at crucial points. The same device is found in part II at least four times.[7] There are also other major stylistic points that indicate the unity of both parts.[8] Furthermore, there are many other features, substantial as well as structural and textual, that hold the two poems together. This should be studied in detail, if only to understand the poems better. Here we give only a few examples. First, the introduction to LB I mentions the glorious days when Enmerkar ruled over Unug; the same theme forms the introduction to Enmerkar's message in LB II. Second, the motif of the victuals (or the *viaticum*) left by the companions for the presumably dying Lugalbanda (LB I lines 85–115) is not only repeated, in a way, by the feast the hero sets before the great gods (LB I lines 371–394), but it is taken up again in LB II in the form of the way in which the hero regales Anzud's young (LB II lines 50–62). Third, the way in which Lugalbanda is abandoned by his companions in LB I is mirrored by the way in which the hero refuses any fellow-traveler on his second heroic journey in LB II. Fourth, while the central part of the story—Lugalbanda alone—is a movement from abandonment to reunion, the "outer frame" is a movement from Unug to Aratta in LB I, and vice versa in LB II.[9]

Yet, be all that as it may, there remains the fact that the two parts are consistently presented by the ancients themselves as two poems—but always as a pair.[10] Therefore, the situation seems to be this: the two parts were regarded as two closely linked installments of one long story, elegantly held together by an outer framework (the campaign against Aratta and Enmerkar's tribulations and ultimate deliverance by the help of the savior saint Lugalbanda). The two parts are then more specifically about Lugalbanda proper. In LB I we see his evolution from an abandoned weakling to the savior of his people, in close alliance with the gods and the powers of light against the powers of darkness. LB II describes the manner in which he acquires the superhuman qualities with which he brings the difficulties, and the full story, to a successful ending.

Lugalbanda in the Wilderness
Introduction

From the viewpoint of the unified outer framework, the first poem contains two parts. The first part deals with Enmerkar's campaign against Aratta, which will be taken up again in The Return of Lugalbanda. The second part, which starts at line 140, is exclusively about Lugalbanda.

In detail we see Enmerkar calling up his troops for an unmotivated campaign against Aratta and the start of this campaign. While the army is marching on, Lugalbanda falls ill in a desolate spot in the mountains. His companions leave him well-provisioned but uncertain of his chances of survival. Lugalbanda's further adventures are apparently presented as three successive night-and-day periods. Lugalbanda prays to the great luminaries (the setting sun, the evening star, the moon, and the rising sun); they save his life. Being left all by himself he (re)invents fire-making, cooking, and trapping; he captures a wild buffalo and some goats. In an ominous dream he is told to sacrifice these animals—and foretold of his special status. The next day he prepares a banquet for the great gods. In the evening (?) there arrives a band of spirits of the night. This poorly understood passage has been interpreted as a cosmic battle between the forces of darkness and the forces of light. These spirits (cosmic forces?) are presented as being both good and evil. A difficult section (lines 422–441) probably describes the exaltation of Lugalbanda as a "herald of heaven," but some of these lines may refer to the sun god himself and are as such subject to further study, as is the whole of the text starting from line 395; however, since the close relationship between the sun god and the heroic kings of Unug pervades the Aratta cycle as well as the Gilgamesh cycle, and since the central part of the double story consists of a graduated ascent to exaltation, culminating in Lugalbanda's manifestation as the holy savior of his people in the latter half of LB II, the hesitations about Lugalbanda's status may well be intentional: at every step he becomes a bit more exalted—or Sun-like. A multitude of stars, called the favorites of Inana, comes out, and it is possible that battle ensues. Then the sun rises. Possibly the battle ends with "a clear sky and numerous stars." The end is lost.

2. Arranged according to its discrete episodes, the story looks like this:

I.	*The Campaign against Aratta*	
[A]	Introduction: in the good old days of Enmerkar...	1–19
[B]	Enmerkar calls up the army.	
	(1) Enmerkar's decision	20–23
	(2) The call-up	24–34
	(3) Enmerkar at the head of the troops	35–41
[C]	The campaign	
	(1) The march	42–58
	(2) The command	59–74

II.	*Lugalbanda's Illness and Recovery*	
[D]	Illness	
	(1) Lugalbanda falls ill.	75–84
	(2) The provisions left for him	85–115
	(3) At the door of death	116–120
	(4) The companions abandon him.	121–140
	(5) He suffers.	141–147
[E]	Recovery (First night and day)	
	(1) Prayer to the setting sun	148–172
	(2) Prayer to the evening star	173–200
	(3) Prayer to the moon	201–227
	(4) Prayer to the rising sun	228–263
	(5) The water of life/fire/cooking	264–299
	(6) Trapping	300–325
[F]	Dream and Banquet (Second night and day)	
	(1) Sleep and ominous dream	326–360
	(2) Fulfillment of the dream	361–370
	(3) Banquet for the gods	371–394
III.	*Cosmic Battle* (?)	
[G]	The spirits arrive.	395–421
[H]	Lugalbanda's exaltation	422–441
[I]	The battle?/Inana's battle array?	442–483
[J]	The sun reappears	484–499

3. The text of this first part of the adventures of Lugalbanda falls naturally into three parts. First, there is the outer framework, which has Enmerkar as its protagonist. Then we have the well-articulated series of episodes in which Lugalbanda falls ill, is saved from death by the gods, recovers and reinvents the necessities of life, is elected for sainthood, and in gratitude sets a banquet before the gods, who apparently accept him as being close to them. Finally, he seems to have to endure a last ordeal during a nightly battle between the spirits of darkness and the spirits of light. This part is still poorly understood, but at the end the forces of light seem to triumph, and the interpretation lies near that the hero is purified or sanctified even further by this cosmic trial. The very end has still not been recovered. It is striking that the whole episode seems to take three nights: the night of Lugalbanda's illness, the following night when he gets the dream[11] that will

change not only his life but also his very nature, and the last night wherein the cosmic battle seems to be fought. Thus the hero is well and truly prepared for his future role as savior by his complete resurrection on the third day. Particularly the middle part (i.e., Lugalbanda's illness, recovery, and acculturation) is a fine piece of writing, replete with cultural pointers as well as with subsurface reflections on the essence of culture versus nature and the singular position of the hero as a middleman between those two. It is ironic that Lugalbanda's very existence, now and for all the future, depends on his liminal position between two essences or two worlds. As to style there are a number of marked departures from straight storytelling. Most striking are, of course, the descriptive/explanatory passages about sleep and dream (lines 326–360). In addition, the series of four prayers (lines 148–263) is a piece of retardation with a decidedly rhythmical character. But the most conspicuous feature is that, apart from the first panel of the outer framework (lines 1–74), the story is exclusively about Lugalbanda. Enmerkar, the companions, Unug, or Aratta are not even mentioned from line 141 onward.

4. The story then tells us of the various stages of trial and purification, which will lead to Lugalbanda's sainthood and his role as a savior.[12] First there is his *lowly status* among his companions (line 71). Second, there is his *weakness,* illness and deprivation (lines 75–84), which is allayed somewhat by the provisions his companions leave for him. But these gifts can be interpreted just as well as a *viaticum,* or a funeral meal. The motif of the meal pervades the stories. There are these provisions, left by his comrades; there is the meal he prepares for the gods; and there is the feasting of the young of Anzud in the second part. In fact, in that second part the poet saw fit to note expressly that on his miraculous journey back to Unug the hero does not want to take any provisions with him. Third, there is his *piety,* beautifully expressed in the series of prayers that follow the journeys of the great luminaries across the skies. Fourth, there is his renewed *confidence* in himself: he reinvents the basic necessities for survival. Fifth, there is his *calling* to sainthood in the form of the dream. Sixth, there is the feast he prepares for the gods,[13] thus enhancing his *association* with them. Seventh and finally, there is his apparent *presence among the stars,*[14] where the battle is fought between light and darkness. Thus the whole first part may be seen as one great *rite de passage* from a weakling to a saint. The second part will be devoted to his acquiring the necessary special powers he needs for effectively saving his people from ruin.

5. The material consists of sixty-four tablets of fragments.[15] Joining reduces this number to perhaps nine "big" editions and no less than forty-three

single-column tablets (imgidas). At present it is unclear whether there were one, two, or three complete editions on a single tablet. There are five fragments of editions of the first half on three-column tablets; curiously, the second half is lacking in this format. There is one piece of a two-column tablet that apparently divided the text over three such tablets, which represents tablet I of such a series. There is no material for tablets II or III. The imgidas are, as usual, uneven in length: they vary from twenty-five to forty-five lines per face. The material is overwhelmingly from Nippur. All the fragments of multicolumn tablets are Nippur. Among the imgidas there is one piece from Ur and five whose provenance is unknown or in doubt.

6. Parts of the text have been edited provisionally by Cohen (1973: introduction), Wilcke (1969: introduction), and Hallo (1983: lines 256–376); there is also a provisional translation in Vanstiphout (1998a: lines 114–129; 1998b: lines 322–365). There is no complete edition.

Lugalbanda in the Wilderness
Composite Text

I. THE CAMPAIGN AGAINST ARATTA

A. INTRODUCTION: IN THE GOOD OLD DAYS OF ENMERKAR. . .

[ud ul an ki-ta ba$_9$-ra$_2$-a-ba]
[. . .] ⸢ul⸣ -e muš$_3$ ⸢keš$_2$⸣-da . . .]
[. . .] ⸢ul?⸣ buru$_{14}$ ul-e še ⸢KAxX⸣-[X]-a-ba

[. . . . . .] ⸢ba⸣-dub-ba ki ba-sur-ra-a-ba
[. . . . . .] ⸢ba⸣-ru$_2$-a-ba mu ba-sar-ra-a-ba
[. . .] ⸢eg$_2$⸣ pa$_5$-re šu-luh ak-a-ba
[. . .] ⸢AD⸣-gin$_7$ X pu$_2$ si sa$_2$-sa$_2$-a-ba
[^{id2}]⸢buranun⸣ id$_2$ ⸢he$_2$⸣-ğal$_2$-la unug^{ki}-ga-⸢ke$_4$⸣ [ki] ⸢in⸣-dar-ra-a-ba

[. . . . . .] NUN BI? TAB du$_3$-a-ba
[. . . . . .] ⸢ha⸣-la UL TAB ğar-ra-ba
[. . . . . .] an kug-ga-ke$_4$ in-zi-zi-ra-a-ba
X [nam]-⸢en⸣ nam-lugal-la-ke$_4$ unug^{ki}-ga-ke$_4$ [(X) pa]-ed$_2$ bi$_2$-in-ak

šibir? ⸢enkara?⸣ kul-ab$_4$^{ki}-ke$_4$ ⸢me$_3$⸣ sağ il$_2$-la-ba
me$_3$ ešemen ^{d}inana-ke$_4$
sağ gig$_2$ zi su$_3$-ud-⸢ba⸣ mi-ni-ib-dug$_3$-ge-eš-ba
in-ti-in-ti-ba ⸢zag-eš⸣-zag-eš-ba
maš$_2$ kur-ra umbin kiğ$_2$-kiğ$_2$-ba
tarah kur-ra aškud sag$_9$-sag$_9$-ba
en-me-er-kar$_2$ dumu ^{d}u-tu-ra mu-na-šum$_2$-mu-uš-ba

B. ENMERKAR CALLS UP THE ARMY

ud-ba lugal-e iri^{ki}-še$_3$ ^{ğiš}mi-tum na-ğa$_2$-ğa$_2$
en-me-er-kar$_2$ dumu ^{d}utu-ra
aratta^{ki} kur me sikil-la-še$_3$ har-ra-an zu na-an-ğa$_2$-ğa$_2$

ki-bal gul-gul-de$_3$ na-an-ğin
en-⸢e iri⸣-a-ni zig$_3$-ga$_{14}$ ba-ni-ğar
niğir kur-kur-ra si gu$_3$ ba-ni-ra
unug[^{ki}] zig$_3$-ga lugal zu ba-ra-ed$_2$-e
kul-ab$_4$^{ki} zig$_3$-ga en-me-kar$_2$-ra he$_2$-us$_2$-e
unug^{ki} zig$_3$-ga-bi a-ma-<ru>-kam
kul-ab$_4$^{ki} zig$_3$-ga-bi an duğu ğar-ra

Lugalbanda in the Wilderness
Translation

I. THE CAMPAIGN AGAINST ARATTA

A. Introduction: In the Good Old Days of Enmerkar...

[In the days long past, when heaven was sundered from earth],[16]
[In the days] long past, [when] all *needs* [*were provided for*],
[In the days] long past, [when] after the *first* harvest barley [*was eaten*],
[When *boundaries*] were laid out, when plots were measured out,
[When *marker stones*] were put up and inscribed with their names,
[When] levees and canals were scoured,
[When] wells were sunk straight as [...],
[When] the bed of the Euphrates, Unug's bountiful river, was cut in the earth,
[When ...] was built,
[When ...] was put in place,
[When] Holy An took *away* [...],
[When] the offices of lord and king of Unug were made brilliantly manifest,
then the scepter and staff of Kulab were held high in battle
—in battle, which is Inana's game—,
Then the Black-headed[17] were long-lived and satisfied
In their ways and within their *means;*
Then mountain goats with *pounding* hooves,
Mountain stags with glorious antlers,
Were (constantly) presented to Enmerkar, son of the Sun.

B. Enmerkar Calls Up the Army

In those days the king set his mace[18] toward a city;
Enmerkar, the son of the Sun,
Conceived a campaign against Aratta, the mound of the inviolate powers.
He would go and destroy the rebel land.
The lord called up his citizenry;
The herald sounded the horn in all countries;
The levy of Unug marched out with the all-wise king;
The levy of Kulab followed Enmerkar.
The levy of Unug was a flood;
The levy of Kulab was a storm cloud.

muru$_9$-gin$_7$ ki he$_2$-us$_2$-sa-ba
⸢sahar] peš-peš-bi an-e mu-un-ši-ib-us$_2$
buru$_4$-dugud^{mušen} numun sağ-še$_3$ zi-zi-i-gin$_7$
lu$_2$-ulu$_3$ zu-ne na-an-ni-pad$_3$-de$_3$
šeš šeš-a-ne giškim na-an-ğa$_2$-ğa$_2$

⸢lugal⸣-bi sağ-ba du-a-ni
⸢lu$_2$ šu-nir⸣ erin$_2$-na-ka di-dam
⸢en⸣-[me-er-kar$_2$] ⸢sağ-ba⸣ du-a-ni
⸢lu$_2$⸣ [... ...]-⸢ka⸣ di-dam
[BIR$^?$⸣ X X X [...] ⸢ki$^?$ sig$_{10}$⸣-ga-ke$_4$
hur-sağ sug nunus gu$_2$ ⸢nu$^?$⸣-gun$_3$-e
gu$_2$ nida-e gu$_2$ me-er-me-er-re-da

C. The Campaign

zid du šag$_4$ kuš$_2$-u$_3$ ^{d}en-lil$_2$-la$_2$-ke$_4$
kul-ab$_4$^{ki} niğin$_2$-na-bi im-ma-an-kar-eš-ba
[...] ⸢kur⸣-ra-ke$_4$ u$_8$-gin$_7$ ba-an-gur-ru-uš

[... ...] ⸢zi-ga⸣ gaba hur-sağ-ğa$_2$-ke$_4$ am-gin$_7$ dug$_3$ bi$_2$-in-ğal$_2$-⸢le⸣
[... ...] zag-še$_3$ i$_3$-kiğ$_2$-e har-ra-an i$_3$-zu-ne
[... ... ...] X i$_3$-kiğ$_2$-e ud-5-am$_3$ ba-zal
[ud 6-kam-ma]-ka a mu-un-⸢tu$_5$-tu$_5$⸣-uš
X [... ...] ud 7-kam-ma kur-ra ba-an-sun$_5$-ne-eš
in-ti-in-ti-a bal-bal-⸢e⸣-da-bi
a-ği$_6$ uru$_{16}$ ambar muš gab gab$_2$ ru-ru-gu$_2$
en-bi ulu$_3$-a u$_5$-a-ni
dumu ^{d}utu kug me-a zid
an-ta ki-gal-še$_3$ gub-ba-am$_3$
niğ$_2$-babbar$_2$-ra sağ mu-na-mu$_2$-mu$_2$
ti zu$_2$ nim-gin$_7$ mu-na-ğir$_2$-ğir$_2$-re
⸢a$_2$⸣-na ŠEN.KAK zabar-ra uri$_3$-na mu-na-mul-lu
ŠEN.KAK-ta ur ad$_6$ gu$_7$-a-gin$_7$ galam mu-na-ta-ed$_2$

ud-bi-a 7 he$_2$-na-me-eš 7 he$_2$-na-me-eš
di$_4$-di$_4$-la$_2$ PEŠ.TUR.ZID kul-ab$_4$^{ki} 7 he$_2$-na-me-eš
7-bi-ne ^{d}uraš-e tud-da šilam ga gu$_7$-me-eš
ur-sağ-me-eš ki-en-gi-ra sig$_7$-me-eš a-la-ba nun-na-me-eš

^{ğiš}banšur an-na-ke$_4$ a$_2$ ed$_2$-a-me-eš
7-bi-ne ugula-a-ke$_4$-eš ugula-a-me-eš
nu-banda$_3$-a-ke$_4$-eš nu-banda$_3$-a-me-eš

Hugging the earth like a heavy fog
Their thick dust reached to heaven.
As to rooks rising to the early *sowing*
He *called* to his people;
From fellow to fellow, the sign was passed on.

Their king's marching at their head
Was [*encouragement to*] the men [. . .] of the army;
Enmerkar's marching at their head
Was [*encouragement to*] the men [. . .] of the army.
[. . .]
[. . .]
To make the emmer-wheat grow abundantly.

C. The Campaign

When the righteous comforter of Enlil's heart
Had thus called up all Kulab,
They wended their way as do the ewes on [*the slopes*] of the mountains,
And like bulls they trampled over the high [. . .] of the foothills.
He sought for [. . .] to the border, *so that they would* know the way;
He sought for [. . .]. Five days went by.
[On the sixth day] they bathed,
[. . .] and on the seventh day[19] they entered the mountains.
Their crossing of the pathways
Was a huge flood rising *upstream to a lake* [. . .].
Their lord, riding a storm,
The son of the Sun, the true refined silver
That came down from heaven to earth—
His head shines brightly;
Barbed arrows flash forth from him as lightning;
The bronze battle-axe, his *coat-of-arms,* glitters at his side;
On that axe there appears, artfully made, a dog devouring a corpse.[20]

Seven they were, seven they were;[21]
Seven were the young lads born in Kulab.
Uraš had born these seven; the Wild Cow had suckled them with milk.
They were heroes, the handsomest in Sumer and princely in their prime.
They grew up at An's high table.
These seven were lieutenants of companies,
They were captains of regiments,

šagina-a-ke$_4$-eš šagina-a-me-eš
ugula lu$_2$ 300 300-ta-a-me-eš
nu-banda$_3$ lu$_2$ 600 600-ta-a-me-eš
šagina erin$_2$ šar$_2$-šar$_2$-šar$_2$-šar$_2$-šar$_2$-šar$_2$-šar$_2$ 7-ta-me-eš
en-ra KA.KEŠ$_2$ igi-bar-ra-ka-na mu-na-sug$_2$-sug$_2$-ge-eš
lugal-ban$_3$-da 8-kam-ma-ne-ne
ERIN$_2$+KIŠIM$_5$ KAxLI a luh-luh-ha-bi
si dug$_4$-dug$_4$-ga-bi ba-ra-ab-ed$_2$
ĝiš tag-ga lugal-la-ke$_4$ ba-da-ab-du$_8$ un-da ba-da-ĝin

II. LUGALBANDA'S ILLNESS AND RECOVERY

D. ILLNESS

kaskal mu-un-sa$_9$ kaskal mu-un-sa$_9$-ba
ki-bi-a tu-ra mu-na-teĝ$_3$ saĝ gig mu-na-teĝ$_3$
muš saĝ-bi gi-TUN$_3$-ra-gin$_7$ e-ne dag i$_3$-si-il-e

maš-da$_3$ ĝiš bur$_2$-ra dab$_5$-ba-din$_7$ ka sahar-ra bi$_2$-us$_2$
šu-ni dab$_5$-ba nu-mu-da-an-gi$_4$-gi$_4$
ĝiri$_3$-ni gu$_2$-ba nu-mu-da-an-ĝa$_2$-ĝa$_2$
lugal zig$_3$-ga šu nu-mu-na-an-ĝal$_2$

kur gal-e muru$_9$-e ki he$_2$-us$_2$-sa-a-ba

unug^{ki} he$_2$-en-tum$_2$-mu-de$_3$ tum$_2$-mu nu-ub-zu
kul-ab$_4$^{ki} he$_2$-en-⸢tum$_2$-mu⸣-de$_3$ tum$_2$-⸢mu⸣ [la]-ba-ni-zu-zu

kur-ra ki šed$_{10}$-bi ⸢zu$_2$-ra-ah i$_3$tuku⸣
ki kum$_2$-ma-⸢bi i$_3$-tum$_4$-tum$_4$⸣ [... ...]
za-ra-ah ⸢ma⸣-[...] ga ah ⸢la⸣ [... ...]
niĝ$_2$-barag$_2$ gud$_3$-gin$_7$ ⸢mu⸣-na-sig$_{10}$-⸢ge⸣-[ne]
zu$_2$-lum ^{ĝiš}peš$_3$ ga-ar$_3$-ga-ar$_3$-ra [...]
ninda gu$_7$-gu$_7$ niĝ$_2$-lu$_2$-tu-ra i$_3$-gu$_7$-⸢u$_3$⸣-ne
kid-da zu$_2$-lum-ma-ka e$_2$ ba-ni-in-du$_3$-du$_3$-uš
i$_3$ hi-a tur$_3$-ra ga-ar$_3$ luh-ha amaš-a
i$_3$ nunuz te nunuz te-a šeg$_6$-ĝa$_2$
^{ĝiš}banšur ki kug ki kal-kal-la-aš sig$_{10}$-ge$_5$-gin$_7$ mu-na-ab-gub-bu-ne

dida naĝ lal$_3$ zu$_2$-lum-ma-ta šar$_2$-ra
ku-bu-ul-lum i$_3$-nun-ta E.KU
igi ^{ĝiš}banšur-ra-ka si ba-ni-in-sa$_2$-sa$_2$-e-eš

They were generals of brigades,
Lieutenants of three hundred men each,
Captains of six hundred men each,
Generals of seven šar[22] of men each.
These served their lord as his elite troops.
Lugalbanda was the eighth of them.
[...] was washed in water.
He went forward in modest silence;
He loosened the [...] of the king, and marched out with the troops.

II. LUGALBANDA'S ILLNESS AND RECOVERY

D. Illness

When they had covered half the way, marched half the way,
An illness befell him there; an affliction of the head befell him.
Like a snake dragged out by the head with a (split) reed, his body was jerking;
Like a gazelle caught in a snare he was biting the dust.
His stricken hand could not return a grip;
His palsied feet he could no longer set down firmly.
Neither the king nor the levy could put out a (helping) hand to him.
In the high mountains, hovering over the earth like a dust cloud,[23] they said:
"He must be brought back to Unug!"—but they did not know how;
"He must be brought back to Kulab!"—but they did not know how to carry him.

In this cold spot in the mountains (his) teeth *were chattering,*
So they brought him to a warm place [...].
Supplies they [...]
They made him a bower like a bird's nest.
Dates, figs, and assorted cheeses [...],
Sweetmeats such as ailing people should eat,
They put in palm baskets and so made him a home.
All kinds of fat from the cow pen, fresh cheese from the sheepfold,
Cold eggs in oil, cold hard-boiled eggs,
All this they set out for him as if laying the table for the holy and precious place.[24]
Strong beer, mixed with date syrup,
Bread loaves with butter ... ...
They arranged for him on top of the table.

^{kuš}maš-li-um-e niğ$_2$-si-sa$_2$-e
^{kuš}A.ĞA$_2$.LA$_2$-e niğ$_2$-sa$_2$-dug$_4$-dug$_4$-ga
šeš-a-ne-ne ku-li-ne-ne
niğ$_2$-gur$_{11}$ ^{ğiš}ma$_2$ ki-buru$_{14}$ ba-al-la-gin$_7$
sağ-ğa$_2$-ni-še$_3$ hur-ru-um kur-ra-ka mu-ni-in-ğar-re-ne
^{kuš}ummud-⸢da⸣-ne-ne a NAM nu-um-ta-X [...]
kaš gig$_2$ kurun ziz$_2$ babbar
geštin na$_8$-na$_8$ gu$_2$ me-ze$_2$ dug$_3$-ga-am$_3$
sağ-ğa$_2$-ni-še$_3$ hur-ru-um kur-ra-[ka] ğiš ^{kuš}ummud-da-gin$_7$ ur$_2$-ba hu-mu-tal$_2$-tal$_2$
i$_3$ šim-gig-ga i$_3$ zi da i$_3$ šim GA i$_3$ ligidba i$_3$ sağ-bi gan-da
si-dug$_4$ sur-ra-ke$_4$ mu-na-ak-eš
sağ-ğa$_2$-ni-še$_3$ hur-ru-um kur-ra-ka mu-ni-ib-la$_2$-e-ne
^{urud}ha-zi-in-na-ni kug-bi nagga
hur-sağ zubi-ta šu-a bal-a
sağ-ğa$_2$-ni-še$_3$ im-ši-ib-ru-gu$_2$-ne
ğir$_2$ ur$_2$-ra-ka-ni an-bar-sug$_4$-ga-am$_3$
hur-sağ gig$_2$-ta šu-a bal-a
ti-ni-ta im-da-ab-sur-ru-ne

igi-ni pa$_5$ mu a-ta dirig-dirig-ga-e
kug ^{d}lugal-ban$_3$-da ba-an-di-ni-ib-bad-bad-de$_3$
nundum-a-na ^{ğiš}ig bar kug ^{d}utu gu$_2$-bi ba-an-gi$_4$
šeš-a-ne-ne nu-mu-un-ne-ba-e
gu$_2$-ni un-zig$_3$-ge-eš zi nu-um-me

šeš-a-ne-ne ku-li-ne-ne
ni$_2$-bi-a ad mi-ni-ib-gi$_4$-gi$_4$-ne
ud šeš-me ^{d}utu [^{ğiš}]nu$_2$-a-gin$_7$ mu-zi-zi-a
diğir niğ$_2$ mu-ni-ra-a-ni bar-ta im-da-gub
ne un-gu$_7$ ne un-⸢nag⸣
ğiri$_3$-ni ğiri$_3$ ki us$_2$-sa ba-an-tah
gar$_3$-gar$_3$ kur-ra-ke$_4$ ⸢he$_2$⸣-en-tum$_2$-mu-de$_3$ sig$_4$ kul-ab$_4$^{ki}-še$_3$

⸢u$_3$⸣ tukum-bi ^{d}utu šeš-me
ki kug ki kal-kal-la-aš gu$_3$ im-ma-an-de$_2$
ğiš-ge-ge-en-na-ka-na ki-us$_2$! he$_2$-en-da-dah
ud me-en-de$_3$ aratta^{ki}-ta i$_3$-re$_7$- me-en-de$_3$-en
ad$_6$ šeš-me sig$_4$ kul-ab$_4$^{ki}-še$_3$ ga-ba-ni-ib-kur$_9$-re-en-de$_3$-en

ab$_2$ kug ^{d}nanna sag$_2$ dug$_4$-ga-gin$_7$
gud ab$_2$-ba nam-sumun-ba šurum-ma tag$_4$-a-gin$_7$

Leather satchels (full of) provisions,
Leather bags (full of) victuals—
His brothers and companions
As if unloading a freighter at harvest time
Placed all that by his head in the mountain cave.[25]
Water [. . .] from their water skins [. . .]
Dark beer, liquor, white beer,
Heavy wine, pleasing to the palate—
They displayed all that by his head in the mountain cave on a water-skin stand.
Incense oil, [. . .] oil, aromatic oil, ligidba oil, and the choicest oils
They *mixed* in pots, and *deep in the cave*
They suspended them by his head in the mountain cave.
His axe, whose precious metal is tin,
Which was imported from the Zubi Mountains,[26]
They *planted* by his head.
His side arm of iron,
Which was imported from the Black Mountains,
They tied to his breast.

His eyes—ditches overflowing with water—
Holy Lugalbanda keeps open, staring at them.[27]
But the door of his lips, like the door of Holy Sun,[28] he kept closed.
He opened it not to his brothers.
They lifted up his neck: there was no breath.

His brothers and companions
Then took counsel together:
"Should our brother rise, like the Sun,[29] from his bed,
"Surely (this is a sign that) the god who smote him will have left.
"When he will have eaten and drunk
"His feet will become stable on the earth again
"And carry him over the high mountain places, back to Kulab, the Brickwork.
"But if the Sun should call our brother
"To the holy precious place,
"All strength of his limbs will *stay here*.
"When we then later return from Aratta,
"We shall have to bring back our brother's corpse to Kulab, the Brickwork."

As do the *migrating cows* of Holy Nanna[30]
When they leave a decrepit breeding bull in the cow-pen,

šeš-a-ne-ne ku-li-ne-ne
kug ^{d}lugal-ban$_3$-da hur-ru-um kur-ra mu-ni-ib-tag$_4$-a-aš
ir$_2$ diš-e a-nir diš-e
ir$_2$-e niğ$_2$-šag$_4$-ne-ša$_4$-ka
šag$_4$ sig$_3$-ge i-si-iš ğa$_2$-ğa$_2$-de$_3$
šeš-gal-šeš-gal ^{d}lugal-ban$_3$-da kur-ra ba-an-sun$_5$-ne-eš

ud-ba lugal-ban$_3$-da tu-ra-am$_3$ ud 2-am$_3$ i-ni-in-zal
ud 2-am$_3$ ud maš-am$_3$ ba-an-tah
^{d}utu e$_2$-a-ni-še$_3$ igi-ni ğa$_2$-ğa$_2$-gin$_7$
maš-anše šurum$_3$-še$_3$ sağ il$_2$-i-gin$_7$
ud šu-niğin$_2$ a$_2$ ud-te-en-na-ra
i$_3$-gin$_7$ su-na mu-na-hal-ha
tu-ra-na nu-um-ta-ab-ed$_3$-de$_3$

E. Recovery (First Night and Day)

^{d}utu-ra an-še$_3$ igi he$_2$-em-ši-ib-il$_2$-ia-ke$_4$
a-a tud-da-na-gin$_7$ ir$_2$ ba-ši-in-pad$_3$
šu sag$_9$-sag$_9$-ga-ni hur-ru-um kur-ra-kam mu-na-ab-zi-zi-zi-i
^{d}utu silim ga-ra-ab-dug$_4$ nam-ba-tu-tu-de$_3$-en
ur-sağ dumu ^{d}nin-gal silim ga-ra-ab-dug$_4$ nam-ba-tu-tu-de$_3$
^{d}utu šeš-mu-ne-ka kur-ra mu-un-ed$_3$-de$_3$
a-a hur-ru-um kur-ra ki šur ki-ka nam-ba-tu-tu-de$_3$

ki ama nu-gub-ba a-a nu-gub-ba
zu-a nu-gub-ba kal-la nu-gub-ba
ama-mu a dumu-mu nu-um-me
šeš-mu a šeš-mu nu-um-me
usar ama-mu e$_2$-a kur$_9$-ra-na ir$_2$-mu nu-še$_8$-še$_8$

diğir ama diğir a-a ul-sug$_3$-ge-eš-a-ta
diğir nam-usar-ke$_4$ lu$_2$ ba-ra-an-ed$_3$-de$_3$ im-me-a
ur nu-zu hul-a lu$_2$ nu-zu huš-am$_3$

kaskal nu-zu gab kur-ra-ka
^{d}utu lu$_2$ nu-zu lu$_2$ hul rib-ba-am$_3$

a-gin$_7$ ki-lul-la nam-ma-e
še-gin$_7$ sahar šeš-a nam-ba-da-gu$_7$-e
ğešpu-gin$_7$ edin ki nu-zu-ğa$_2$ nam-ba-e-de$_3$-šub-bu-de$_3$-en
mu in-na šeš-mu-ne-ka nam-ba-an-ku$_4$-ku$_4$-de$_3$-en
su-lum-mar du$_{10}$-sa-mu-ne-ka nam-ba-an- ku$_4$-ku$_4$-de$_3$-en

His brothers and companions
Abandoned Holy Lugalbanda in the mountain cave.
In tears and sighs,
In tears and wailing,
In grief and weeping
Lugalbanda's older brothers took to the mountains again.

Lugalbanda lay ill for two days,
And half a day was added to those two days.
Then, when the Sun was already looking toward home,
When the animals lifted their heads toward their cow-pens,
At the end of the day, the cool of the evening
Flowed over his flesh like balm—
But his illness had not yet gone.

E. Recovery (First Night and Day)

He lifted his eyes to the Sun in the sky,
Wept to him as to his bodily father.
In the mountain cave he raised his fair hands, praying:
"Sun, I salute you! Let me no longer be ill!
"Hero, Ningal's son, I salute you! Let me no longer be ill!
"Sun, my brothers are now ascending the mountains—
"O father, let me not stay ill in the mountain cave, the most dismal place on earth!
"A place where there is no mother nor father,
"Nor an acquaintance, nor a loved one!
"My mother is not here to say: 'Woe! My child!';
"My brother is not here to say: 'Woe! My brother!';
"My mother's neighbor who frequents our house is not here to wail for me.
"If mother god and father god were standing here,
"The god of neighborliness would say: 'This man should not perish!'
"A dog unknown to anyone is sad; a man unknown to anyone is dreadful.
"And here, on this unknown road at the edge of the mountains,
"O Sun, there now is such a man unknown by anyone: this is unbearable!
"Let me not be poured away like water in this dismal place;
"Let me not yet eat bitter dust instead of barley;[31]
"Let me not be thrown away like a throwstick in the desolate plain!
"Let not my name be scorned by my brothers;
"Let me not be made into a jest among my comrades;

dim$_3$-ma-gin$_7$ kur-ra muš$_3$ nam-ba-an-tum$_2$-mu
^{d}utu ir$_2$-na šu ba-an-ši-in-ti
zi-šag$_4$-ğal$_2$-la-ni hur-ru-um kur-ra-ka mu-ni-ib-e$_{11}$-de$_3$

uku$_2$-e NE.NE ğa$_2$-ğa$_2$-da ešemen dug$_3$-ga-am$_3$

kar-kid eš$_2$-dam-še$_3$ ed$_2$-da ki-nu$_2$ dug$_3$-dug$_3$-ge-da
uku$_2$-e niğ$_2$-gu$_7$-da-ni
^{d}inana dumu ^{d}suen-na-ke$_4$
gud-gin$_7$ kalam-ma sağ mu-na-il$_2$
me-lam$_4$-ma-ni kug ^{d}šara$_2$-gin$_7$
muš$_3$-a-ni hur-ru-um kur-ra-ka ud mu-un-na-ğa$_2$-ğa$_2$
^{d}inana-ra an-še$_3$ igi he$_2$-en-ši-ib-il$_2$-i-a-ka
a-a tud-da-na-gin$_7$ ir$_2$ ba-an-ši-in-pad$_3$
šu sag$_9$-sag$_9$-ga-ni hur-ru-um kur-ra-ka ⸢mu⸣-na-zi-zi-i-zi
^{d}inana e$_2$-mu he$_2$-me-a iri^{ki}-mu he$_2$-me-a
iri ama-mu tud-da kul-ab$_5$^{ki} [. . .]
muš-gin$_7$ kankal-mu he$_2$-me-[a]
ğiri$_2$-gin$_7$ ki-in-dar-mu ⸢he$_2$⸣-[me-a]
un gal-gal-la-mu-ne ma-ra-⸢an⸣-[. . .]
nin gal-gal-la-mu-ne ma-ra-⸢an⸣-[. . .]
a-⸢a⸣ [. . .] ⸢e$_2$⸣-an-na-še$_3$ ma-[. . .]
damaged
KA.NI KA.NI KA SI im-me
na$_4$ tur-tur-bi na$_4$ gi-rin hi-li-ba
an-ta na$_4$ sağ-kal-e ki-ta IRIxX.IRIxX-e
akkil-bi-ta iši za-bu-e
gu$_3$-bi-ta sur ğal$_2$ tak$_4$-e
a$_2$-ur$_2$ kur ha-šu-ur$_2$-ra-ke$_4$ muš nam-ba-an-tum$_2$-mu
^{d}inana ir$_2$-na šu ba-an-ši-in-ti
zi-šag$_4$-ğal$_2$-la ^{d}utu u$_3$-sa$_2$-gin$_7$ ba-an-ku
šag$_4$ hul$_2$-la ^{d}inana-ke$_4$ tug$_2$-gin$_7$ mu-un-dul-dul
i-gi$_4$-in-zu sila gibil sig$_4$ kul-ab$_4$^{ki}-še$_3$ na-gin

gud-de$_3$ tu$_7$ gig$_2$-ga gu$_7$-da
mul amar kug en-nu-un-še$_3$ am$_3$-ši-ri
mul ud zal-le-da-ke$_4$ an-e im-sar-re
ud babbar-re ği$_6$-a bi$_2$-ib-bur$_2$-re
^{d}suen ud-sakar-e silim dug$_4$-ga
a-a ^{d}nanna ^{d}utu ed$_2$-a-ra si sa$_2$ mu-na-an-šum
en giri$_{17}$-zal men-na tum$_2$-ma
^{d}suen dumu ki ağ$_2$-ğa$_2$ ^{d}en-lil$_2$-la$_2$
diğir si-un$_3$-na me-te-aš bi$_2$-ib-ğal$_2$

"Let me not come to my end in the mountains like a fool!"
The Sun accepted his tears;
He sent down his encouragement into the mountain cave.

She whose playing is sweet even to the poor,[32]
The harlot who goes out to the tavern, who makes the bedroom a delight,
Who is food for the needy,
Inana, daughter of Suen,
Raised her head up to him like the bull of the Land.
Her radiance, shining like that of Holy Šara,[33]
Her bright face lit up the mountain cave.
Lugalbanda lifted his eyes to Inana in the sky,
Wept to her as to his bodily father.
In the mountain cave he raised his fair hands (praying):
"Inana, if only this were my home, my city!
"If only this were Kulab, the city where my mother bore me [. . .]!
"If only this were even as the wasteland is to a snake![34]
"If only this were even as the crevice is to a scorpion!
"My mighty people [. . .] me/I [. . .]
"My great ladies [. . .] me/I [. . .]
"[. . .] to the Eana . . .
"[. . .]
". . .
"Its small stones, shining stones in their splendor;
"On top, sagkal stones, below [. . .]
"From its clamor in the Zabu region,
"From its voice [. . .] open!
"Let my body not perish in the Cypress Mountains!"
Inana accepted his tears.
With her encouragement she made him sleep like the slumbering Sun;
She covered him with *solace*[35] as with a woolen cloth.
Then, as if . . . she went back to Kulab, the Brickwork.

The bull that devours the *mass* of darkness,
The star "Holy Calf" then took up his watch.[36]
He shines in the skies as (brightly as) the star that *announces the day;*
He spreads bright light in the night.
Suen, addressed as the new moon,
Father Nanna, who gives direction to the rising Sun,
The glorious Lord whom his crown[37] befits,
Suen, beloved son of Enlil—
This god reached the zenith, *his glorious token.*

me-lam$_4$-ma-ni kug ^{d}šara$_2$-gin$_7$
muš$_3$-a-ni hur-ru-um kur-ra-ka ud mu-na-ğa$_2$-ğa$_2$
^{d}suen-ra an-še$_3$ igi he$_2$-en-ši-ib-il$_2$-i-a-ka
a-a tud-da-na-gin$_7$ ir$_2$ ba-an-ši-in-pad$_3$
šu sag$_9$-sag$_9$-ga-ni hur-ru-um kur-ra-ka mu-na-zi-zi-zi-i
lugal an sud-ra$_2$ nu-mu-ra-teğ$_3$-ğe$_{26}$-da
^{d}suen an sud-ra$_2$ nu-mu-ra-teğ$_3$-ğe$_{26}$-da
lugal-e niğ$_2$-si-sa$_2$-e ki ağ$_2$ niğ$_2$-erim$_2$-e hul gig
^{d}suen-e niğ$_2$-si-sa$_2$-e ki ağ$_2$ niğ$_2$-erim$_2$-e hul gig
niğ$_2$-si-sa$_2$-e šag$_4$ hul$_2$-la si-sa$_2$-bi ša-ra-da-a-de$_6$
^{ğiš}asal di-hi gal-am$_3$ u$_3$-luh-bi ša-ra-mu$_2$-mu$_2$
niğ$_2$-si-sa$_2$-e KA.KEŠ$_2$-bi e-du$_8$-u$_3$
niğ$_2$-erim$_2$ KA.KEŠ$_2$-bi nu-e-du$_8$
niğ$_2$-erim$_2$-e sağ-bi um-DU.DU eğir-bi-še$_3$ IM bi$_2$-ib-tum$_3$
ud šag$_4$-zu i-im-il$_2$-i-am$_3$
niğ$_2$-erim$_2$-e muš ze$_2$ gur$_5$-e-gin$_7$ ⸢uš$_{11}$⸣-zu ši-im-ri-e
^{d}suen-e ⸢ir$_2$⸣-na šu ba-an-ši-in-ti nam-ti mu-na-šum$_2$
ğiri$_3$-ni ğiri$_3$ ki us$_2$-sa ba-an-tah

min$_3$-kam-ma-še$_3$ gud babbar an-ur$_2$-ta ed$_2$-a
gud ha-šu-ur$_2$-ra nam-e-a ak-e
^{kuš}gur$_{21}$^{ur3}-ra ki-us$_2$-sa igi tab unkin-na
^{kuš}gur$_{21}$^{ur3}-ra e$_2$ niğ$_2$-gur$_{11}$-ta ed$_2$ igi tab ğuruš-a
⸢šul⸣ ^{d}utu si muš$_3$ kug-ga-na an-ta mu-ta-la$_2$
kug ^{d}lugal-ban$_3$-da hur-ru-um kur-ra-⸢ka⸣ mu-na-šum
[^{d}]⸢udug⸣ sag$_9$-ga-ni an-ta im-ta-la$_2$
^{d}lama sag$_9$-ga-ni eğir-a-na ba-e-gin
diğir niğ$_2$ mu-ra-ni bar-ta ba-gub

^{d}utu-ra an-še$_3$ igi he$_2$-en-ši-ib-il$_2$-ia-ka
a-a tud-da-ni-gin$_7$ er$_2$ ba-an-ši-in-pad$_3$
šu sag$_9$-sag$_9$-ga-ni hur-ru-um kur-ra-ka mu-na-zi-zi-i-zi
^{d}⸢utu⸣ sipad kalam-ma a-a sağ gig$_2$-ga
nu$_2$-a-zu-ne un ši-mu-e-da-nu$_2$
šul ^{d}utu zi-zi-da-zu-ne un ši-mu-e-da-zi-zi-i
^{d}utu za-e-da nu-me-a
mušen-e gu nu-DU sağ LU$_2$xKAR$_2$-še$_3$ nu-di
lu$_2$ dili du-ur$_2$ šeš-tab-ba-ni-me-en
^{d}utu lu$_2$ 2 du 3-kam-ma-bi za-e-eme-en
ulul la$_2$ ^{ğiš}igi-tab-ba-ni-me-en
uku$_2$-re lu$_2$ lul-e lu$_2$ tug$_2$ nu-tuku-e
gaba ud-da-zu ^{tug2}zulumbi kug-gin$_7$ ša-mu$_4$-mu$_4$
e$_2$ ur$_5$-ra tug$_2$ siki babbar bar-ba im-dul

His halo was like that of Holy Šara,
His face brought light into the mountain cave.
Lugalbanda lifted his eyes to Suen in the sky,
Wept to him as to his bodily father;
In the mountain cave he raised his fair hands (praying):
"King whom one cannot reach in the distant sky,
"Suen, whom one cannot reach in the distant sky,
"King, lover of justice, hater of evil,
"Suen, lover of justice, hater of evil,
"Justice *satisfies*[38] your joyful heart.
"The poplar, the great staff, *is a scepter for you*!
"You loosen the fetters of the righteous,
"But you do not loosen the shackles of the bad!
"In chasing away the *origin* of evil, you also drive off its *effect*.[39]
"When your heart rises (in anger),
"You spit poison at evil like a venomous snake!"
Suen accepted his tears and gave him life
And made his feet stand up again.

And then the bright bull rose again from the horizon,
The bull that abides between the cypresses,
The firmly standing shield *admired* by the assembly,
The shield from the treasury *admired* by the troops.
Youthful Sun shot his holy brilliant rays down from heaven
And gave them to Holy Lugalbanda in the mountain cave.
His (Lugalbanda's) protecting spirit hovered in front of him;
His guardian angel walked behind him.
The god who had smitten him went away.[40]

To the Sun in heaven he lifted his eyes and
Wept to him as to his own father.
In the mountain cave he raised his fair hands (praying):
"O Sun, shepherd of the Land, father of the Black-headed,
"When you go to sleep, all people go to sleep with you;
"Ever youthful Sun, when you rise, all people rise with you!
"O Sun, without you
"No bird is ever netted, no slave is ever caught.
"To him who walks alone you are the companion,
"O Sun, and you are the third of those who travel in pairs;
"You are the helmet of him who holds the reins.
"The poor, the destitute, the naked—
"Your sunshine clothes them like a woolen robe,
"And like a white woolen cloth it covers even the slaves!

ab-ba-ab-ba gu$_2$ tuku-gin$_7$
bur-šu-ma-e-ne gaba ud-da-zu
a-ar$_3$ ud ul-li$_2$-a-aš ši-im-dug$_3$-dug$_3$-ge-ne
gaba ud-da-zu i$_3$-gin rib-ba-am$_3$
am gal-gal-e dug$_3$ am$_3$-mi-ğal$_2$
niğ$_2$ DUR$_2$-ba kaš$_3$ niğ$_2$ DI i$_3$-ib-sur-ra
ur-sağ dumu ^{d}nin-gal-la bur$_2$-bur$_2$ babbar ši-mu-e-ši-ib-za
⸢ki⸣-ba lu$_2$ lu$_2$ gud su$_8$-ba-ke$_4$
X ⸢du$_8$⸣-a-ni X X X [. . .]
⸢šeš šeš-a-ni-a⸣ ba-ši-in-la$_2$
⸢apin⸣-a-ni ki-a$_2$-ba-ka am$_3$-mi-ni-in-gub-gub-bu
i-lu-zu dug$_3$-ga dug$_3$-ga-am$_3$ an-e mu-un-ši-ib-us$_2$
ur-sağ dumu ^{d}nin-gal-ka me-teš am$_3$-i-i-ne

kug ⸢lugal⸣-ban$_3$-da hur-ru-um kur-ra-[ta] im-ma-da-ra-ta-ed$_2$
ud-bi-a zid du šag$_4$ kuš$_2$-u$_3$ ^{d}en-lil$_2$-la$_2$-ka u$_2$ nam-til$_3$-la i-im-tud

id$_2$ hal-hal-la ama hur-sag-ğa$_2$-ke$_4$ a nam-til$_3$-la im-tum$_3$

u$_2$ nam-til$_3$-la-ka zu$_2$ nam-mi-in-gub
a nam-til$_3$-la-ka UM nam-mi-in-rig$_7$
u$_2$ nam-til$_3$-la-ka zu$_2$ he$_2$-em-gub-bu-a-aka
a nam-til$_3$-la UM he$_2$-em-rig$_7$-a-ka
gu$_2$-e-ta umbin diš-a-ni ki mu-un-dab$_5$-dab$_5$
ki-bi-ta anše kur-kur-ra-gin$_7$ am$_3$-GUL-e
dur$_3^{ur3}$ AŠ.DU-e ^{d}šakkan$_2$-na-ke$_4$ hur-sağ i$_3$-⸢si-il⸣-[le]
dur$_3^{ur3}$ uru$_{16}$ gal-gin$_7$ kušum i$_3$-tag-tag-ge
dur$_3^{ur3}$ sal-la kaš-e kiğ$_2$-ğa$_2$-am$_3$ kaš im-mi-dar-dar
ği$_6$-bi-ta ud-te-en-⸢še$_3$⸣ na-gin
hur-sağ šag$_4$ sig ^{d}suen-ne-ka kaš mi-ni-ib-kar-kar-re
diš-a-ni-im lu$_2$ igi niğin lu$_2$ nu-mu-un-da-bar-re
^{kuš}maš-li-um-e niğ$_2$ si sa$_2$-e
^{kuš}A.ĞA$_2$.LA$_2$-e niğ$_2$ sa$_2$ dug$_4$-dug$_4$-ga
šeš-a-ne-ne ku-li-ne-ne
a šed$_{10}$-gin$_7$ ninda ki-a mu-un-da-an-du$_8$-uš-am$_3$
kug ^{d}lugal-ban$_3$-da hur-ru-um kur-ra-ta im-ma-ra-an-il$_2$-il$_2$
gu$_2$ ne-mur-⸢ra⸣-ka ba-an-še$_{21}$
^{ğiš}buniğ$_2$ X ⸢NE⸣ a bi$_2$ in-ra
igi-ni-še$_3$ mu-un-ta-ğar-ra mu-un-si-⸢il⸣
⸢NA$_4$ SUR⸣ šu im-ma-an-ti X
teš$_2$-bi he$_2$-em-ra-ra-a-⸢ta⸣
u$_3$-dub$_2$ dar-dar-ra gu$_2$ edin-e ba-ni-in-⸢nu$_2$⸣
^{na4}zu$_2$ sal-la izi bi$_2$-in-[. . .]

"Old rich men
"And poor old women alike praise your sunshine
"Sweetly until their final days!
"Your sunshine is as powerful as any balm;
"It even comforts the great wild bulls.
"...
"Hero, son of Ningal, you spread sheen and brilliance
"Wherever people and cattle dwell.
"[...]
"Brother [...] his brother;
"He places his plow in the *proper* place.[41]
"Your praise, rising up to heaven, is sweet!
"Hero, son of Ningal, they praise you as you deserve!

Holy Lugalbanda came out of the mountain cave.
Thereupon the fertile one,[42] who appeases Enlil's heart, begot the plant of life;
The rolling river, the mother of the hills, brought down the water of life.
Lugalbanda nibbled at the plant of life;
He sipped of the water of life.
When he had nibbled at the plant of life
And sipped of the water of life,
From the slope he put one hoof[43] on the ground:
And from that place he speeds like the mountain ass;
Like a wild ass of Šakkan he races over the hills;
Like a large and powerful ass he charges;
Like a slender ass, eager to run,[44] he bounds along.
From nightfall until the cool of the evening he keeps running
Through the hills; alone in the moonlight he races on
He is all alone; however much he looks around, nobody is to be seen.
The things that had been stocked in the packs,
That had been kept in the leather satchels,
That his brothers and companions,
With fresh water, used for baking bread in the open[45]—
Holy Lugalbanda brought all that out of the mountain cave
And put it among the embers.[46]
He filled a bucket with water
And crumbled in it what he had in front of him.
He took hold of some flints
And struck them together.
He had placed charcoal[47] in an open space on the ground;
The fine flint made a spark

izi-bi šag$_4$ sig-ga ud-gin$_7$ mu-na-an-⸢ed$_2$⸣
ninda gug$_2$ du$_8$ nu-zu ^{im}tinur nu-zu
ne-mur 7-ta ninda gi-izi-eš-ta-a ba-ra-an-du$_8$
ninda ni$_2$-bi-a en-na am$_3$-šeğ$_6$-šeğ$_6$
gi šul-hi kur-ra ur$_2$-ba mi-ni-in-bu-bu pa-ba mi-ni-in-suh-suh

gu$_2$-en gug$_2$-ga-ka PAD.UD-še$_3$ KA ba-ni-in-KEŠ$_2$-KEŠ$_2$
ninda gug$_2$ du$_8$ nu-zu ^{im}tinur nu-zu
ne-mur 7-ta ninda gi-izi-eš-ta ba-ra-an-du$_8$
⸢lal$_3$⸣ zu$_2$-lum-ma niğ$_2$ ku$_7$-ku$_7$-da hi-li ba-ni-in-du$_8$-du$_8$

am su$_4$ am sig$_7$ am si gur$_3$-gur$_3$
am šag$_4$ sig-ga nam-a-a ak
am su$_4$-su$_4$ hur-sağ ki sikil-la akkil-bi kiğ$_2$-ğa$_2$

u$_3$-ur$_5$-re šim-gig še-am$_3$ i$_3$-tukur$_2$-re

ğiš ha-šu-ur$_2$-ra U$_2$.NUMUN$_2$.BUR i$_3$-ma$_5$-ma$_5$
pa ^{ğiš}še-nu U$_2$.KI.KAL-gin$_7$ u$_2$ kiri$_4$-ba mu-un-si-im-me
a id$_2$ hal-hal-la-ka i-im-na$_8$-na$_8$-ne
^{u2}i-li-in-nu-uš u$_2$ sikil kur-ra-ka bu-lu-uh$_3$ mu-un-si-il-si-il-le
am su$_4$ am kur-ra u$_2$-a sub$_2$-ba-bi

diš-am$_3$ ⸢du$_{10}$⸣-ba-na im-ma-ra-an-dab$_5$
^{ğiš}še-du$_{10}$ kur-ra ur$_2$-ba mi-ni-in-bu-bu pa-ba mi-ni-in-suh-suh
^{ğiš}i-ri$_9$-na-bi ^{u2}A.GUG$_4$ gid$_2$-da a-šag$_4$-ga-ke$_4$
kug ^{d}lugal-ban$_3$-da ğiri$_2$-ta ba-ra-an-šab
am su$_4$ am kur-ra saman-e bi$_2$-in-la$_2$
maš su$_4$ maš-ud$_5$ ⸢maš sa⸣la$_2$ maš sa KEŠ$_2$.KEŠ$_2$ sa maš gu$_2$-ed$_2$-gu$_2$-ed$_2$

u$_3$-ur$_5$-re šim-gig še-am$_3$ i$_3$-tukur$_2$-re
ğiš ha-šu-ur$_2$-ra U$_2$.NUMUN$_2$.BUR-gin$_7$ i$_3$-ma$_5$-ma$_5$
pa ^{ğiš}še-nu U$_2$.KI.KAL-gin$_7$ u$_2$ kiri$_4$-⸢ba⸣ mu-un-si-im-me
a id$_2$ hal-hal-la-ka i-im-na$_8$-na$_8$-ne
^{u2}i-li-in-nu-uš u$_2$ sikil kur-ra-ka bu-⸢lu-uh$_3$⸣ mu-un-si-il-si-il-le
maš su$_4$ [maš]-⸢ud$_5$⸣ u$_2$-a sub$_2$-[ba]-bi

2-am$_3$ [du$_{10}$-ba]-na im-ma-ra-an-dab$_5$
<^{ğiš}še-du$_{10}$ kur-ra ur$_2$-ba mi-ni-in-bu-bu pa-ba mi-ni-in-suh-suh>
^{ğiš}i-ri$_9$-na-bi ^{u2}A.GUG$_4$ gid$_2$-da a-šag$_4$-ga-ke$_4$
kug ^{d}lugal-ban$_3$-da ğiri$_2$-ta ba-ra-an-šab
maš$_2$ su$_4$ maš$_2$-ud$_5$ maš$_2$ 2-abi HUR.GAM-še$_3$ bi$_2$-in-[la$_2$]

And soon the first flame flared up over the wasteland like sunlight.
He had never learnt to bake bread; he did not know what an oven is;
Yet with just seven embers he baked gizi-ešta bread.
While the bread was baking,
He pulled out mountain šulhi-reeds, roots and all, and stripping off the leaves
Packed the loaves into daily rations.
Not knowing how to bake bread, not knowing what an oven is,
With just seven embers he had baked gizi-ešta bread,
Which he then garnished with dates and sweet syrup.

Now there was a brown buffalo, a sleek buffalo tossing its horns;
This hungry buffalo, *lying down,*
Was calling and bellowing to the brown buffaloes of the hills, the pure place.
This animal chews *myrtle* like grain,[48]

Grinds the bark of the cypresses like halfa-grass,
Sniffs at the foliage of the šenu-tree like grass,
Drinks the water of the rolling streams,
And belches from the soapwort, the pure plant of the highlands.
While the brown buffaloes of the highlands were thus browsing among the verdure,
Lugalbanda caught one in a trap.
He pulled up a mountain juniper and stripped off its branches;
Its roots, which are like the tallest rushes in the meadows,
Holy Lugalbanda cut off with a knife.
He tethered the brown buffalo, the highland buffalo with them.
The brown goat and the nanny goat—flea-bitten goats, lousy goats, goats covered in sores—
Are also like this. They too chew *myrtle* like grain,
Grind the bark of the cypresses like halfa-grass,
Sniff with their noses at the foliage of the šenu-tree like grass,
Drink the water of the rolling streams,
And belch from soapwort, the pure plant of the highlands.
While the brown goat and the nanny goat were thus browsing among the verdure,
He caught them both in a trap.
He pulled up a mountain juniper and stripped off its branches;
Its roots, which are like the tallest rushes in the meadows,
Holy Lugalbanda cut off with a knife.
Both these goats, the brown goat and the nanny goat, he shackled with them.

F. Dream and Banquet (Second Night and Day)

diš-a-ni lu$_2$ igi niğin nu-mu-un-da-ab-bar-re

lugal-ra u$_3$-sa$_2$-ge sa$_2$ nam-ga-mu-ni-ib-dug$_4$
u$_3$-sa$_2$-ge kur nam-du$_2$-ga-ke$_4$
KU.KUR galam-ma-gin$_7$ šu e$_2$-gar$_8$-gin$_7$ gul-la
šu-bi galam-am$_3$ ğiri$_3$-bi galam-am$_3$
niğ$_2$ igi-bi-ta lal$_3$ šu$_2$-šu$_2$-e
igi-bi-ta ⸢lal$_3$⸣ dirig-dirig-ga-e
ugula nu-zu-e nu-banda$_3$ nu-zu-e
niğ$_2$ ur-sağ-ra a$_2$ ğal$_2$-la$_2$-e
^{ğiš}da-ha-ša ^{d}nin-ka-si-ka-ke$_4$
^{d}lugal-ban$_3$-da u$_3$-sa$_2$-ge sa$_2$ nam-ga-mu-ni-ib-dug$_4$
^{u2}i-li-in-nu-uš u$_2$ sikil kur-ra-ka ki-nu$_2$-ğar-še$_3$ mu-un-ğar
^{tug2}zulumhi-e mu-un-dag gada babbar bi$_2$-in-bur$_2$
e$_2$-ur$_5$-ra a tu$_5$-tu$_5$ nu-ğal$_2$-la ki-bi-še$_3$ sa$_2$ im-dug$_4$
lugal u$_3$-sa$_2$-ge la-ba-an-nu$_2$-a ma-mu$_2$-de$_3$ ba-nu$_2$
ma-mu$_2$-da ^{ğiš}ig-e nu-gi$_4$-e za-ra nu-gi$_4$-e
lul-da lul di-da zid-da zid di-dam
lu$_2$ hul$_2$-hul$_2$-le-de$_3$ lu$_2$ šir$_3$-šir$_3$-re-de$_3$
^{gi}pisan kad$_5$ diğir-re-e-ne-kam
unu$_2$ igi sag$_9$ ^{d}nin-lil$_2$-la$_2$-kam
ad gi$_4$-gi$_4$ ^{d}inana-kam
ga-bi$_2$-ib$_2$-lu-lu nam-lu$_2$-ulu$_3$-ka gu$_3$ lu$_2$ nu-til$_3$-la
^{d}za-an-gar$_3$-ra diğir ma-⸢mu$_2$-da⸣-ke$_4$
^{d}lugal-ban$_3$-da ni$_2$-te-ni gud-⸢gin$_7$⸣ [. . .]-⸢ša$_4$⸣
amar ab$_2$-šilam-ma-gin$_7$ gu$_3$-nun ⸢im-me⸣
am su$_4$-e ğa$_2$-a-ra a-ba-a ma-ra-ab-⸢TAG⸣-[. . .]
i$_3$-li$_2$-udu-bi ğa$_2$-a-ra a-ba-a ma-ra-ab-zal-X-e
^{urudu}ha-zi-in-ğa$_2$ kug-bi nagga šu im-⸢ma⸣-[(X)]-⸢tiğ$_4$⸣
ğiri$_2$ ur$_2$-ra-ğa$_2$ an-bar-sug$_4$-am$_3$ im-ma-da-X [X]
am su$_4$ am kur-ra-ke$_4$ lu$_2$-ğešpu$_2$-gin$_7$ ga-am$_3$-[ma-DU.DU]

⸢lu$_2$⸣-lirum-⸢gin$_7$⸣ ga-am$_3$-ši-gam-gam
lipiš-bi he$_2$-em-ta-ab-zig$_3$ ^{d}utu ed$_2$-a-ra u$_3$-mu-na-ğar
maš$_2$ su$_4$ maš$_2$-ud$_5$ maš$_2$ 2-a-bi sağ-du-bi še-gin$_7$ um-⸢ta-a⸣-dub
uš-bi si-dug$_4$-ga um-ma-ni-in-de$_2$-de$_2$
ir edin-na DU.DU-a-bi
muš ul$_4$ kur-ra-ke$_4$ si-im he$_2$-em-ši-ak-de$_3$

^{d}lugal-ban$_3$-da i-im-zi ma-mu$_2$-da im-bu-lu-uh$_3$ u$_3$-sa$_2$-ga-am$_3$

F. Dream and Banquet (Second Night and Day)

Still he was all alone; however much he looked around, nobody was to be seen.
Sleep then overwhelmed the king.
Sleep is the realm of darkness;
It is a towering flood; like the hand that demolishes a brick wall
Its hand is overpowering, its foot is overpowering;
It covers all that it finds before it like syrup;
It overflows all that it finds before it like runny honey;[49]
It knows no lieutenant, no captain,
Yet it strengthens the warrior.
By means of Ninkasi's wooden cask[50]
Sleep finally overcame Lugalbanda.
He patted down soapwort, the pure herb of the highland, as a bed,
Spread out a linen garment, unfolded a linen sheet;
There being no convenience for bathing, he prepared one there.
But the king lay not down to sleep: he lay down to a dream!
Dream—a door cannot hold it back, nor can the pivot;
To the liar it speaks lies, to the truthful the truth;[51]
It may make one happy or sad
But it remains the closed tablet-basket of the gods.
It is the bridal chamber of fair Ninlil
But also the counsellor of Inana.[52]
The multiplier of humankind, the voice of one not alive,[53]
Zangara, god of dreams,
In person bellowed to Lugalbanda like a bull;
Like the heifer to the mother-cow he lowed:
"The brown buffalo, who will slaughter it for me?
"Who will melt its fat for me?
"He must carry my axe, whose metal is tin;
"He must wield my dagger of iron;
"Like a *bullfighter* he must take on the brown buffalo, the highland buffalo; like a wrestler he must subdue it.[54]
"Its strength will leave it. When he sacrifices it before the rising Sun
"He must also crush the heads of both the brown goat and the nanny goat like barleycorns.
"When he has poured out their blood in the pit
"So that the smell wafts over the plain,
"The alert snakes of the highlands will sniff it."[55]

Lugalbanda awoke—it had been a dream; he shivered—he had slept.[56]

igi-ni šu bi$_2$-in-kiğ$_2$ niğ$_2$-me-ğar sug$_4$-ga-am$_3$
^{urudu}ha-zi-in-na-ni kug-bi nagga šu im-ma-an-tiğ$_4$
ğiri$_2$ ur$_2$-ra-ka-ni an-bar-sug$_4$-am$_3$ im-ma-da-SUH$^?$
am su$_4$ am kur-ra-ke$_4$ lu$_2$-ğešpu$_2$-gin$_7$ ga-am$_3$-ma-DU.DU lu$_2$-lirum-ma-gin$_7$ im-ma-ši-gam
lipiš-bi im-ta-an-zig$_3$ ^{d}utu ed$_2$-a-ra mu-na-an-ğar
maš$_2$ su$_4$ maš$_2$-ud$_5$ maš$_2$ 2-a-bi sağ-du-bi še-gin$_7$ im-ta-an-dub

uš-bi si-dug$_4$-ga im-ma-ni-in-de$_2$-de$_2$
ir-bi edin-na DU.DU-a-bi
muš ul$_4$ kur-ra-ke$_4$ si-im im-ši-ak-de$_3$

^{d}utu nam-ta-ed$_2$-aš X [. . .]
lugal-ban$_3$-da mu ^{d}en-lil$_2$-le zi [. . .]
an ^{d}en-lil$_2$ <^{d}en-ki> ^{d}nin-hur-sağ-ğa$_2$-ke$_4$
si-dug$_4$-ta ğišbun-na im-ma-ni-in-dur$_2$-ru
kur-ra ki-ğar-ra mu-un-ak-a
ğišbun ba-ni-in-ğar ne-sağ ba-ni-in-de$_2$
kaš gig$_2$ kurun ziz$_2$ babbar
geštin na$_8$-na$_8$ gu$_2$ me-ze$_2$ dug$_3$-ga
edin-na a šed$_{10}$ ki-še$_3$ im-ma-ni-in-de$_2$-de$_2$
uzu maš su$_4$-ke$_4$ ğiri$_2$ bi$_2$-in-ak
ur$_5$ niğ$_2$-gig$_2$ izi im-mi-ni-in-si
na izi sig$_9$-ga-gin$_7$ i-bi$_2$-⸢bi⸣ bi$_2$-in-mu$_2$
i-gi$_4$-in-zu ^{d}dumu-zid ir dug$_3$-⸢ga⸣ amaš-a kur$_9$-ra-a
niğ$_2$ šu dug$_4$-ga lugal-ban$_3$-da
an ^{d}en-lil$_2$ ^{d}en-ki ^{d}nin-hur-sağ-ğa$_2$-ke$_4$ dug$_3$-ga-bi mu-un-gu$_7$-uš
a$_2$ sikil-la ki dadag-ga-bi
barag ^{d}suen-na kug-gin$_7$ mi-ni-in-ri
⸢barag⸣ ^{d}utu barag ^{d}suen-na-ka igi-nim-še$_3$ ba-du$_3$
barag 2-a-bi KA ⸢ŠU⸣ za-gin$_3$ ^{d}inana-ka še-er-ka-an ba-ni-in-dug$_4$
^{d}suen-e ĞIŠ DA ŠU KA NI[57]
a$_2$-an-kar$_2$ a ba$^?$-an-tu$_5$-tu$_5$
iri an-na a tu$_5$-a-ni
gu$_2$-en gug$_2$-ga-ka me-te-aš bi$_2$-ib-ğar
X X ⸢zi ^{d}en-ki a-a diğir-re-e-ne an-da-ak-ak-eš⸣

III. COSMIC BATTLE (?)

G. The Spirits Arrive

an ğal$_2$ tak$_4$-a X ⸢mu-un-dib$_2$-ba nam SU BAR⸣ DUR.SAR in-ğal$_2$-le-eš
X X BU MAŠ DUR.SAR-gin$_7$ sağ ⸢ŠU$^?$⸣ mu-ni-in-ğal$_2^?$-le$^?$-eš$^?$

He rubbed his eyes: it had been gruesome.
He took hold of his axe, whose metal is tin;
He wielded his dagger of iron;
Like a *bullfighter* he took on the brown buffalo, the highland buffalo; like a wrestler he subdued it.
Its strength left it. He sacrificed it before the rising Sun.
He crushed the heads of both the brown goat and the nanny goat like barleycorns.
He poured out their blood in the pit
So that the smell wafted over the plain;
The alert snakes of the highlands sniffed it.

At the rising of the Sun
Lugalbanda, invoking the name of Enlil,
Made An, Enlil, Enki, and Ninhursag
Sit down for a banquet at the slaughtering pit,
The place in the highlands he had prepared.
The banquet was set, the *libations* poured out;
Dark beer, strong drinks, white beer,
Wine, drinks pleasing to the palate,
He poured out over the plain as a libation.
He cut the meat of the brown goats
And roasted the dark livers;
Like incense put on the fire, he let the smoke rise.
As if Dumuzid himself had brought the *tastiest bits* from the cattle-pen,
So the food prepared by Lugalbanda
Was eaten with relish by An, Enlil, Enki, and Ninhursag.
He *prepared the place* like that gleaming place of pure strength,
The holy altar of Suen.[58]
An altar for Utu and for Suen he built on top;
These two altars he decorated with lapis lazuli of Inana.
Suen bathed his *side-weapon,*[59]
The a-ankara weapon.
Having lustrated *this heavenly city,*
He set out all the breads properly.
They made [... *for/to*?] ... Enki, father of the gods.

III. COSMIC BATTLE (?)

G. The Spirits Arrive

The heaven having been *opened,* now there came [...];[60]
They are [...]

^{ğiš}peš$_3$ še-er-gu hi-li bur-ra-gin$_7$
a$_2$-ne-ne-a mu-un-de$_3$-la$_2$-la$_2$
maš-da$_3$ kas$_4$ kar-re ^{d}suen-na-me-eš
niğ$_2$-ur$_2$*-limmu* sag$_9$-sag$_9$ ^{d}nin-lil$_2$-la$_2$-me-eš
^{d}iškur-ra a$_2$-tah-a-ni-me-eš
gu dub$_2$-bu-me-eš še dub$_2$-bu-me-eš
maš$_2$-anše ğiš-haš ak-a-me-eš
ki-bal hul gig ^{d}suen-na-še$_3$ ud-de$_3$ DU.DU-e-me-eš
lu$_2$ ud-de$_3$ DU.DU-e e-ne-ne he$_2$-en-na-me-eš
ud gid$_2$-da ud šu$_4$-še$_3$ im-mi-ib-nu$_2$-u$_3$-ne
ği$_6$ lugud$_2$-da e$_2^?$ DU$_3^?$ ba mu-⸢ni-ib-TU.TU⸣ [. . .]
ud gid$_2$-da ği$_6$ lugud$_2$-da-⸢dam ğiš-nu$_2$⸣-a mi-ni-ib-⸢nu$_2$-u$_3$-ne⸣
ud ⸢ga⸣ LAM$^?$ niğ$_2$ giri$_{17}$-zal [im]-ma-ab-šum$_2$-mu-ne
⸢ği$_6$⸣-u$_3$-na muš$_3$ za-gin$_3$ im-⸢ši⸣-ib-šir$_3$-re-de$_3$-ne
si-si-ig sim^{mušen}-sim^{mušen} ^{d}utu-ka ur$_2$-ba šu mi-ni-in-TE
e$_2$-e$_2$-a i-im-ku$_4$-ku$_4$-ne
e-sir$_2$-e-sir$_2$-ra gu$_2$ mu-un-gid$_2$-gid$_2$-i-ne
ga-ab-dug$_4$ inim dug$_4$-ga-ab šu-a ga-bi$_2$-ib$_2$-gi$_4$-me-eš
ama-ra kiğ$_2$ dug$_4$-ga nin gal-ra inim gi$_4$-a
⸢da⸣ ğiš-nu$_2$-da-ka ki-nu$_2$ ak-a
X si-ga-⸢a$^?$⸣ sağ ğiš ra-ra
[X] gig$_2$-gig$_2$-ga zuh-ha-a-ba
[X] ^{ğiš}ig ^{ğiš}banšur nam-lu$_2$-ulu$_3$-ta ba-ta-an-ed$_2$
[. . .] X šu-a mi-ni-ib-bal-e-ne
⸢teš$^?$⸣-bi za-ra-za-ra KA mu-ne-KEŠ$_2$

H. Lugalbanda's Exaltation

⸢ur$^?$⸣-sağ uš gid$_2$-da lu$_2$-še$_3$ ⸢nu$_2$-nu$_2$⸣ X
^{d}utu uš gid$_2$-da lu$_2$-še$_3$ ⸢nu$_2$-nu$_2$-u$_3$⸣-a
ur-sağ šul ^{d}utu inim$^!$ zid-da-kam
šir$_3^?$ zu KA [X]-⸢a$^?$⸣ šag$_4$ inim-ma-zu-a
an ⸢ki⸣ [X] ⸢gi⸣ KA inim-ma-bi si um-mi-in-sa$_2$
⸢ka$^?$ inim-ma⸣ X DI šul ^{d}utu-kam
^{d}a-nun-na diğir gal-gal-e-ne nu-mu-un-zu-uš-a$^?$
ud ri-ta [(X)] ^{d}utu UNU ^{d}en-lil$_2$-la$_2$
nam-niğir gal an-na [X X] mu-na-an-šum
⸢DI$^?$⸣ kur-kur-ra ⸢X X⸣ mu-na-an-tah
PA SI TE X [. . .] diğir-re-e-ne-ke$_4$
ab-ba iri gal-⸢zu⸣ [X X] ⸢ed$_2^?$⸣ AB gal an kug-ga
an ⸢ki⸣ [X] ⸢gi⸣ KA ⸢inim$^?$-ma$^?$⸣-bi si im-mi-in-sa$_2$-ta
⸢ka⸣ inim-ma-ke$_4$ ⸢si⸣- [sa$_2$] ⸢šul⸣ d[utu]-kam
⸢^{d}⸣a-nun-na diğir gal-gal-⸢e-ne⸣ nu-mu-⸢un-zu⸣-uš-a

As if with strings of figs, dripping with lusciousness,
Their arms are laden.
They are gazelles of Suen, running and fleeing;
They are the finest creatures of Ninlil;
They are the helpers of Iškur.
They heap up flax; they pile up grain;
They are wild animals on the rampage;
Like a tempest, they batter the rebel lands, hateful to Suen;
Indeed, they batter like a storm; such are they!
Every day they lie asleep for the whole length of the day,
But during the short night they enter the built-up houses.
During the long day and the short night they lie in beds.[61]
By day [. . .]; they promise luxury;
At night they chant over the *gleaming plain.*
They *touch off* the breezes, the swallows of the Sun.
House after house they enter;
Street after street they haunt.
They jabber constantly, and still they prompt: "Talk to us!"
They seek words with the mother, they answer back to the great Lady.
They nestle at the bedside;
They smite the [*strong and the*] weak.
Having stolen the dark . . .
They take away the [. . .], doors, and tables from humankind.
They change [. . .] . . .
They shackle together the door-pivots.

H. Lugalbanda's Exaltation

The hero *is now shining on the whole length of that man;*[62]
The Sun *is now shining upon the whole length of that man*
Youthful hero Utu of the true word
. . . who understands the meaning,
Having directed its incantation *in* heaven and on earth. . . .
The incantation . . . of the youth Utu,
Which even the Anuna, the great gods, do not know,
From that time, Utu, the . . . of Enlil
Granted to him (Lugalbanda) the great office of herald of heaven,
And he added the . . . jurisdiction over all the countries,
And the . . . of the gods.
The wise elders of the city . . .
After in heaven and on earth . . . its incantation was directed,
The incantation directed by youthful Sun,
Which even the Anuna, the great gods, do not know,

X kug BAD.BAD-e-ne-kam me$_{3}^{?}$ kug$^{?}$ X [. . .] X X [. . .]
X X X sağ šu ak$^{?}$ nu-mu-su-⸢bu⸣-[X X]-ne
BAD am [X] ⸢da⸣ BAD si$^{?}$ X [. . .]
BAD.⸢BAD⸣ X X NIĞIN$_{2}$ gu$_{2}$ ba$^{?}$-ab$^{?}$-[. . .]
eğir [X] X šu ni$_{2}$-ba gi$_{4}$-gi$_{4}$ [. . .]

I. The Battle?/Inana's Battle Array?

^{d}utu-ra ^{d}en-lil$_{2}$-la$_{2}$ diğir ki-mah-a [. . .]
su$_{6}$ mu$_{2}$ dumu ^{d}nin-gal-la mu-na-da-⸢an⸣-ku$_{4}$-ku$_{4}$
^{d}suen X X mu-na-an-šum-mu-uš šen mu-na-ab-tah-e-me-eš
nam kur-kur-ra-ke$_{4}$ šu$^{?}$-ne-a mu-un-na-ni-in-gi-ne$_{2}$-me-eš
ği$_{6}$-u$_{3}$-na-ka šah gig$_{2}$ mu-un-zu-uš
an-bar$_{7}$-gana$_{2}$-ka ^{d}utu-ur$_{2}$ ka inim-ma-ka-ni igi-⸢še$_{3}$⸣ [X]-bi mu-un-da-ğal$_{2}$
an-na ⸢šir$_{3}$ zu⸣ igi-ni X mu-un-ğal$_{2}$
^{d}UDUG$^{?}$ nin MU X X diğir nu-mu-un-da-sa$_{2}$
⸢niğ$_{2}$ X⸣-ne-ne igi-ne-ne-⸢kam⸣
an ^{d}en-lil$_{2}$ X X ^{d}inana diğir ⸢mu-un-ne⸣-en-⸢kur$_{9}$⸣
X X ra ⸢mu⸣ [. . .] sa šar$_{2}$-ra mu-un-zu-uš
⸢DA⸣ X DU.DU ⸢AH⸣ DA X nu-KEŠ$_{2}$ gir$_{5}$-gir$_{5}$-re-de$_{3}$ igi bi$_{2}$-in-du$_{8}$-ru-uš
⸢KA ŠEŠ⸣ niğ$_{2}$ ŠEŠ mul-la-ba ab-lal$_{3}$-ta mu-un-ne-RU$_{2}$
^{ğiš}ig ⸢kur šuba⸣ ğiš-gan kur šuba
mi-tum [X] X ^{d}KAL.KAL an-na
har-ra-⸢an⸣ [X X] X ⸢NUN$^{?}$⸣ ^{d}inana U GA lil$_{2}$-ta ed$_{2}$-a
^{ğiš}taskarin X X kur šuba-ta ed$_{2}$-a
AN X X AN kug-sig$_{17}$ ban$_{3}$-da
ma X [X] X ⸢LU AN⸣ [X X X] me$_{3}$ ba-sug$_{2}$-ge-eš
me$_{3}$ X [. . .] X ra-gin$_{7}$
šag$_{4}$ [. . .] X ^{d}inana eš$_{2}$ za-gin$_{3}$ ⸢mi-ni⸣-ib-sar-sar-e-ne
lu$_{2}$ šag$_{4}$ ^{d}inana sag$_{9}$-ge-me-eš me$_{3}$ ba-sug$_{2}$-ge-eš
me$_{3}$ izi-ğar-bi 14-me-eš nu-ga-mu-rib-⸢ba-me⸣-eš
ği$_{6}$ sa$_{9}$-a e$_{2}$ sağ ğar-ra ⸢šu$^{?}$⸣ [. . .]
ği$_{6}$ u$_{3}$-na-ka izi-gin$_{7}$ mu-un-sar-sar-re-de$_{3}$-eš
KA.KEŠ$_{2}$-da nim-gin$_{7}$ mu-un-na-ğir$_{2}$-ğir$_{2}$-re-de$_{3}$-eš
MIR šag$_{4}$ sig$_{10}$-ga me$_{3}$-ka
a mah ed$_{2}$-a-gin$_{7}$ gu$_{2}$ nu mi-ni-ib-be$_{2}$
lu$_{2}$ šag$_{4}$ ^{d}inana sag$_{9}$-ge-me-eš me$_{3}$ ba-sug$_{2}$-ge-eš
izi-ğar me$_{3}$ 7-me-eš nu-ga-mu-rib-ba-me-eš
an sig$_{7}$-ga men sağ il$_{2}$-la-gin$_{7}$ ul-la ba-an-sug$_{2}$-ge-[eš]
sağ-ki-ne-ne igi-ne-ne an-usan$_{2}$ sig$_{7}$-ga-me-eš
ğeštug$_{2}$-ne-ne ^{ğiš}ma$_{2}$ X [. . .]-la$_{2}$-me-eš
KA-ne-ne šah ğiš-gi nam-a-a ak-me-eš
ka me$_{3}$-ka gub-ba-ne-ne

...
...
...
...
...

I. The Battle?/Inana's Battle Array?

Into the presence of the Sun, the Enlil god of the grave, ...
Of the bearded son of Ningal they are allowed to enter.
To Suen they give ... and add battle;
The fate of the foreign countries they enforce with their force.
At midnight, they know the black wild boar;
At noon his incantation is *set up* before the Sun;
In heaven your song is set up before him.
... no god *can rival* ...
Their ..., which are before them.
They enter before An, Enlil, [...], and Inana, the gods;
They know ...
They watch ...
They ... from the window ...
The door of the shining mountain, the lock of the shining mountain,
The mace ... of KAL.KAL of heaven,
The road ... Inana ... gone with the wind;
The boxwood ... growing out of the shining mountain
... golden and fierce
... they stand;
Like ...
They chase ... Inana from the gleaming shrine;
They are favored by Inana's heart, steadfast in battle,[63]
They are the fourteen torches of battle, which are ...
At midnight they ...
At the dead of night they dart about like wildfire;
In a band they flash together like lightning;
In the *most violent* ... heart of battle
Roaring loudly like the rising of the mighty flood.
They are favored by Inana's heart, steadfast in battle,
They are the seven[64] torches of battle, which are ...
They stand joyfully as she dons the crown under the clear sky;
Their foreheads and eyes light up the evening;
Their ears ... a boat;
Their mouths are wild boars *resting* in the reed thicket;
They stand in the thick of battle;

zi-šag$_4$-ğal$_2$-bi ⸢sağ DU$_3$⸣ sig$_3$-ge-ne
zi-ir-bi ud ru te ⸢ğa$_2$ ke$_4$ ki mu-un⸣-ne-hul$^?$-uš
lu$_2$ šag$_4$ ^{d}inana sag$_9$-ge-me-eš me$_3$ ba-sug$_2$-ge-eš
^{d}nin-tud an-na šar$_2$-šar$_2$-me-eš
zi an-na šu bi$_2$-in-du$_8$-uš
šita$_3$ kug mul-mul zag an ki-še$_3$ mu-un-ne-de$_3$-ğal$_2$

^{d}nin-TAB.KU.LIBIR mu-un-ne-de$_3$-ğal$_2$

J. The Sun Reappears

mul ud zal-le-da-ke$_4$ an-⸢na mul⸣ mu-un-ne-ur$_4$$^!$-re$^!$
^{d}utu ğa$_2$-nun-ta ed$_2$-a-ni
šita$_3$ kug an-na-ke$_4$ si mu-un-na-ab-sa$_2$
diğir si-sa$_2$ nita$_2$-da nu$_2$-a
diğir erim$_2$ du šag$_4$ niğ$_2$-erim$_2$ ğal$_2$
diğir X X ŠAR$_2$.ŠAR$_2$-me-eš
e-ne-ne-ne ^{d}nanna-gin$_7$ ^{d}utu-gin$_7$ ^{d}inana me ninnu-gin$_7$
an ki zag-ba ğiš mu-un-ni-kam
niğ$_2$-erim$_2$ dug$_4$-ga ensi-bi-me-eš
niğ$_2$-a$_2$-zig$_3$-ga igi du$_8$-bi-me-eš
[X] ⸢mu⸣-un-e$_{11}$* šu mah mu-un-e$_{11}$*
⸢HA$^?$ nu$^?$⸣ mu-un-e$_{11}$* bur-šum-ma ba-e$_{11}$*
an sig$_7$-ga-am$_3$ mul šar$_2$-ra bi$_2$-in-e$_{11}$*-X
mas-sum* ğiš-bur$_2$-gin$_7$ bal-e-de$_3$ mul ^{ğiš}gigir bi$_2$-in-e$_{11}$*
^{ğiš}erin duru$_5$ kur ha-šu-ur$_2$-ra-ke$_4$ ki [. . .]-⸢un⸣-ak
an-ur$_2$ an-pa sa-par$_3$ [. . .]

Unknown number of lines missing

Their life force is . . . ;
. . .
They are favored by Inana's heart, steadfast in battle;
They are (made) numerous by Nintud of heaven;
The life of heaven they hold.
The holy starry battle-mace she carries to the confines of heaven and earth;
Yea, divine nin.TABKULIBIR carries it!

J. The Sun Reappears

The star that makes the day go by flares up in the sky;
The Sun, appearing from his chamber,
Readies the holy battle-mace of the sky,
The righteous god who lies with a man.[65]
They are evil gods with sinful hearts;
They are . . . gods.
Like Nanna, like the Sun, like Inana of the fifty powers,
They are the *door* of the edge of heaven and earth;
They are the *interpreters* of evil words;
They are the spies of righteousness.[66]
. . . rose[67] . . . rose
. . . rose, the matriarch[68] made (them) rise.
(In) a clear sky the numerous stars rose;
The Sieve,[69] *to turn over like a trap,* the Chariot[70] rose.
Fresh cedars in the cypress mountains . . .
A battle net from horizon to zenith . . .
Unknown number of lines missing

The Return of Lugalbanda
Introduction

1. The second part of Lugalbanda's adventures starts after the cosmic battle between the forces of light and the spirits of darkness, the battle that the hero has survived and that has sanctified him further.[71] He is now stranded at the edge of the inhabited world, a mysterious region in the highlands under the rule of the gigantic thunderbird Anzud. The hero decides to invoke the bird's help in returning to his comrades. While the bird and his wife are away foraging, Lugalbanda treats Anzud's young very kindly, plying it with food and all kinds of luxury, so that it probably falls asleep. When Anzud returns he is upset at not hearing his young's usual answering call. Lugalbanda comes forward and shows how well he has treated the fledgling. Anzud, wanting to reward the hero, tempts him with wealth, power, and high status. Lugalbanda refuses all gifts and instead asks for miraculous speed. This being granted, he suddenly alights in the midst of his amazed companions. Meanwhile, the siege of Aratta, which was begun in the first half of the story, has proven unsuccessful. Enmerkar asks for a runner to travel back to Inana in Unug and to ask for her help. Only Lugalbanda volunteers, but he insists on traveling alone. His companions try to dissuade him but to no avail. After a wondrously swift journey (he arrives in the Eana before the evening meal has been served!) he puts Enmerkar's request to Inana. Her reply consists in prescribing a magical cure: a magic fish must be caught; then all will end well, with war no longer necessary. Aratta is praised for its abundant wealth.

2. The text can be broken down into three discrete main parts, and in coherent episodes, as follows:

I.	*Lugalbanda and Anzud*	
[A]	Lugalbanda's stratagem	
	(1) Lugalbanda's loneliness; his plan	1–14
	(2) The Ninkasi interlude	15–27
	(3) Description of Anzud's dwelling	28–49
	(4) Lugalbanda takes care of the young bird.	50–62
[B]	The meeting with Anzud	
	(1) Anzud returns; his fears	63–89
	(2) Anzud's joy and gratitude	90–110
	(3) Lugalbanda praise and supplication to Anzud	111–131
	(4) Anzud's offers; Lugalbanda's refusals	132–166
	(5) Lugalbanda's request: miraculous speed	167–202
		(168–183 = 185–200)

II.	*Lugalbanda's Return to His Brothers*	
[C]	Effects of the return	
	(1) The journey; Anzud advises secrecy.	203–219
	(2) Effects of Lugalbanda's return	220–250
	(3) Discomfiture of Enmerkar's campaign	251–266
III.	*The Solution*	
[D]	Problem solving	
	(1) Enmerkar requests a runner.	268–289
	(2) Enmerkar's message to Inana	290–321
	(3) Lugalbanda insists on going all alone.	322–337
[E]	The ultimate message	
	(4) His journey and arrival in Unug	338–349
	(5) He delivers Enmerkar's message.	350–387 (360–87=294–321)
	(6) Inana's reply: catch the magic fish!	388–412
IV.	*Epilogue*	
	Praise to Aratta and Lugalbanda!	413–417

3. It is obvious that the text consists of two main parts: the Anzud episode and the journey to Unug. It is also obvious that the second follows from the first. The interlude, consisting of the hero's return to his comrades, has two functions: first, it is the realization of Lugalbanda's specific wish; second, it harkens back to Lugalbanda's tribulations in the first part in overt terms. The end is peculiar: the solution to Enmerkar's problem is given to Lugalbanda by Inana—but the text omits the journey back to Aratta, the repetition of the message, and Enmerkar's acting upon it. These things are merely implied, since the epilogue sings the praise of Aratta. In fact, the poem uses straight repetition only sparingly. On a small scale there is the episode describing Anzud's fears at not finding his young (lines 70–77), where the repetition is cleverly used to bring about an effect of climax. On a larger scale there is the (usual) repetition of Enmerkar's message to Inana (lines 294–320 = 359–386); as mentioned above, the omission of the repetition of Inana's answer is highly unusual. There are also a few instances of "formula repetition," by which I mean a series of statements that while not being identical as to contents are so in style. Lines 70–77 show this tactic as well; the best example is the "temptation scene" in which Anzud wants to reward Lugalbanda with lavish gifts (lines 135–157). Lastly, this second installment of the story also shows some instances of longish descriptive or explanatory matter that is not necessarily germane to the main story line—a device that was also used in the first part. As such we

can point to the Nin-kasi paragraph (lines 15–22) but also to the description of Anzud (lines 115–124), Unug's camp before Aratta (lines 255–265), and the state of Unug before Enmerkar started to renovate it (lines 294–299//360–365).

4. This second poem represents the final stage and apogee of Lugalbanda's development into the (saintly) savior of his nation.[72] This happens in several stages, all of them recognizable in traditional saints' lives. First, there is the meeting with a potentially dangerous creature. The hero by means of subterfuge, but which takes the form of an act of charity, gains the unfailing gratitude and support of this creature. In fact, Lugalbanda's luxurious treatment of the young of Anzud duplicates in a way the feast that he had offered the gods in the first poem. Lugalbanda's reward is somewhat negotiated, in that he spurns worldly power, riches, and success but asks instead for the one thing that is necessary to him: the ability to rejoin his people. The fact that this selfsame property of miraculous speed will later be used to act as the savior of his people cannot as yet be foreseen, but it is there nevertheless. Also, this gift makes the hero somewhat akin to the Thunderbird itself, since Lugalbanda will now be able to travel as fast as the bird. The notion that he must keep silent about his newly acquired miraculous power is a motif one often meets in saints' lives: by their sainthood and their wondrous powers they and they alone are able to work miracles, and so from the moment when they obtain sainthood they are forever set apart from the common people. The disbelief and indeed mistrust of his brothers is also a theme often met in saints' lives: it takes dire circumstances before the skeptical people will admit that they are in the presence of sanctity. However, soon Lugalbanda claims that he is the one to save his people from their impossible predicament—and this without unveiling what his strange power is and how he got it. It is probably important that his miraculous speed impresses even Inana, who immediately treats him more or less as an equal, or at least as someone who is fit to associate with higher powers such as herself. That the story is turned inside out is illustrated by the fact that the story ends with Inana advising Lugalbanda about what Enmerkar should do. The return to Enmerkar and the realization of the advice is not even mentioned. Lugalbanda, not Enmerkar, is the hero of both poems. The outer frame and the inner plot have been blended into a whole, and they come together in the person of Lugalbanda.

5. The text is known at present from fifty-five tablets and/or fragments thereof.[73] There were at least five recensions containing the whole composition on one tablet, with three or four columns per side. Two of these are well preserved and give us an almost complete text. Eleven exemplars

are recensions on two or three tablets, which may well represent volumes 1 and 2 (and 3) of a complete edition. The proper sequence of such series will have to be decided by further epigraphic study. As expected, the first part of the composition is better represented than the latter part. The rest of the material consists of single-column tablets containing from thirty to fifty lines per side. There are no obvious "early exercise" tablets, although a small number of extract tablets[74]—all of them fragmentary—are executed with much less care than the rest. Only seven pieces come from outside Nippur. Kish is represented by two partial editions on two-column tablets. Ur has one such edition. The provenance of an extract tablet in the Louvre is unknown, but it is possibly also from Kish. All this material, from Nippur or not, is Old Babylonian. The most exciting pieces, however, are not, since they are from the British Museum K collections found at Nineveh: we have two extracts and one larger edition. These are bilingual, which is highly important on two counts. First, they are proof that the high literary tradition of the Old Babylonian curriculum was preserved until well into the first millennium. Second, they bothered to translate them, which implies an interest at some level in the texts as literature.

6. The first and well-nigh complete edition of the text is Wilcke 1969, which after more than three decades is still a model of the craft. Important material was added in Falkowitz 1983. Later translations are Römer and Edzard 1993 and Black 1998: 58–64. One might also consult Vanstiphout 1998a: 130–46.

The Return of Lugalbanda
Composite Text

I. LUGALBANDA AND ANZUD

A. Lugalbanda's Stratagem

lugal-ban$_3$-da kur ki su$_3$-ra$_2$ ğa$_2$-la ba-ni-in-dag
iši za-bu^{ki}-a nir ba-ni-in-ğal$_2$
ama nu-mu-un-da-an-ti na nu-mu-un-ri-ri
a-a nu-mu-un-da-an-ti inim nu-mu-un-di-ni-ib-be$_2$
zu-a kal-la-ni nu-mu-un-da-an-ti
lu$_2$ inim šag$_4$-ga-na-ke$_4$ inim nu-um-mi-ib$_2$-sig$_{10}$-sig$_{10}$-ge
šag$_4$ ni$_2$-te-na-ka inim am$_3$-mi-ib$_2$-sig$_{10}$-ge
mušen nam-me-te-a ba-ni-in-ak
anzud^{mušen} nam-me-te-a ba-ni-in-ak
dam-a-ni-da gu$_2$-da ba-ni-in-la$_2$
dam anzud^{mušen}-de$_3$ dumu anzud^{mušen}-de$_3$
ğišbun-na um-ma-ni-in-dur$_2$-ru-un
an-ne$_2$ nin-gu$_2$-en-na-ka
hur-sağ-ğa$_2$-ni-ta um-ma-da-an-ri
munus tuku-tuku ama-ra me-te ğal$_2$
^{d}nin-ka-si tuku-tuku ama-ra me-te ğal$_2$
^{na4}gakkul-a-ni ^{na4}za-gin$_3$ dur$_5$-ru
^{gi}lam-sa$_2$-a-ni kug-me kug-sig$_{17}$
kaš-a gub-ba-a-ni niğ$_2$-giri$_{17}$-zal
kaš-ta tuš-a-ni mud$_5$-me-ğar-ra
sagi-a kaš sa$_2$-sa$_2$-da-ni DU.DU nu-kuš$_2$-u$_3$
^{d}nin-ka-si ^{ğiš}buniğ zag-ga-ta ib$_2^{?}$-ba-ta
ğeštin ne-sağ-ğa$_2$-mu me-te-a-aš he$_2$-em-mi-ib-ğal$_2$
mušen kaš nağ-ğa$_2$ ul ti-a
anzud^{mušen} kaš nağ-ğa$_2$ ul ti-a
ki unug^{ki} ba-ğin-na ha-ma-an-pad$_3$-de$_3$
anzud^{mušen}-de$_3$ har-ra-an šeš-mu-ne-ka he$_2$-em-mi-ib-sig$_{10}$-sig$_{10}$-ge

ud-ba giri$_{17}$-zal ğiš hu-ri$_2$-in ^{d}en-ki-ke$_4$
hur-sağ ^{na4}gug igi-gun$_3$ ^{d}inana-ka
ugu-ba u$_{18}$-ru-gin$_7$ ki he$_2$-us$_2$-sa-ba
a-ru-gin$_7$ siki la$_2$-la$_2$-a-ba
kur-ra ğissu-bi ki-mah-ba
tug$_2$-gin$_7$ i-im-dul gada-gin$_7$ i-im-bur$_2$
^{ğiš}i-ri$_9$-na-bi muš sağ-kal-gin$_7$
id$_2$ ka 7 ^{d}utu-ka šag$_4$-ba mu-un-še$_{21}$-še$_{21}$

The Return of Lugalbanda
Translation

I. LUGALBANDA AND ANZUD

A. Lugalbanda's Stratagem

Lugalbanda is stranded in the farthest highlands
Ever since he ventured into the Zabu region.
No mother is with him to give him advice;
No father is with him to speak to him;
No valued acquaintance is with him,
No trusted person he can consult.
Therefore he speaks to himself:[75]
"I shall treat the bird as befits him;
"I shall treat Anzud as befits him,
"And I shall embrace his wife.
"Anzud's wife and child
"I shall seat at a banquet.
"An shall fetch me Ninguenaka
"from her hilly country.
"And that knowing woman, her mother's pride,
"Ninkasi, that knowing woman, her mother's pride—
"Her brewing vat is of gleaming lapis lazuli;
"Her cask is of refined silver and gold;
"When she stands by the beer, there is joy;
"When she sits down after (drawing) the beer, there is applause;
"Untiringly Ninkasi the cup-bearer mixes drinks and serves them
"From the kegs at her side and on her lap—
"That Ninkasi shall surely help me to serve fine and fitting drinks!
"When the bird has drunk the beer he will be happy;
"When Anzud has drunk the beer he will be happy,
"And he will find me the place where Unug went.
"Anzud will put me on the track of my brothers!"

Now there was a splendid eagle-tree of Enki;[76]
On top of the many-hued carnelian hill of Inana
It stood—fixed in the earth like a tower it was
And scraggly like an A.RU.[77]
Its shade covers the highest peaks in the highlands
Like a cloth, spreads over them like a linen sheet.
Its roots, like sagkal-snakes,
Repose in the Sun's seven-mouthed river.

da-da-ba ha-šu-ur$_2$ nu-zu kur-ra-ka
muš nu-un-sul-sul ğir$_2$ nu-sa-sa
šag$_4$-ba buru$_5$-az^{mušen}-e
gud$_3$ im-ma-ni-ib-us$_2$ nunus-bi ba-ab-ğar
da-da-ba mušen anzud^{mušen}-de$_3$
gud$_3$ im-ma-ni-ib-ğar amar-bi ba-e-šeg$_{11}$
ğiš-bi ğiš-li ğiš ^{ğiš}taskarin-na-kam
mušen-e pa mul-mul-la-bi an-dul$_3$-še$_3$ ba-ab-ak
mušen-e a$_2$ ud zal-le-da-ka ni$_2$ un-gid$_2$
anzud^{mušen}-de$_3$ ^{d}utu ed$_2$-a-ra šeg$_{11}$ un-gi$_4$
šeg$_{11}$ gi$_4$-bi-še$_3$ kur-ra lu$_5$-lu$_5$-bi-a ki mu-un-ra-ra-ra
umbin kušu$_2$$^{\text{ku6}}$-e hu-ri$_2$-in^{mušen}-na-kam
ni$_2$-bi-ta am-e kur ur$_2$-še$_3$ ni$_2$-bi im-sar-re
tarah-e kur-bi-še$_3$ zi-bi im-sar-re

lugal-ban$_3$-da gal in-zu gal in-ga-an-tum$_2$-mu
ninda mu-ud-gi diğir-re-e-ne-ke$_4$
sağ-sig$_{10}$-ga-ba sağ-sig$_{10}$ ba-an-tah
ninda gi-ze-eš-ta-ba lal$_3$ ba-an-du$_8$-du$_8$ lal$_3$ ba-an-tah-tah
amar-gud$_3$ amar anzud^{mušen}-da-ka igi-bi-še$_3$ mu-un-ğar
amar-e ^{uzu}sul$_2$ bi$_2$-in-gu$_7$ ^{uzu}i$_3$-udu bi$_2$-in-peš$_5$
ninda-i$_3$-de$_2$-a ka-bi-še$_3$ sa$_2$ bi$_2$-in-dug$_4$
amar anzud^{mušen}-da-ka gud$_3$-ba mi-ni-šeg$_{11}$
igi-bi šim-bi-zid-da mi-ni-gun$_3$
sağ-ba ^{ğiš}erin bar$_6$-bar$_6$ bi$_2$-in-du$_3$-du$_3$
mu-du-li-a šu gur-gur-ra-bi sağ-bi-še$_3$ mu-un-ğar
gud$_3$ anzud^{mušen}-da-ka ba-ra-zig$_3$
ha-šu-ur$_2$-ra nu-zu kur-ra-ka ki-gub mu-un-na-ak-en

B. The Meeting with Anzud

ud-ba mušen-e am kur-ra-ka gu$_2$ mi-ni-ib-gur-gur
anzud^{mušen}-de$_3$ am kur-ra-ka gu$_2$ mi-ni-ib-gur-gur
am ti-la šu-bi-še$_3$ i-im-la$_2$
am ug$_5$-ga gu$_2$-ba i-im-la$_2$
a 10$^{!}$ gur$^{!}$-am$_3$ ze$_2$$^{!}$-bi mu-un-de$_2$
mušen zag diš am$_3$-ma-da-lu-ga
anzud^{mušen} zag diš am$_3$-ma-da-lu-ga
mušen-e gud$_3$-bi-še$_3$ šeg$_{11}$ un-gi$_4$
anzud^{mušen}-de gud$_3$-bi-še$_3$ šeg$_{11}$ un-gi$_4$
amar-bi gud$_3$-bi-ta inim nu-um-ma-ni-ib-gi$_4$
2-kam-ma-še$_3$ mušen-e gud$_3$-bi-še$_3$ šeg$_{11}$ un-gi$_4$
amar-bi gud$_3$-bi-ta inim nu-um-ma-ni-ib-gi$_4$

Nearby in this highland that knows no cypress,[78]
Where no snake slithers, no scorpion scurries—
In the midst thereof only the buru-az bird
Builds its nest and lays its eggs.
There the bird Anzud
Had made his nest and settled his young.
The nest was made of juniper and boxwood:
The bird had woven their bright twigs into a shade.
At daybreak, when the bird stretches himself,
At sunrise, when Anzud cries out,
The earth in the Lulubi Mountains shakes at his cry.
He has shark's teeth and eagle claws;
In terror of him buffaloes[79] scatter into the foothills;
Stags flee into their mountains.

Lugalbanda, being clever and cunning,
Added to the sweetmeats fit for gods[80]
The choicest ingredients.
Into the gizi-ešta dough he kneaded honey, adding it steadily.
Then he set (the cake) before the nestling, the young of Anzud.
He gave the young salted meat to eat, fed it on sheep's fat;
He set out more cakes at its beak.
Then he put the young of Anzud back in its nest,
Painted its eyes with kohl,
Dabbed its head with cedar scent,
And set out spicy sausages at its head.
He then withdrew from Anzud's nest
And waited for him[81] in the highland that knows no cypress.

B The Meeting with Anzud

Just then the bird was herding the highland buffaloes,
Anzud was herding the highland buffaloes.
He held a live buffalo in his talons
And carried a dead buffalo on his shoulders.
He spit bile like gallons of water.
The bird circled around once,
Anzud circled around once.
When the bird called out to his nest,
When Anzud called out to his nest,
His fledgling did not call back from the nest.
When the bird called out to his nest again,
His fledgling did not call back from the nest.

ud na-an-ga-ma mušen-e gud$_3$-bi-še$_3$ šeg$_{11}$ un-gi$_4$
amar-bi gud$_3$-bi-ta inim ba-ni-ib-gi$_4$-gi$_4$
i$_3$-ne-še$_3$ mušen-e gud$_3$-bi-še$_3$ šeg$_{11}$ un-gi$_4$
amar-bi gud$_3$-bi-ta inim nu-um-ma-ni-ib-gi$_4$
mušen-e a-nir i-im-ğar an-e ba-teğ$_3$
dam-bi u$_8$ bi$_2$-in-dug$_4$ engur-ra ba-teğ$_3$
mušen-e u$_8$ dug$_4$-ga-bi-še$_3$
dam-bi a-nir ğar-ra-bi-še$_3$
^{d}a-nun-na diğir hur-sağ-ğa$_2$
kiši$_8$-gin$_7$ ki-in-dar-ra ba-an-di-ni-ib-kur$_9$-re-eš-am$_3$
mušen-e dam-bi-ir gu$_3$ am$_3$-ma-de$_2$-e
anzud^{mušen}-de$_3$ dam-bi-ir gu$_3$ am$_3$-ma-de$_2$-e
gud$_3$-mu-ta tur$_3$ gal ^{d}nanna-gin$_7$ ni$_2$ huš he$_2$-em-da-ri
piriğ kur-ra teš$_2$-bi du$_7$-du$_7$-gin$_7$ su-zi he$_2$-em-du$_8$-du$_8$
amar-mu gud$_3$-ba a-ba-a ba-ra-ab-tum$_3$
anzud^{mušen} gud$_3$-ba a-ba-a ba-ra-ab-tum$_3$

mušen-e gud$_3$-bi-še$_3$ he$_2$-em-ma-teğ$_3$-ğa$_2$-da-ka
anzud^{mušen}-de$_3$ gud$_3$-bi-še$_3$ he$_2$-em-ma-teğ$_3$-ğa$_2$-da-ka
ki diğir til$_3$-la-gin$_7$ im-ak giri$_{17}$-zal im-du$_8$-du$_8$
amar-bi gud$_3$-bi-a i-im-šeg$_{11}$
igi-bi šim-zid-da mu-un-gun$_3$
sağ-ba ^{giš}erin bar$_6$-bar$_6$ mu-un-du$_3$-du$_3$
mu-du-li-a šu gur-gur-ra-bi sağ-bi-še$_3$ mu-un-ğar
mušen-e ni$_2$-bi silim-e-še$_3$ iri in-ga-am$_3$-me
anzud^{mušen}-de$_3$ ni$_2$-bi silim-e-še$_3$ iri in-ga-am$_3$-me

id$_2$ hal-hal-la nun nam tar-re-bi-me-en
zid du šag$_4$ kuš$_2$-u$_3$ ^{d}en-lil$_2$-la$_2$-ka ^{giš}igi-tab-bi-me-en
a-a-mu ^{d}en-lil$_2$-le mu-un-de$_6$-en
kur-ra ^{giš}ig gal-gin$_7$ igi-ba bi$_2$-in-tab-en
nam u$_3$-mu-tar a-ba-a šu mi-ni-ib-bal-e
inim u$_3$-bi$_2$-dug$_4$ a-ba-a ib$_2$-ta-bal-e
lu$_2$ gud$_3$-ğa$_2$ ne-en ba-e-a-ak-a
diğir he$_2$-me-en inim ga-mu-ra-ab-dug$_4$
ku-li-ğa$_2$ nam-ba-e-ni-kur$_9$-re-en
lu$_2$-ulu$_3$ he$_2$-me-en nam ga-mu-ri-ib-tar
kur-re gaba šu ğar nam-mu-ri-in-tuku-un
mes anzud^{mušen}-de$_3$ a$_2$ šum$_2$-ma he$_2$-me-en

lugal-ban$_3$-da ni$_2$ diš-ta hul$_2$-la diš-ta
ni$_2$ diš šag$_4$ hul$_2$-la diš-ta
mušen-e mi$_2$ iri im-me

Up until then, whenever the bird called out to his nest
His fledgling had always called back from the nest,
But now, when the bird called out to his nest,
His fledgling did not call back from the nest.
The bird shrieked in grief; the cry rose up to heaven;
His wife cried out "Woe!"; the cry descended into the Abzu.
The bird with his cry of "Woe!"
His wife with her cry of grief
Made the Anuna, the gods of the hills,
Crawl into crevices like ants.
The bird spoke to his wife,
Anzud spoke to his wife:
"My nest, vast like the cattle-pen of Nanna,[82] spells disaster!
"As if mountain lions are *advancing,* it spreads fear!
"Who stole my fledgling from its nest?
"Who stole (young) Anzud from his nest?"

But when the bird came near to his nest,
When Anzud came near to his nest,
It seemed to him like a divine dwelling, so brilliantly it was adorned.
The fledgling was lying in the nest,
Its eyes painted with kohl,
Its head sprinkled with cedar scent,
And a roll of salted meat set out at its head.
The bird rejoiced in his good fortune;
Anzud rejoiced in his good fortune:

"I am the Prince who decides the destiny of the rolling rivers;
"I am the *helmet* of the fertile one who soothes Enlil's heart.
"My father Enlil brought me here;
"He made me bar the entrance to the highland like a great door.
"A fate decided by me—who can alter that?
"A decree uttered by me—who can change that?
"Whoever you are who has done this to my nest,
"If you are a god, I want to talk to you;
"I will let you enter in amity!
"If you are a man, I will decide your fate;
"I shall not suffer you to have a rival in the highlands;
"'Hero-made-strong-by-Anzud' you(r name) shall be!"[83]

Lugalbanda, partly in awe, partly in joy,
Partly in awe, partly in great joy,
Praises the bird,

anzud^{mušen}-de$_3$ mi$_2$ iri im-me
mušen šu-ur$_2$ sig$_7$ niğin$_5$-a tud-da
anzud^{mušen} šu-ur$_2$ sig$_7$ niğin$_5$-a tud-da
sug-a a tu$_5$-tu$_5$-zu-a a-ne dug$_4$-dug$_4$
pa-bil$_2$-ga-zu nun hal-hal-la-ke$_4$
an šu-zu-še$_3$ mu-un-ğar ki ğiri$_3$-zu-še$_3$ mu-un-ğar
pa-zu an-na sa am$_3$-ši-im-la$_2$-la$_2$-en nu-mu-[. . .]
ki-še$_3$ umbin-zu am kur-ra šilam kur-ra ^{ğiš}es$_2$-ad$^!$-am$_3$ ba-nu$_2$

murgu-zu dub sar-sar-re-me-en
ti-ti-zu ^{d}nirah dar-a-me-en
šag$_4$-su$_3$-zu kiri$_6$ sig$_7$-ga u$_6$-e gub-ba-me-en
ša-dug$_4$-ga-ta zi-mu mu-ri-de$_6$ zag-mu mu-ri-us$_2$
dam-zu ama-mu he$_2$-am$_3$ bi$_2$-in-dug$_4$
za-e ad-da-mu he$_2$-me-en bi$_2$-in-dug$_4$
di$_4$-di$_4$-la$_2$-zu-ne šeš-mu-ne-ka nam-ba-e-ni-in-ku$_4$-ku$_4$
ša-dug$_4$-ga-ta ha-šu-ur$_2$-ra nu-zu kur-ra-ka ki-gub mu-ra-ak-e
dam-zu silim-ğa$_2$ he$_2$-mu-e-da-gub
silim-mu ga-mu-ra-dug$_4$ nam tar-ra-mu ga-mu-ra-ab-[bur$_2$]-ra-a

mušen-e ni$_2$-bi mu-un-na-ra-ba-e ul mu-un-ši-ak-e
anzud^{mušen}-de$_3$ ni$_2$-bi mu-un-na-ra-ba-e ul mu-un-ši-ak-e
anzud^{mušen}-de$_3$ kug lugal-ban$_3$-da-ar gu$_3$ mu-na-de$_2$-e
ğa$_2$-nu lugal-ban$_3$-da-mu
^{ğiš}ma$_2$ kug-gin$_7$ ^{ğiš}ma$_2$ še-gin$_7$
^{ğiš}ma$_2$ ^{ğiš}hašhur bal-bal-e-gin$_7$
^{ğiš}ma$_2$ ukuš$_2$-a an-dul$_3$ ak-a-gin$_7$
^{ğiš}ma$_2$ ki buru$_{14}$ hi-li du$_8$-du$_8$-a-gin$_7$
sig$_4$ kul-ab$_4$^{ki}-še$_3$ sağ il$_2$-la ğin-na
lugal-ban$_3$-da lu$_2$ numun-e ki ağ$_2$-am$_3$ šu nu-um-<ma>-gid$_2$-de$_3$
^{d}šara$_2$ dumu ki ağ$_2$ ^{d}inana-gin$_7$
ti zu$_2$-zu-a ud-gin$_7$ ed$_2$-i$_3$
GIL.AK iti$_6$-gin$_7$ ed$_2$-i$_3$
ti zu$_2$ lu$_2$ ra-ra-bi muš šag$_4$-tur$_3$ he$_2$-e
ku$_6$ ^{urudu}dur$_{10}$-ra-gin$_7$ tu$_6$ kud he$_2$-e
ad ^{urudu}dur$_{10}$-ra-gin$_7$ niğ$_2$-KEŠ$_2$ he$_2$-ak-e
lugal-ban$_3$-da lu$_2$ numun-e ki ağ$_2$-am$_3$ šu nu-um-ma-gid$_2$-de$_3$
^{d}nin-urta dumu ^{d}en-lil$_2$-la$_2$-ke$_4$
^{tug2}sağšu piriğ me$_3$-a ugu-za he$_2$-eb-dul
LUM$^?$ BU TUKU kur gal-la gaba nu-gi$_4$ gaba-za he$_2$-eb-tab

kur-ra sa u$_3$ NE$_2$ KA sa UŠ [. . .]
iri im-ši-du-u$_5$ ki X [. . .]

Praises Anzud.
"O bird with the sparkling eyes, born in this region,
"O Anzud with the sparkling eyes, born in this region,
"You frolic as you bathe in the pools.
"Your father, Prince of all *domains,*
"Placed heaven at your hands and earth at your feet.
"Your wingspan is a net stretched across the sky; *it cannot* [. . .]
"On the earth your talons are a trap laid for the bulls and cows of the highland;
"Your spine is straight enough to write tablets;[84]
"Your breast is Nirah parting the waters;
"As to your back you are a verdant garden, a wonder to behold.
"Yesterday I put my life in your hands, entrusted my being to you.
"Saying 'May your wife become my mother,'
"And saying 'May you become my father!'
"I shall treat your little ones as my brothers.
"Since yesterday I have waited in the highland that knows no cypress.
"Your wife is included in my salutations;
"My salutations to you! Now I would like you to decide my fate."

The bird spoke, being pleased with him;
Anzud spoke, being pleased with him;
Anzud spoke to Lugalbanda:
"Well now, Lugalbanda,
"Like a ship full of precious metal, a ship full of grain,
"A ship delivering the apple harvest,
"A ship piled up with cucumbers, so high that it casts shade,
"A ship laden lavishly at the harvest fields—
"Return proudly in this manner to the brickwork of Kulab!"
But Lugalbanda, who loves his descendants, would not accept.
"Like Šara, the beloved son of Inana,
"Shoot forth your barbed darts like sunbeams;
"Shoot forth your reed arrows like *moonrays.*
"Let your barbed darts be a horned viper to those they hit;
"Let them cut with magic power, as one cuts fish with a cleaver;
"May they be bound together like logs hewn with the axe!"[85]
But Lugalbanda, who loves his descendants, would not accept.
"May Ninurta, Enlil's son,
"Set the helmet 'Lion of Battle'[86] on your head;
"May he put the *breastplate* 'In the Great Highland No Retreat!' on your breast!
"May he *give you* [. . .] the battle-net [. . .] in the highland;
"And when you march against a city, *may he* [. . .]!"

lugal-ban$_3$-da lu$_2$ numun-e ki [ağ$_2$-am$_3$ šu nu]-⸢um⸣-ma-⸢gid$_2$⸣-[de$_3$]
he$_2$-ğal$_2$ ^{dug}šakir kug ^{d}dumu-zid-da-[ka-ka]
i$_3$-bi ki-šar$_2$-ra-ke$_4$ ša-ra-X [. . .]
gara$_2$-bi ki-šar$_2$-ra-ke$_4$ ša-ra-X [. . .]
lugal-ban$_3$-da lu$_2$ numun-e ki ağ$_2$-am$_3$ šu nu-um-ma-gid$_2$-de$_3$
ki-ib^{mušen} ki-ib^{mušen} eğur-ra sug gid$_2$-i-gin$_7$ inim-ma ⸢mu⸣-[na]-ni-ib-gi$_4$

mušen-e ğeštug$_2$ mu-un-ši-ğa$_2$-ar
anzud^{mušen}-de$_3$ kug lugal-ban$_3$-da-ar gu$_3$ mu-na-de$_2$-e
ğa$_2$-nu lugal-ban$_3$-da-mu
inim šag$_4$-ga sig$_{10}$-ge ur$_5$-gim-ma-am$_3$
gud erim$_2$ du-us$_2$-a sig$_{10}$-ge$_5$-dam
anše dug$_3$ guz-za har-ra-an si sa$_2$ dab$_5$-be$_2$-dam inim-inim ma-gub ga-ri-gub
nam tar-ra šag$_4$-ge gur$_7$-a-zu ga$_2$-e ga-mu-ri-ib-tar

kug lugal-ban$_3$-da mu-na-ni-ib-gi$_4$-gi$_4$
zag-še-ğa$_2$ kas$_4$ he$_2$-ğal$_2$ nam-ba-kuš$_2$-u$_3$-de$_3$-en
a$_2$-ğa$_2$-a lirum he$_2$-ğal$_2$
a$_2$-mu ga-sud-sud a$_2$-mu na-an-gig-ge
ud-gin$_7$ du ^{d}inana-gin$_7$
ud 7-e ud ^{d}iškur-ra-gin$_7$
izi-gin$_7$ ga-il$_2$ nim-gin$_7$ ga-ğir$_2$
igi du$_8$-a bar-ra-ğa$_2$ ga-ğin
igi il$_2$-la-ğa$_2$ ğiri$_3$-mu ga-ab-gub
šag$_4$-ge gur$_7$-ğa$_2$ an-ta ga-ab-gi$_4$
ki šag$_4$-mu na-an-ga-ma-ab-be$_2$-a ^{kuš}e-sir$_2$-[mu] ga-du$_8$
^{d}utu iri-mu kul-ab$_4$^{ki}-še$_3$ am$_3$-ku$_4$-ku$_4$-de$_3$-ne-a
lu$_2$ aš$_2$ dug$_4$-ga-mu nam-ba-e-ši-hul$_2$-e-en
lu$_2$ du$_{14}$ mu$_2$-a-mu he$_2$-du-mu nam-me
alan-zu ğiš-dim$_2$-ba um-mi-dim$_2$ u$_6$-e gub-ba-me-en

mu-zu ki-en-gi-ra pa ed$_2$ ha-bi$_2$-ak
e$_2$ diğir gal-gal-e-ne-ka me-te-aš bi$_2$-[ib]-ğal$_2$

anzud^{mušen}-de$_3$ kug lugal-ban$_3$-da -ra ⸢gu$_3$⸣ [mu-na]-de$_2$-e
za$_3$-še-za kas$_4$ he$_2$-ğal$_2$ nam-[ba-kuš$_2$-u$_3$-de$_3$]-⸢en⸣

a$_2$-zu-a lirum [he$_2$-ğal$_2$]
a$_2$-zu sud-sud-a a$_2$-[zu na-an-gig-ge]
ud-gin$_7$ du d[inana-gin$_7$]
ud 7 ^{d}[iškur-ra]-⸢gin$_7$⸣
izi-gin$_7$ il$_2$-la nim-gin$_7$ ğir$_2$-a

But Lugalbanda, who loves his descendants, would not accept.
"The bounty of the churn of Holy Dumuzid,
"Whose fat is the fat of the whole world, may it also [. . .];
"Its milk is the milk of the whole world; may it also [. . .]."
But Lugalbanda, who loves his descendants, would not accept.
Like the kib bird, the sweetwater kib bird flying over the swamp, he answers.[87]
The bird listens to him.
Anzud then spoke to Lugalbanda:
"Well now, my Lugalbanda,
"May it[88] then be as your own heart wishes!
"A willful plowing ox must be kept on the track;
"A braying donkey must be kept on the straight path—I will grant your wish![89]
"I will decide your destiny according to your own desire!"

Holy Lugalbanda replied:
"May the strength of running abound in my thighs, so that I never tire.
"Let there be power in my arms;
"May my arms stretch wide, may my force not weaken.
"Traveling like the Sun, like Inana,
"Like the seven storms of Iškur,
"May I leap like the flame, jump like lightning!
"I want to be able to go wherever I choose,
"Set my feet wherever I cast my eyes,
"Arrive wherever my heart prompts me,
"And loosen my sandals only where my heart tells me!
"If the Sun allows me to reach my city Kulab,
"May those who despise me not rejoice!
"May those who have a quarrel with me not say, 'Come on then!'
"Then I shall have the sculptors make statues of you, a wonder to behold!
"Your name shall be revered throughout Sumer,
"And the statues will become an emblem in every great temple!"[90]

Anzud replied to Holy Lugalbanda:
"The strength of running shall abound in your thighs, so that you never tire.
"There shall be power in your arms;
"Your arms shall stretch wide, your force shall not weaken.
"Traveling like the Sun, like Inana,
"Like the seven storms of Iškur,
"You shall leap like the flame, jump like lightning!

igi du$_8$-a bar-ra-za ğin-na
igi il$_2$-la-za ğiri$_3$-zu gub-bi$_2$-ib
šag$_4$-ge gur$_7$-a-zu an-ta gi$_4$-bi$_2$
ki šag$_4$-zu na-an-ga-ra-ab-be$_2$-e-a ^{kuš}e-sir$_2$-zu du$_8$-a
^{d}utu iri-zu kul-ab$_4$^{ki}-še$_3$ am$_3$-ku$_4$-ku$_4$-de$_3$-en-na-a
lu$_2$ aš$_2$ dug$_4$-ga-zu nam-ba-e-ši-hul$_2$-le-en
lu$_2$ du$_{14}$ mu$_2$-a-zu he$_2$-du-zu nam-me
[alan]-mu ğiš-dim$_2$-ba um-mi-dim$_2$ u$_6$-e um-mi-gub
[mu]-mu ki-en-gi-ra pa ed$_2$ ba-ni-ak
[e$_2$]⸢diğir⸣ gal-gal-e-ne-ka me-te-aš im-mi-ib-ğal$_2$
[X] X ^{kuš}e-sir$_2$-gin$_7$ ni$_2$-ba hu-mu-ra-an-dub$_2$-dub$_2$-be-eš
[X] $^{\text{id2}}$buranun-na pa$_5$ ubur-gin$_7$ ğiri$_3$-zu pa$_4$-pa$_4$ mi$_2$ am$_3$-me

II. LUGALBANDA'S RETURN TO HIS BROTHERS

C. Effects of the Return

[ninda] kaskal-la-ka-ni nu-um-ka-aš
^{ğiš}tukul-a-ni diš-bi šu im-ma-an-ti
anzud^{mušen} an-ta i$_3$-ğin
lugal-ban$_3$-da ki-ta i$_3$-ğin
[mušen-e an]-ta igi mi-ni-in-il$_2$ erin$_2$-e igi bi$_2$-in-du$_8$-ru
[lugal]-⸢ban$_3$⸣-da ki-ta igi mi-ni-in-il$_2$ sahar erin$_2$-e du$_8$-a igi bi$_2$-in-du$_8$-ru
mušen-e kug lugal-ban$_3$-da-ar gu$_3$ mu-na-de$_2$-e
ğa$_2$-nu lugal-ban$_3$-da-mu
na ga-e-ri na-ri-mu he$_2$-e-dab$_5$
inim ga-ra-ab-dug$_4$ ğizzal he$_2$-em-ši-ak
gu$_3$ i-ri-de$_2$-a nam i-ri-tar-ra
ku-li-zu-ne-er nam-mu-ni-ib-be$_2$-en
šeš-zu-ne-er pa nam-bi$_2$-ib-ed$_2$-en
sag$_9$-ga hul šag$_4$-ga ğal$_2$-la ur$_5$ he$_2$-na-nam-ma
ğa$_2$-e gud$_3$-mu-še$_3$ he$_2$-me-en za-e erin$_2$-zu he$_2$-me-en
mušen-e gud$_3$-bi-še$_3$ šu am$_3$-ma-niğin
lugal-ban$_3$-da ki šeš-a-ne-ne-še$_3$ ğiri$_3$ im-ma-gub-be$_2$

u$_5$^{mušen} ğiš-gi kug-ta ed$_2$-a-gin$_7$
la-ha-ma abzu-ta re$_7$-e-gin$_7$
lu$_2$ an-ta ki-a gub-ba-gin$_7$
lugal-ban$_3$-da ka KEŠ$_2$ ğar-ra šeš-a-ne-ne-ka murub$_4$-ba ba-an-gub?
šeš-a-ne-ne gu$_3$ ba-ab-ra-ra-ra-⸢aš⸣ [X] erin$_2$-e gu$_3$ ab-ra-ra-aš
šeš-a-ne-ne ku-li-ne-ne
en$_3$ tar-re im-mi-in-kuš$_2$-u$_3$-ne
ğa$_2$-nu lugal-ban$_3$-da-mu za-e ğal$_2$-la-zu-ne

"You shall be able to go wherever you choose,
"Set your feet wherever you cast your eyes,
"Arrive wherever your heart prompts you,
"And loosen your sandals only where your heart tells you!
"If the Sun allows you to reach your city Kulab,
"Those who despise you shall not rejoice!
"Those who have a quarrel with you shall not say, 'Come on then!'
"Have the sculptors make statues of me, a wonder to behold!
"My name shall be revered throughout Sumer,
"And my statues will become an emblem in every great temple!
"Of themselves [*the rough places*] shall become [*plain*] as a street for you!
"The [*width*] of the Euphrates shall be but an irrigation ditch to your feet!"

II. LUGALBANDA'S RETURN TO HIS BROTHERS

C. Effects of the Return

The travel provisions he had not eaten,
And his weapons, one by one, he took in hand.
Anzud flew above, in the air,
And Lugalbanda ran below, on the earth.[91]
Looking from above [the bird] spied the troops;
Looking from below Lugalbanda saw the dust raised by the troops.
The bird told Lugalbanda:
"Now, then, my Lugalbanda,
"I will give you some advice—heed it!
"I will tell you something—listen!
"What I promised you, the destiny I fixed for you,
"Do not tell that to your companions,
"Do not make it known to your brothers!
"Good fortune causes bad feelings—so it has ever been!
"Now I am for my nest; you go to your troops!"
And the bird *turned around* to his nest
As Lugalbanda set out for the place where his brothers were.

Like the U-bird rising from the holy reed thicket,
Like a lahama-spirit shooting up from the Abzu,
Like one landing on earth from heaven,
Lugalbanda suddenly stepped into the midst of the troop of his brothers.
His brothers started to chatter, the troop began to babble.
His brothers and companions
Weary him with questions:
"Well now, Lugalbanda, (how is it that) you are here again?

lu$_2$ me$_3$-a ğiš ra-gin$_7$ erin$_2$-e he$_2$-en-tak$_4$-nam
i$_3$ dug$_3$-a tur$_3$-ra ba-ra-mu-un-gu$_7$
ga luh-ha amaš-a ba-ra-mu-un-gu$_7$
hur-sağ gal lu$_2$ dili nu-du-u$_3$-da
lu$_2$-bi lu$_2$-ra nu-gi$_4$-gi$_4$-da a-gin$_7$ im-da-du-de$_3$-en
2-kam-ma-še$_3$ šeš-a-ne-ne ku-li-ne-ne
en$_3$ tar-re im-mi-in-kuš$_2$-u$_3$-ne
id$_2$ kur-ra ama he$_2$-nun-na-ra
peš$_{10}$-peš$_{10}$-bi peš$_{10}$-ta sur-ra-am$_3$
a-bi a-gin$_7$ mu-e-nağ a-gin$_7$ mu-e-bal-e

kug lugal-ban$_3$-da mu-un-na-ni-ib-gi$_4$-gi$_4$
id$_2$ kur-ra ama he$_2$-nun-na-ra
peš$_{10}$-peš$_{10}$-bi peš$_{10}$-ta sur-ra-am$_3$
zag-še-ğa$_2$ ki um-ma-ni-us$_2$ a ^{kuš}ummud-gin$_7$ u$_3$-mu-nağ
ur-bar-ra-gin$_7$ gum$_3$-ga-am$_3$ mi-ni-za u$_2$-sal i$_3$-gu$_7$-en
tu-gur$_4$^{mušen}-gin$_7$ ki im-ri-ri-ge-en i-li-a-nu-um kur-ra i$_3$-gu$_7$-[en]

lugal-ban$_3$-da šeš-a-ne-ne ku-li-ne-ne
inim in-ne-en-dug$_4$-ga šag$_4$-ga-ne-ne-a ba-an-šub-bu-uš
i-gi$_4$-in-zu buru$_5$^{mušen}-e ud gid$_2$-da teš$_2$-bi KEŠ$_2$-da-gin$_7$
gu$_2$-ni gu$_2$-da im-da-la$_2$-e-ne ne mu-un-su-su-ub
amar gam$_3$-gam$_3$^{mušen} gud$_3$-ba tuš-a-gin$_7$
mu-ni-ib-gu$_7$-u$_3$-ne mu-ni-ib-na$_8$-na$_8$-ne
kug lugal-ban$_3$-da tu-ra-ni mu-un-ta-ab-ed$_3$-ne

ud-ba unug^{ki}-ga lu$_2$ dili-gin$_7$ eğir-bi-ir bi$_2$-ib-us$_2$
muš zar-ra-gin$_7$ hur-sağ-ta im-me-re-bal-bal
iri danna 1-am$_3$ am$_3$-da-ğal$_2$-la-ba
dim-dim-e aratta^{ki}-ka
unug^{ki} kul-ab$_4$^{ki}-bi ur$_2$ ba-an-dun-dun
iri-ta gi-bar-bar-re im-gin$_7$ im-šeğ$_3$
im-dug-ge im mu-a ğin-na-gin$_7$
bad$_3$ aratta^{ki}-ka gu$_3$-nun-bi im-me
ud ba-zal-zal iti ba-sud-sud mu ama-bi-ir ba-gi$_4$
buru$_{14}$ sig$_7$-ga an-na ba-e-a-ed$_3$-de$_3$
a-šag$_4$-ga igi ba-ab-hul ni$_2$ su-e bi$_2$-ib-us$_2$
im-dug-ge im mu-a ğin-na-gin$_7$
kaskal-la ki ba-ni-ib$_2$-u$_2$-us$_2$
^{ğiš}U$_2$.ĞIR$_2$ kur-ra-ke$_4$ ka ba-ni-ib$_2$-KEŠ$_2$
ušumgal teš$_2$-bi mu-un-tag-tag-ge
lu$_2$ iri-še$_3$ du-u$_3$ nu-um-zu
kul-ab$_4$^{ki}-še$_3$ du-u$_3$ sağ nu-mu-da-ab-šum$_2$-mu

"The troop had left you like one fallen in battle;
"You were no longer eating the good fat of the herd;
"You were no longer eating the fresh cheese from the fold!
"From the high hills where no one can walk alone,
"Whence no one can return to humankind, how did you come back?"
And again his brothers and companions
Weary him with questions:
"The highland streams, though mothers of plenty,
"Have *very steep* banks.
"How did you drink, how did you draw (water)?"

Holy Lugalbanda replied:
"The highland streams, though mothers of plenty,
"Have *very steep* banks.
"Lying on my side, I drank as from the water skin;[92]
"I *growled* like the wolf, I grazed the water-meadows;
"I pecked the earth like the wood-pigeon, I ate *wild* acorns."

Lugalbanda's brothers and companions
Accepted the words he had spoken to them.
As small birds flocking together all day
They embrace and kiss him.
As if he were a gamgam-chick in its nest
They feed him and give him to drink.
Thus they drove away the illness of Holy Lugalbanda.[93]

Then they again followed (the host of) Unug as one man;[94]
They wound their way over the hill like a snake over a grain pile.
When the city (Aratta) was but one league distant,
By the *watchtowers* of Aratta,[95]
Unug and Kulab pitched camp.
From the city javelins were raining down as from a cloud;
Slingstones, numerous as the raindrops falling in a whole year,
Were whizzing down from the wall of Aratta.
Days went by and lenghtened into months; a whole year *passed*.
The harvest grew yellow beneath the skies.
Worrying, they looked at the fields; they grew uneasy.
Slingstones, numerous as the raindrops falling in a whole year,
Kept falling on the roads.
Mountain thorns hemmed them in,
Dragons[96] closed up on them;
Nobody knew how to get back to the city;
Nobody could hasten back to Kulab.

III. THE SOLUTION

D. Problem Solving

šag$_4$-ba en-me-er-kar$_2$ dumu ^{d}utu-ke$_4$
ni$_2$ ba-ni-in-te zi ba-ni-in-ir za-pa-ağ$_2$-bi ba-ni-in-BAD
lu$_2$ iri-še$_3$ mu-un-gi$_4$-gi$_4$-a ki mu-ši-kiğ$_2$-kiğ$_2$
kul-ab$_4$^{ki}-še$_3$ mu-un-gi$_4$-gi$_4$-a ki mu-ši-kiğ$_2$-kiğ$_2$
lu$_2$ iri-še$_3$ ğa$_2$-e ga-ğin nu-mu-un-na-ab-be$_2$
kul-ab$_4$^{ki}-še$_3$ ğa$_2$-e ga-ğin nu-⸢mu⸣-[un-na-ab]-⸢be$_2$⸣
ugnim kur-kur-ra-ka ⸢mu⸣-[un-ed$_2$]
lu$_2$ iri-še$_3$ ğa$_2$-e ga-ğin nu-mu-⸢na⸣-[ab- be$_2$]
kul-ab$_4$^{ki}-še$_3$ ğa$_2$-e ga-ğin nu-mu-na-⸢ab⸣-[be$_2$]
ka-KEŠ$_2$ igi bar-ra-ka mu-un-ed$_2$
lu$_2$ iri-še$_3$ ğa$_2$-e ga-ğin nu-mu-na-ab- be$_2$
kul-ab$_4$^{ki}-še$_3$ ğa$_2$-e ga-ğin ⸢nu⸣-[mu-na-ab- be$_2$]
2-kam-ma-še$_3$ ugnim kur-kur-ra-ka mu-un-ed$_2$
lu$_2$ iri-še$_3$ ğa$_2$-e ga-ğin nu-mu-na-ab-be$_2$
kul-ab$_4$^{ki}-še$_3$ ğa$_2$-e ga-ğin nu-⸢mu⸣-[na-ab- be$_2$]
ka-KEŠ$_2$ igi bar-ra-ka mu-un-ed$_2$
lugal-ban$_3$-da dili-ni un-ğa$_2$ mu-na-an-zi gu$_3$ mu-na-de$_2$-e
lugal-mu ğa$_2$-e iri-še$_3$ ga-ğin lu$_2$ nam-mu-da-an-du
kul-ab$_4$^{ki}-še$_3$ dili-mu-ne ga-ğin lu$_2$ nam-mu-da-an-du

Enmerkar

ud-da iri-še$_3$ i$_3$-du-un lu$_2$ nu-mu-e-da-du-u$_3$
ud-da kul-ab$_4$^{ki}-še$_3$ i$_3$-du-un lu$_2$ nu-mu-e-da-du-u$_3$
zi an-na zi ki-a i$_3$-pad$_3$ me gal-gal kul-ab$_4$^{ki}-a šu-zu ba-ra-ba-ra-ed$_2$

unkin ğar-ra si sa$_2$-a-na
šag$_4$ e$_2$-gal-la kur gal-gin$_7$ ki he$_2$-us$_2$-a-ba
en-me-er-kar$_2$ dumu ^{d}utu-ke$_4$
eme sig ^{d}inana ba-ni-in-gu$_7$
ki ud-ba nin$_9$ e$_5$-mu kug ^{d}inana-ke$_4$
kur šuba$^{?}$-ta šag$_4$ kug-ga-ni-a he$_2$-em-ma-ni-pad$_3$-de$_3$-en
sig$_4$ kul-ab$_4$^{ki}-še$_3$ he$_2$-em-[ma-ni]-in-kur$_9$-re-en
unug^{ki}-e sug he$_2$-me-am$_3$ a he$_2$-em-de$_2$-a
bar$_2$-rim$_4$ he$_2$-me-am$_3$ ^{ğiš}asal he$_2$-mu$_2$-a
ğiš-gi he$_2$-me-am$_3$ gi-uš$_2$ gi-henbur he$_2$-<mu$_2$-a>
^{d}en-ki lugal eridug^{ki}-ga-ke$_4$
gi-uš$_2$-bi ha-ma-an-ze$_2$ a-bi ha-ma-an-uš$_2$
mu ninnu-uš hu-mu-du$_3$ mu ninnu-uš hu-mu-di
ki-en-gi ki-uri niğin$_2$-na-a-ba

III. THE SOLUTION

D. Problem Solving

In their midst Enmerkar, son of the Sun,
Grew anxious and despondent by the unceasing noise.[97]
He sought someone to travel back to the city,
He sought someone to travel back to Kulab,
But no one said, "I will travel back to the city!"
No one said, "I will travel back to Kulab!"
He went to the foreign troops,
But no one said, "I will travel back to the city!"
No one said, "I will travel back to Kulab!"
He went to the *guides*'[98] regiment,
But no one said, "I will travel back to the city!"
No one said "I will travel back to Kulab!"
Again he went to the foreign troops,
But no one said "I will travel back to the city!";
No one said, "I will travel back to Kulab!"[99]
As he went again to the *guides*' regiment,
Only Lugalbanda among the throng stood up and said:
"My king, I will go to the city, but no one may come with me!
"I alone will go to Kulab, no one may come with me!"
Enmerkar
"When you go to the city no one shall go with you!
"When you go to Kulab no one shall go with you!"
He (Lugalbanda) swore by the life of heaven and earth: "The powers of Kulab shall not elude you!"

Standing straight before the gathered assembly
In the *palace*[100] that rests on earth as a tall mountain
Enmerkar, son of the Sun,
Spoke harsh words to Inana:
"Once upon a time my noble sister, Holy Inana,
"From her bright mountain chose me in her holy heart
"And made me enter Kulab, the Brickwork.
"Unug then was a mere marsh, oozing water.
"Where there was dry land Euphrates poplars grew.[101]
"Where there was a reed thicket old and young reeds grew together.
"Enki, king of Eridug,
"Made me tear out the old reeds and made me drain the water.
"Fifty years I was building, fifty years I was working.
"So now, if eventually in all of Sumer and Akkad

mar-tu lu$_2$ še nu-zu hu-mu-zig$_3$
bad$_3$ unug^{ki}-ga gu mušen-na-gin$_7$ edin-na he$_2$-ni-la$_2$-la$_2$

i-da-al-la-ba ki-ğal$_2$-la-ba hi-li-mu ba-til
^{ab2}šilam amar-bi la$_2$-a-gin$_7$ erin$_2$-mu mu-da-la$_2$
dumu ama-ni-ir hul gig-ga iri-ta ed$_2$-a-gin$_7$
nin$_9$ e$_5$-mu kug ^{d}inana-ke$_4$
sig$_4$ kul-ab$_4$^{ki}-še$_3$ šu ma-ra-an-dag
ud-da iri-ni ki ha-ba-an-ağ$_2$ ğa$_2$-a-ra hul ha-ba-an-gig
iri ğa$_2$-da a-na-aš am$_3$-da-la$_2$-e
ud-da iri-ni hul ha-ba-an-gig ğa$_2$-a-ra ki ha-ba-an-ağ$_2$
ğa$_2$-e iri-da a-na-aš am$_3$-da-la$_2$-e-en
nu-gig-ge anzud^{mušen} amar-ra-gin$_7$
ni$_2$ te-a-ni sag$_2$ um-ma-an-di$^{!}$
bar kug-ga-ni-a um-ma-an-šub-be$_2$-en
sig$_4$ kul-ab$_4$^{ki}-še$_3$ he$_2$-em-ma-ni-in-kur$_9$-en
^{ğiš}gid$_2$-da-mu ud ne ba-an-de$_6$
^{kuš}E.IB$_2$.UR$_2$-mu ud ne e-ne ba-an-zur-zur-re
nin$_9$ e$_5$-mu kug ^{d}inana-ra ur$_5$-gin$_7$ dug$_4$-mu-na-ab

kug lugal-ban$_3$-da e$_2$-gal-ta im-ma-da-ra-ta-ed$_2$
šeš-a-ne-ne ku-li-ne-ne
ur gir$_5$ ur-ra kur$_9$-ra-gin$_7$ hu-un-ha mu-un-ši-ib-za-na-aš
dur$_3$ gir$_5$ dur$_3$-a kur$_9$-ra-gin$_7$ galam mu-un-na-ta-ed$_2$

companions
en-ra unug^{ki}-še$_3$ gi$_4$-mu-un-ši-ib
en-me-er-kar$_2$ dumu ^{d}utu-ra

Lugalbanda
kul-ab$_4$^{ki}-še$_3$ dili-mu-ne ga-ğin lu$_2$ nam-mu-da-du a-gin$_7$ mu-un-ne-dug$_4$

companions
me-na-am$_3$ dili-zu-ne kaskal-e sağ ba-ra-mu-ri-ib-us$_2$
^{d}udug sag$_9$-ga-me nam-ba-e-de$_3$-gub-ba
^{d}lama sag$_9$-ga-me nam-ba-e-de$_3$-ğin-na
ki-gub-ba-me-a nam-ba-e-de$_3$-gub-bu-nam
ki-tuš-a-me-a nam-ba-e-de$_3$-tuš-u$_3$-nam
sahar ğir i$_3$-me-a ğiri$_3$ nam-ba-e-de$_3$-us$_2$-e
hur-sağ gal lu$_2$ dili nu-du-u$_3$-dam
lu$_2$-bi lu$_2$-ra nu-gi$_4$-gi$_4$-da ba-ra-gi$_4$-gi$_4$-nam

Lugalbanda
ud zal-le in-zu-ta ki-gal-la ba-ra-da-ni-in-sug$_2$-ge-en-za-na

"The Martu, who know no grain,[102] should rise up,
"There stands the wall of Unug, extended across the desert like a bird net!
"But here, in this place, my power[103] seems to be finished!
"My troops are bound to me as a calf to its mother.
"Yet, like a child that hates its mother and leaves the city
"My noble sister, Holy Inana,
"Has run back to Kulab, the Brickwork!
"Could she love her city, yet hate me?
"She should link the city to me!
"Could she hate her city, yet love me?
"She should link the city to me![104]
"Should the nu-gig[105]—as happened to the Anzud chick—
"Reject me in person
"And abandon me by keeping to her holy chamber,
"Let her at least bring me back to Kulab, the Brickwork!
"Only on that day my spear shall be laid aside;
"On that day my shield shall be broken![106]
"Speak thus to my noble sister, Holy Inana!"

Thereupon Holy Lugalbanda left the *palace.*
His brothers and companions
Barked to him as to a strange dog trying to enter the pack,
while he (Lugalbanda) was prancing proudly like a donkey-foal trying to enter the herd.

companions

"Send someone else to Unug for the lord,
"For Enmerkar, son of the Sun!"

Lugalbanda

"I alone will go to Kulab; no one may come with me!" he said.

companions

"Why do you insist on traveling this road all alone?
"If our guardian angel does not go with you,
"If our benevolent spirit does not march with you,[107]
"You will never again stand here with us;
"You will never again sit here with us;[108]
"You will never again set your feet on the earth with us!
"From the high hills where no one can walk alone,
"Whence no one can return to humankind, you cannot return!"

Lugalbanda

"I know that time flies; there is none of you who can keep up with me traveling over the broad earth!"

E. The Ultimate Message

lugal-ban$_3$-da šag$_4$ gu$_3$ di šeš-a-ne-ne-ta
šag$_4$ sig$_3$ ku-li-ne-ne-ta
ninda kaskal-la-ka-ni nu-um-ka-aš
^{ğiš}tukul-a-ni diš-bi diš-bi šu im-ma-an-ti
kur ur$_2$-ra kur bad$_3$-da ma-du-um-e

zag an-ša$_4$-na-ta sağ an-ša$_4$-an^{ki}-na-še$_3$
hur-sağ 5 hur- sağ 6 hur-sağ 7 im-me-re-bal-bal
ği$_6$-sa$_9$-a ^{ğiš}banšur kug ^{d}inana-ke$_4$ nu-um-ma-teğ$_3$-a-aš

sig$_4$ kul-ab$_4$^{ki}-še$_3$ ğiri$_3$ hul$_2$-la mi-ni-in-gub
nin-a-ni kug ^{d}inana-ke$_4$
ša$_3$-da-ga-na mu-na-an-tuš
i$_3$-gur$_2$ ki-a mu-na-ab-za

su$_8$-ba ^{d}ama-ušumgal-an-na mu-na-ši-bar-gin$_7$
kug lugal-ban$_3$-da igi mu-na-ši-bar-re
dumu-na en ^{d}šara mu-na-de$_2$-a-gin$_7$
kug lugal-ban$_3$-da gu$_3$ mu-un-na-da-de$_2$-e
ğa$_2$-nu lugal-ban$_3$-da -mu
iri-ta a$_2$ ağ$_2$-ğa$_2$ a-na-aš mu-e-de$_6$
aratta^{ki} dili-zu-ne a-gin$_7$ im-da-ğin-ne-en
kug lugal-ban$_3$-da mu-na-ni-ib-gi$_4$-gi$_4$
šeš-zu a-na bi$_2$-in-dug$_4$ a-na bi$_2$-in-tah
en-me-er-kar$_2$ dumu ^{d}utu-ke$_4$ a-na bi$_2$-in-dug$_4$ a-na bi$_2$-in-tah
ki ud-ba nin$_9$ e$_5$-mu kug ^{d}inana-ke$_4$
kur šuba$^{?}$-ta šag$_4$ kug-ga-ni-a he$_2$-em-ma-ni-pad$_3$-de$_3$
sig$_4$ kul-ab$_4$^{ki}-še$_3$ he$_2$-em-ma-ni-in-kur$_9$-re-en
unug^{ki}-e sug he$_2$-me-am$_3$ a he$_2$-em-de$_2$-a
bar$_2$-rim$_4$ he$_2$-me-am$_3$ ^{ğiš}asal he$_2$-mu$_2$-a
ğiš-gi he$_2$-me-am$_3$ gi-uš$_2$ gi-henbur he$_2$-mu$_2$-a

^{d}en-ki lugal eridug^{ki}-ga-ke$_4$
gi-uš$_2$-bi ha-ma-an-ze$_2$ a-bi ha-ma-an-uš$_2$
mu ninnu-uš hu-mu-du$_3$ mu ninnu-uš hu-mu-di
ki-en-gi ki-uri niğin$_2$-na-a-ba
mar-tu lu$_2$ še nu-zu hu-mu-zig$_3$
bad$_3$ unug^{ki}-ga gu mušen-na-gin$_7$ edin-na he$_2$-ni-la$_2$-la$_2$
i-da-la-ba ki-ğal$_2$-la-ba hi-li-mu ba-til
^{ab2}šilam amar-bi la$_2$-a-gin$_7$ erin$_2$-mu mu-da-la$_2$
dumu ama-ni-[ir] hul gig-ga iri-ta ed$_2$-a-gin$_7$

E. The Ultimate Message

Lugalbanda, *in spite of* the pounding hearts of his brothers,
In spite of the dejection of his companions,
Took no provisions for the journey;
He only took his weapons, one by one.
From the foot of the highlands, through the mountain ranges, to the plains,
From the far border of Anšan to the upland of Anšan
He crossed five, six, seven mountain ranges.
That same night, before they had even brought in the evening meal for Holy Inana,
He stepped joyfully into Kulab, the Brickwork!
His lady, Holy Inana,
Was sitting there on her *cushion.*
He bowed and prostrated himself before her.

As she is wont to look at Ama-ušumgalana,[109] the shepherd,
She looked upon Holy Lugalbanda;
As she is wont to speak to her son Šara,
She spoke to Holy Lugalbanda:
"Well now, my Lugalbanda,
"Why do you bring news from the city?
"Why did you come from Aratta, all by yourself?"
Holy Lugalbanda replied:
"Your brother, this is what he said, what he spoke;
"This is what Enmerkar, son of the Sun, said, what he spoke:
"'Once upon a time my noble sister, Holy Inana,
"'from her bright mountain chose me in her holy heart,
"'and made me enter Kulab, the Brickwork.
"'Unug then was a mere marsh, oozing water.
"'Where there was dry land Euphrates poplars grew.
"'Where there was a reed thicket old and young reeds grew together.
"'Enki, king of Eridug,
"'Made me tear out the old reeds and made me drain the water.
"'Fifty years I was building, fifty years I was working.
"'So now, if eventually in all of Sumer and Akkad
"'The Martu, who know no grain, should rise up,
"'There stands the wall of Unug, extended across the desert like a bird net!
"'But here, in this place, my power seems to be finished!
"'My troops are bound to me as a calf to its mother.
"'Yet, like a child that hates its mother and leaves the city

nin$_9$ e$_5$-mu kug ^{d}inana-ke$_4$
sig$_4$ kul-ab$_4$^{ki}-še$_3$ šu ma-ra-an-dag
ud-da iri-ni ki ha-ba-an-ağ$_2$ ğa$_2$-a-ra hul ha-ba-an-gig
iri ğa$_2$-da a-na-aš am$_3$-da-la$_2$-e
ud-da iri-ni hul ha-ba-an-gig ğa$_2$-a-ra ki ha-ba-an-ağ$_2$
ğa$_2$-a iri-da a-na-aš am$_3$-da-la$_2$-e-en
nu-gig-ge anzud^{mušen} amar-ra-gin$_7$
ni$_2$ te-a-ni sag$_2$ um-ma-an-di$^{!}$
bar kug-ga-ni-a um-ma-an-šub-be$_2$-en
sig$_4$ kul-ab$_4$^{ki}-še$_3$ he$_2$-em-ma-ni-in-kur$_9$-re-en
^{ğiš}gid$_2$-da-mu ud ne ba-an-de$_6$
^{kuš}E.IB$_2$.UR$_2$-mu ud ne e-ne ba-an-zur-zur-re
nin$_9$ e$_5$-mu kug ^{d}inana-ra ur$_5$-gin$_7$ dug$_4$-mu-na-ab

kug ^{d}inana-ke$_4$ mu-na-ni-ib-gi$_4$-gi$_4$
i$_3$-ne-še$_3$ id$_2$ šen-na id$_2$ a šen-na-ka
id$_2$ ^{kuš}ummud za-gin$_3$ ^{d}inana-ke$_4$
kun-ba peš$_{10}$-peš$_{10}$-ba u$_2$-sal-u$_2$-sal-ba
suhur-maš^{ku6}-e u$_2$ lal$_3$ i$_3$-gu$_7$-e
kiğ$_2$-tur^{ku6}-e ^{u2}i-li-a-nu-um kur-ra i$_3$-gu$_7$-e
ĞIŠ.ŠEŠ^{ku6} diğir suhur-maš$_2$^{ku6}-a-ke$_4$
šag$_4$-ba a-ne hul$_2$-la mu-un-e kun-bi mu-un-sud-e
kun šika ri-ba gi-uš$_2$ ki kug-ga im-mi-ib$_2$-us$_2$-e
^{ğiš}šinig ma-da a-na-me-a-bi
ambar-bi-a a ib$_2$-na$_8$-na$_8$
dili-bi i$_3$-du$_3$ dili-bi i$_3$-du$_3$
^{ğiš}šinig-e bar-ta dili-bi i$_3$-du$_3$
en-me-<er>-kar$_2$ dumu ^{d}utu-ke$_4$
^{ğiš}šinig-bi un-sig$_3$ ^{ğiš}buniğ-še$_3$ un-dim$_2$
gi-uš$_2$ ki kug-ga ur$_2$-ba mi-ni-bu šu im-ma-an-ti

ĞIŠ.ŠEŠ^{ku6} diğir suhur-maš$_2$^{ku6}-a-ke$_4$ šag$_4$-ba u$_3$-ba-ra-ed$_2$-a

ku$_6$-bi un-dab$_5$ un-šeğ$_6$ un-sud
a$_2$-an-kar$_2$ a$_2$ me$_3$ ^{d}inana-ka u$_3$-bi$_2$-in-gu$_7$
erin$_2$-na-ni šu-bi he$_2$-en-di-ni-ib-sud-sud
zi aratta-ka engur-ra he$_2$-ni-in-til

iri kug dim$_2$-bi kug-dim$_2$ u$_3$-bi$_2$-in-dab$_5$
za dim$_2$-ma-bi za-dim$_2$ u$_3$-bi$_2$-in-dab$_5$
iri-da u$_3$-gibil-la$_2$ um-ma-an-di-ni-ib-ğar-ğar
aratta^{ki} agarin$_4$-agarin$_4$-ba šu hu-mu-na-niğin

"'My noble sister, Holy Inana,
"'Has run back to Kulab, the Brickwork!
"'Could she love her city, yet hate me?
"'She should link the city to me!
"'Could she hate her city, yet love me?
"'She should link the city to me!
"'Should the nu-gig—as happened to the Anzud chick—
"'Reject me in person
"'And abandon me by keeping to her holy chamber,
"'Let her at least bring me back to Kulab, the Brickwork!
"'Only on that day my spear shall be laid aside;
"'On that day my shield shall be broken!
"'Speak thus to my noble sister, Holy Inana!'"

Holy Inana replied to him:
"Now then, at the end of the clear river, of the clear watercourse,
"Of the river that is the gleaming water skin of Inana,
"Where at the banks and in the water meadows
"The suhur-maš fish eats the honey herb,
"The kin-tur fish eats wild acorns,
"There the ĞIŠ.ŠEŠ fish, the god of all suhur-maš fish,
"Is playing happily and darting about,
"Touching with its scaly tail the old reeds in that holy place.
"Tamarisks, many of them,
"Draw water from that pool.
"One stands alone, one stands alone;[110]
"One tamarisk stands there all alone, beside (the pool).
"Now, when Enmerkar, son of the Sun,
"Has cut that tamarisk and made a bucket from it,
"He must tear out the old reeds of that holy place and take them away.
"When he has thus chased the ĞIŠ.ŠEŠ fish, god of all suhur-maš fish, from (that pool),
"Caught it, cooked it, and served it
"And so fed the a-ankara, Inana's battle strength,
"Then his army shall succeed;
"Then he will be able to end the life force Aratta draws from the subterranean waters!
"If he then carries off from the city its worked metal and its smiths,
"If he carries off its worked stones and its jewelers,
"If he renovates and resettles the city,
"All the moulds of Aratta shall be his forever!"

IV. EPILOGUE

aratta^{ki} zag-ed$_2$-bi ^{na4}za-gin$_3$ dur$_5$-ru-am$_3$
bad$_3$-bi sig$_4$ sağ-zi-bi huš-am$_3$
im-bi im nagga
kur ha-šu-ur$_2$-ra-ta im-kid$_2$-a
kug lugal-ban$_3$-da zag-mi$_2$

IV. EPILOGUE

Aratta's battlements are of greenish lapis lazuli;
Its wall and its towering brickwork are bright red;
Its bricks are of tinstone
Excavated in the hills where the cypress grows!
Praise be to Holy Lugalbanda!

Notes

[1] The text is not explicit on this point, nor on the point whether the "seven heroes" (LB I lines 59–71) are really Lugalbanda's brothers.

[2] The text is difficult. It is not clear whether they are good spirits or bad demons—or both.

[3] The main reason for doing so is that there is still some hesitation on this point in the relevant scholarly literature. A secondary but equally legitimate reason is that the "one-story thesis" enlightens the structure of both poems as we have them, while the "two-stories thesis" has serious drawbacks precisely on this point.

[4] Gilgamesh and Aka. See Katz 1993.

[5] See Vanstiphout 1996b and 2002b for Lugalbanda as the archetype of the Christian saints.

[6] To wit, lines 300–307//314–319 (the sacrificial animals); 327–334 (sleep); 341–347 (dream); 395–421 (the ghosts).

[7] Lines 15–22 (Ninkasi); 115–124 (Anzud); 255–265 (Unug's camp before Aratta); 294–299 (Unug before Enmerkar started to build). The latter is repeated as 360–365. Note that the first such passage in LB I (see previous note) is repeated, as is the last one in LB II. Close reading reveals that the composer has a penchant for explanatory verse anyway, and many more examples of this technique may be found.

[8] See Black 1998, passim.

[9] In fact, this may be the poetical reason why Lugalbanda's return, with Inana's solution, to Enmerkar and the army laying siege to Aratta is not mentioned at all in the text.

[10] See the catalog texts (20 n. 72 above) and Vanstiphout 2003: 19–26.

[11] For the dream passage, see Vanstiphout 1998b.

[12] See Vanstiphout 2002b for a treatment in detail.

[13] In this respect he may be compared to Zid-udsudra/Ut-napištim after he had weathered an even greater crisis.

[14] It is interesting to note that that other great cosmic traveler, Dante, ends his three books with the words *le stelle*.

[15] The ETCSL site www-etcsl.orient.ox.ac.uk/section1/b1821.htm gives particulars and indications of publication, but many fragments are still unpublished. Wilcke 1987 may also be consulted for the manuscripts. Hallo 1983 gives a good but partial analysis of the material.

[16] Only the Lugalbanda story opens with a "cosmogonical" introduction. Such introductions, which should not be taken too seriously as cosmogony, occur elsewhere, such as in a few mythological and heroic narratives and some disputations.

There seems to be no strong or even explicit relationship between them and the type of text they introduce. If one insists, the rationale in this case may have been to emphasize the venerable age of the House of Unug.

17 "Black-headed" is a common epithet for "Sumerians." The expression undoubtedly derives from the ideological imagery, which represents humanity as a flock of sheep—that are black-headed to this day—under the care and protection of their divine and royal *pastor bonus*.

18 "Setting the mace toward" means "to intend to conquer."

19 The number seven recurs in most of the cycle. In ELA there are seven journeys to be made by the messenger, who has to cross seven mountain ranges.

20 We know of a large number of undoubtedly ceremonial bronze weapons adorned with images of wild animals. A number of them seem to be falsifications, and provenance is but rarely assured. The general opinion is that—if genuine—they come from Luristan, i.e., the part of the Zagros Mountains to the northeast of Mesopotamia, which happens to be the general direction of Enmerkar's campaign. Even so, they appear to be considerably later than our poems.

21 See above, note 19.

22 The šar is the number 36,000—or infinity, since the sign is originally a full circle.

23 It is not altogether clear what or who is "hovering over the earth": the mountains or the Urukean army?

24 "The holy and precious place" is a common euphemism for the grave.

25 This whole passage should consistently be read simultaneously on two levels: that of the food left by the companions so that Lugalbanda will be able to survive, and that of a rich assemblage of burial gifts. Even the references to traveling provisions are ambiguous, for the possibility, even probability, exists that Lugalbanda will soon have to undertake the most difficult ultimate journey: to the underworld.

26 The Zubi Mountains and the Black Mountains (line 114) are to be sought due east from Unug, in the trans-Tigridian southern end of the Zagros Range. Note the use of "imported," Sumerian šu-a bal-a. Since ELA explicitly states that trading (bala) did not yet exist, this qualification—if not a mere oversight—would seem to imply that, in the minds of author(s) and public, the three stories represent three separate and different attempts by Enmerkar to impose his supremacy over Aratta. This can be argued from the contents of the stories as well: in EE and ELA an ultimatum is used, in LB a military campaign. However, since the shock and awe of Enmerkar's invasion turns out to be a damp squib, all three attempts depend on cleverness, magic, and, wittingly or unwittingly, a little help from Enmerkar's divine friends. Also, if the stories are meant to be separate and different, can we put them in chronological order?

27 Perhaps because he fears that he will never again be able to use these precious weapons.

28 The simile is not clear to me. In any case, the opposition between "open" and "closed" is intended.

29 Or "at sunrise." But "like the sun" may be defended as meaning "as the sun will surely do tomorrow," hinting at the sun's constant protection of the heroic rulers of Unug, such as Gilgamesh.

[30] The "cows of Nanna," the moon god, might well be an expression for the stars in general or even for the Milky Way—which term could ultimately depend upon this usage, at least if they recognized the Milky Way as stars. Their "migrating" probably points to the movement of the stars.

[31] An allusion to the common notion that dust is the only food available in the underworld.

[32] Inana, whose name is only mentioned as such in line 176, is presented here in her role of provider of sexual delight, for the delectation of which no great riches are necessary. Her "playing" usually denotes war, but here it must mean sex.

[33] Šara is Inana's son. Note that the radiance (or halo) of Inana as the evening star is thought to be her face.

[34] Snakes and scorpions, lowly and despicable though they are, have at least a home, be it mere wasteland or a crevice in the earth. Lugalbanda has nothing.

[35] Literally "a satisfied heart."

[36] It is not clear why Nanna or Suen (his name in Akkadian) should be called here "Holy Calf" (amar kug). The preceding verse calls him "bull," and in line 133 he is presented as tending the heavenly herds. The only divine "calf" of any special significance is Amar-Utu-ka, better known as Marduk. Perhaps the name of the third king of the Ur III dynasty, Amar-Suen, is of relevance here.

[37] Nanna's "crown" is the crescent, which in Mesopotamia lies down as it still does on the early mosques.

[38] Literally "sets straight."

[39] The text has "head" for *origin* and "back" for *effects*. It is somewhat strange that Nanna is presented here as the guarantor of justice, an office that otherwise belongs to Utu.

[40] See above, line 123.

[41] Unclear to me.

[42] As suggested ingeniously by Jerry Cooper (private communication), the Sumerian term zid-du, usually translated "righteous one," is probably the fertile soil, bringing forth the plant of life. That Sumerian zid can mean "productive, fertile" in various contexts has been suggested before. See below, LB II, lines 99–100, where the zid-du and the rolling rivers are said to be under the protection of Anzud. In contrast to the magical plant in the Gilgamesh epic, this plant is truly and literally the "plant of life." The food and water of life also appear—in a very important way—in the Akkadian Adapa story.

[43] "Hoof" (umbin) is used in anticipation of the similes in the next lines.

[44] "Fit for racing" might also be considered.

[45] Instead of baking it in an oven.

[46] Probably these "embers" are the dead coals left over from the brothers' fire, which he now reignites. This might explain why he has only seven pieces of coal, as is said in line 293.

[47] Although a different term is used, this coal is apparently a synonym of the embers of line 284.

[48] I regard lines 303–307 as an explanatory notice inserted into the story and breaking or diverging from the narrative thread. This stylistic device seems typical for the poet of both Lugalbanda stories.

[49] Actually, Sumerian uses the same term (lal$_3$) for "runny honey" and "(date) syrup," whence the freedom I have taken in translating.

[50] Ninkasi is the goddess of beer. The contents of her cask put Lugalbanda to sleep.

[51] The point being made here seems to be that, contrary to the venerable technique or "science" of oneirocriticism, one cannot put one's complete trust in a dream. For this dream sequence, see Vanstiphout 1998b.

[52] The contrast between lines 345 and 346 seems to be that dreams can be as sedate and staid as Ninlil, the matron goddess who watches over orderly family life, but also as wild and violent as Inana's destructive sexuality.

[53] This verse is not very clear. Does Zangara speak in a ghostly voice? And why should he be the multiplier of humankind?

[54] Perhaps an allusion to the episode of the Bull of Heaven in the Gilgamesh stories. For "bullfighter" the text uses a term with the general meaning of athlete.

[55] One may well ask why. Perhaps this is an allusion to the flood episode in the Gilgamesh epic, where the gods sniff the scent of Ut-napištim's sacrifice and gather above it like flies. The snakes might then be either an intentionally obscure term for the gods or a straight lie. See lines 371–375.

[56] This double expression occurs also elsewhere. To our understanding the verbs "to wake up" and "to shiver" are linked to the wrong nouns, namely, "dream" and "sleep." Is this intended as a deliberate and artful chiasm?

[57] Read perhaps ^{ğiš}šu-da-ka-ni?

[58] The meaning of this reference, perhaps to an existing place, escapes us.

[59] Reading ^{ğiš}šu-da-ka-ni for GIŠ DA ŠU KA NI. Still, the term as such is unknown.

[60] From this verse onward the text is hard to understand, although the Sumerian is not especially abstruse. It needs much more study.

[61] This verse seems to contradict the preceding couplet.

[62] Lines 422–423 are still somewhat uncertain. The proposed translation of the lines was inspired by a remark of Jerry Cooper. First, "that man" is taken to be Lugalbanda; "shining upon" stands for what is literally "lying upon, covering"; the "whole length" is literally "the long length." The terms uš and gid$_2$ are known as terms used in measuring real estate. Therefore an alternative, but less attractive, rendering might be "The hero, whose breadth and length lies upon everybody," alluding to the notion that the sunshine envelops the whole body. However, there is here the distinct possibility of punning. As noted above (note 42 to line 265), the term zid, used in the line that immediately follows, can mean "true, loyal" but also "fertile." Since uš can also be read as giš$_3$ "penis," and nu$_2$ is one of the common expressions for coitus, the pun, questionable in taste as it is, seems unavoidable. So a third possible rendering would be "The hero, whose long penis 'sleeps with' that man." However, this does not seem to be very informative in context.

[63] Again, line 463 seems to contradict line 462.

[64] Why only seven here, as against fourteen in line 464?

[65] Rather than regarding the "holy battle-mace of the sky" as personified (and homosexual), the sentence might mean that the divine weapon/righteous god lies next to a man at night in order to protect him.

[66] Does this mean that they inform the gods of the evil words of others and that they are thus spying for righteousness?

[67] In lines 494–497 the reading of the verbs as e_{11} is a conjecture for the incomprehensible zu-ub$_3$ of the manuscript, which is in need of collation. In addition, the reading mas-sum is a conjecture for MAŠ.TE. In any case the passage is about stars and constellations.

[68] "Matriarch" (bur-šum-ma) is an epithet of Inana, who here seems to cause the stars and constellations to rise.

[69] A constellation.

[70] A constellation.

[71] See already the introduction to the Lugalbanda poems and to LB I.

[72] This theme is treated in some detail in Vanstiphout 2002b.

[73] See the Oxford on-line presentation www-etcsl.orient.ox.ac.uk/section1/b1822.htm for the full list of tablets/fragments. The number is not absolute: some of the fragments join others.

[74] These are the fragments with a 3N-T siglum.

[75] Literally "to his own heart/mind."

[76] Perhaps this reference to the "splendid tree" is a hidden announcement of the "single tree" or the "tree standing alone" occurring at the very end of the poem (lines 397–402 below). The motif of the single tree appears elsewhere, such as in the tale about Inana and Šukaletuda. The best-known instance is the tree that Gilgamesh felled and used to make furniture for Inana, and subsequently his own playthings, in the first part of Gilgamesh, Enkidu, and the Netherworld. Note that here this tree is inhabited by eagle-like Anzud and that in Gilgamesh, Enkidu, and the Netherworld the tree is inhabited by an eagle and Lilith. This also happens in a way in the folktale about *Šamšum al-Jabbar* (see Vanstiphout 2000), while in the Addadian Etana story the single tree of the central fable houses an eagle and a snake. Another important "single tree" is, of course, the giant cedar Gilgamesh and Enkidu brought back from the cedar forest.

[77] A.RU is unknown as to reading and meaning. It is possible that it is an Akkadian loanword: *aru* is a term for the foliage of the palm tree. However, a palm tree seems out of place in this mountain region. Still, the term could refer to foliage.

[78] I.e., " where the cypress does not grow," meaning that this is above the ordinary tree line. Only the eagle-tree grows there.

[79] It is not clear precisely which species is meant here. There were three distinct species in Mesopotamia: the wild bull, or aurochs (am [bull] or sun$_2$ [cow] in Sumerian; *bos primigenius*), the bison (*kusarikku* in Akkadian), which was probably already extinct in historic times but is well known from art, and the water buffalo, which still lives in the southern marshes.

[80] A clear allusion to the sumptuous meal that Lugalbanda had prepared for the gods in the first part of the story.

[81] I.e., Anzud.

[82] The "cattle-pen of Nanna" is a kenning for the sky, where Nanna tends his cattle, which are the stars, as is mentioned in the first part of the story. It is tempting to speculate that this image is at the origin of our "Milky Way."

[83] Granting a name that ensures a fortunate destiny seems otherwise to be the privilege of the gods. It is the topic of the short story Enlil and Namzitarra (see Civil 1974). Note that many kings bore names of this kind.

[84] The precise meaning of this line escapes me. Could it be "as straight as a stylus"?

[85] I.e., may they fly so thickly that they are like a bundle of logs tied together.

[86] As in medieval romance, weapons of great heroes and/or gods sometimes bear names and can even have lives of their own.

[87] We do not know what Lugalbanda answers. Is his answer a simple refusal?

[88] I.e., your destiny.

[89] The relevance of these two obviously proverbial statements is not altogether clear to me. Perhaps they simply mean that Anzud consents to be guided by Lugalbanda in the matter.

[90] There are a number of early temple friezes—a monumental one at Al-Ubaid—and smaller wall plaquettes representing Anzud.

[91] One is tempted to interpret this couplet as meaning that Lugalbanda has somehow become the shadow of Anzud, which travels over the ground with the same speed as Anzud in the air.

[92] Lugalbanda's "explanation" is, of course, nonsense.

[93] What illness is this? Lugalbanda has long since been healed.

[94] At which point in the campaign has Lugalbanda reappeared? The following lines seem to imply that the army of Unug is only just beginning to invest Aratta and that the siege remains fruitless for a whole year (line 262).

[95] It is possible that these "watchtowers" refer to small and temporary structures erected in the outlying fields to protect them from predatory animals (or humans).

[96] The Sumerian term is u š u m g a l, which has no precise translation since it seems to be a mythical animal, perhaps somewhat like the much later *mušhuššu* of Babylon's Ištar gate. Jacobsen translates—elegantly—as "basilisk."

[97] Presumably of the javelins and slingstones raining down on the besieging army.

[98] Literally "the regiment of the open-eyed." The term has also been understood as meaning "elite troops."

[99] The motif of the repeated demand for help or approval occurs elsewhere. See Gilgamesh and Aka and Gilgamesh and Huwawa—and Thucydides' description of Alcibiades' Sicilian venture!

[100] This is what the text says. Enmerkar's palace is in Unug/Kulab; at this point Enmerkar is still laying siege to Aratta. Is "palace" merely a somewhat grand term for Enmerkar's headquarters in the field?

[101] They still do.

[102] The expression "who know no grain" refers to the lack of civilization on the part of the Martu bedouins. It occurs as part of the catalogue of their uncivilized ways in the Curse of Agade (see Cooper 1983) and in the Marriage of Martu (see Klein 1996).

[103] Here, as elsewhere when referring to a personal attribute, "power" (Sumerian m e) might best be understood as *charisma* or *karma* or *baraka*.

[104] The argument seems to be that Inana has always loved Enmerkar, and she has always loved her city. So why does she treat Enmerkar like this? "To link" can best be taken as "to identify," although I cannot offer any philological underpinning.

[105] I.e., Inana. The reference is to the opening episode of the story, where the young Anzud has been left alone by his parents.

[106] This means probably "to lay down arms."

[107] It is possible that by the "guardian angel" and the "protective spirit" the *esprit de corps* of the troop, or the band of brothers, is meant.

[108] The coupled verbs "to stand" and "to sit down" are used elsewhere (Gilgamesh and Aka; see Katz 1993) as an expression for life in the services.

[109] Another name for Dumuzid, the lover and spouse of Inana.

[110] See above, note 76.

Bibliography

Alster, Bendt. 1973. "An Aspect of 'Enmerkar and the Lord of Aratta.'" *RA* 67:101–10.

———. 1975a. "Paradoxical Proverbs and Satire in Sumerian Literature." *JCS* 27:201–30.

———. 1975b. *Studies in Sumerian Proverbs*. Copenhagen Studies in Assyriology 3. Copenhagen: Akademisk Forlag.

———. 1976. "Early Patterns in Mesopotamian Literature." Pages 13–24 in *Kramer Anniversary Volume: Cuneiform Studies in Honor of Samuel Noah Kramer*. Edited by Barry L. Eichler, with the assistance of Jane W. Heimerdinger and Åke W. Sjöberg. AOAT 25. Kevelaer: Butzon & Bercker.

———. 1983. "Dilmun, Bahrain, and the Alleged Paradise in Sumerian Myth and Literature." Pages 39–74 in *Dilmun: New Studies in the Archaeology and Early History of Bahrain*. Edited by Daniel T. Potts. BBVO 2. Berlin: Reimer.

———. 1990. "Lugalbanda and the Early Epic Tradition in Mesopotamia." Pages 59–72 in *Lingering over Words: Studies in Ancient Near Eastern Literature in Honor of William L. Moran*. Edited by Tzvi Abusch, John Huehnergard, and Piotr Steinkeller. HSS 37. Atlanta: Scholars Press.

———. 1991. "Two Sumerian Short tales Reconsidered." *ZA* 82:186–201.

———. 1993. "The Sumerian Folktale of the Three Ox-Drivers from Adab." *JCS* 43–45:27–38.

———. 1995. "Epic Tales from Ancient Sumer: Enmerkar, Lugalbanda, and Other Cunning Heroes." *CANE* 4:2315–26.

Alster, Bendt, and Herman L. J. Vanstiphout. 1987. "Lahar and Ashnan: Presentation and Analysis of a Sumerian Disputation." *AS* 9:1–43.

Attinger, Pascal. 1984. "Enki et Nin-hursaga." *ZA* 74:1–52.

Bahrani, Zainab. 2001. *Women of Babylon. Gender and Representation in Mesopotamia*. London: Routledge.

Behrens, Hermann. 1978. *Enlil und Ninlil: Ein sumerischer Mythos aus Nippur.* Studia Pohl: Series Maior 8. Rome: Biblical Institute Press.

———. 1983–84. Review of Adele Berlin, *Enmerkar and Ensuhkeshdanna: A Sumerian Narrative Poem. AfO* 29–30:98–103.

Berlin, Adele. 1979. *Enmerkar and Ensuhkeshdanna: A Sumerian Narrative Poem.* Occasional Publications of the Babylonian Fund 2. Philadelphia: University Museum.

Bernhardt, Inez, and Samuel Noah Kramer. 1956–57. "Götter-Hymnen und Kult-Gesänge der Sumerer auf zwei Keilschrift-'Katalogen' in der Hilprecht-Sammlung." *WZJ* 6:389–95.

Black, Jeremy. 1996. "The Imagery of Birds in Sumerian Poetry." Pages 23–46 in *Mesopotamian Poetic Language: Sumerian and Akkadian.* Edited by Marianna E. Vogelzang and Herman L. J. Vanstiphout. Cuneiform Monographs 6. Proceedings of the Groningen Group for the Study of Mesopotamian Literature 2. Groningen: Styx.

———. 1998. *Reading Sumerian Poetry.* Athlone Publications in Egyptology and Ancient Near Eastern Studies. London: Athlone.

———. 2002. "The Sumerians in Their Landscape." Pages 41–61 in *Riches Hidden in Secret Places: Ancient Near Eastern Studies in Memory of Thorkild Jacobsen.* Edited by Tzvi Abusch. Winona Lake, Ind. Eisenbrauns.

Charpin, Dominique. 1986. Pages 455–58 in idem, *Le clergé d'Ur au siècle d'Hammurabi: (XIXe–XVIIIe siècles av. J.-C.).* Genève: Librairie Droz.

Civil, Miguel. 1974. "Enlil and Namzitarra." *AfO* 25:65–71.

———. 1983. "Enlil and Nin-lil: The Marriage of Sud." *JAOS* 103:43–66.

Cohen, Sol. 1973. "Enmerkar and the Lord of Aratta." Ph.D. diss., University of Pennsylvania.

Cooper, Jerrold S. 1972–75. "Heilige Hochzeit. B. Archäologisch." *RlA* 4:259–69.

———. 1983. *The Curse of Agade.* Baltimore: Johns Hopkins University Press.

———. 1997. "The Incipit of Enmerkar and Ensuhkesdana." *NABU* 118.

Edzard, Dietz Otto. 1994. "Sumerian Epic: Epic or Fairy Tale?" *BCSMS* 27:7–14.

Empson, William. 1935. *Some Versions of Pastoral.* London: Chatto & Windus.

Falkowitz, Robert S. 1983. "Notes on 'Lugalbanda and Enmerkar.'" *JAOS* 103:103–11.

Flückiger-Hawker, Esther. 1999. *Urnamma of Ur in Sumerian Literary Tradition.* OBO 166. Fribourg: Universitätsverlag; Göttingen: Vandenhoeck & Ruprecht.

Foster, Benjamin R. 1993. *Before the Muses: An Anthology of Akkadian Literature.* Bethesda, Md.: CDL.

———. 2001. *The Epic of Gilgamesh.* New York: Norton.

George, Andrew. 1999. *The Epic of Gilgamesh: A New Translation*. New York: Barnes & Noble.

Glassner, Jean-Jacques. 1993. *Chroniques mésopotamiennes*. Paris: Les belles lettres.

———. 2000. *Écrire à Sumer: L'invention du cunéiforme*. Univers historique. Paris: Seuil.

Grayson, A. K. 1970. *Assyrian and Babylonian Chronicles*. Texts from Cuneiform Sources 5. Locust Valley, N.Y.: Augustin.

Green, Margaret W. 1978. "The Eridu Lament." *JCS* 30:127–67.

———. 1984. "The Uruk Lament." *JAOS* 104:253–79.

Gurney, Oliver E. 1977. "A Note on the Babel of Tongues." *AfO* 25:170–71.

Hallo, W. W. 1966. Review of UrET 6/1. *JCS* 20:89–93.

———. 1983. "Lugalbanda Excavated." *JAOS* 103:165–80.

Hansman, J. 1978. "The Question of Aratta." *JNES* 37:331–36.

Heimpel, Wolfgang. 1981. Adele Berlin, *Enmerkar and Ensuhkeshdanna: A Sumerian Narrative Poem*. *JAOS* 101:404–7.

Jacobsen, Thorkild. 1939. *The Sumerian King List*. AS 11. Chicago: University of Chicago Press.

———. 1987. *The Harps That Once. . . : Sumerian Poetry in Translation*. New Haven: Yale University Press.

———. 1992. "The Spell of Nudimmud." Pages 403–416 in *Sha'arei Talmon: Studies in the Bible, Qumran, and the Ancient Near East Presented to Shemaryahu Talmon*. Edited by Michael Fishbane and Emanuel Tov. Winona Lake, Ind.: Eisenbrauns.

———. 1997. "Enmerkar and the Lord of Aratta." *COS* 1.170:547–50.

Jestin, Raymond-Riec. 1957. "Le poème d'En-me-er-kar." *RHR* 151:145–220.

Katz, Dina. 1993. *Gilgamesh and Akka*. LOT 1. Groningen: Styx.

Klein, Jacob. 1971. Review of Claus Wilcke, *Das Lugalbandaepos*. *JAOS* 91:295–99.

——— 1996 "The Marriage of Martu: The Urbanization of the 'Barbaric' Nomads." *Michmanim* 9:83–96.

Komoróczy, Geza. 1975. "Zur Ätiologie der Schrifterfindung im Enmerkar-Epos." *AF* 3:19–24.

Kramer, Samuel Noah. 1940. *Lamentation over the Destruction of Ur*. AS 12. Chicago: University of Chicago Press.

———. 1942. "The Oldest Literary Catalogue: A Sumerian List of Literary Compositions Compiled about 2000 B.C." *BASOR* 88:10–19.

———. 1943. "Man's Golden Age: A Sumerian Parallel to Genesis XI.1." *JAOS* 63:191–94.

———. 1952. *Enmerkar and the Lord of Aratta: A Sumerian Tale of Iraq and Iran*. Museum Monographs. Philadelphia: University Museum, University of Pennsylvania.

———. 1961. "New Literary Catalogue from Ur." *RA* 55:169–76.

———. 1968. "The Babel of Tongues: A Sumerian Version." *JAOS* 88:108–11.

———. 1969. The Sacred Marriage Rite: Aspects of Faith, Myth and Ritual in Ancient Sumer. Bloomington: University of Indiana Press.

———. 1990. "The 'Barnett' Enmerkar Tablet: A New Sumerian Dialect (?)." Pages 7–25 in *De la Babylonie à la Syrie, en passant par Mari: Mélanges offerts à Monsieur J.-R. Kupper à l'occasion de son 70e anniversaire*. Edited by. Ö. Tunca. Liège: Université de Liège.

Kramer, Samuel Noah, and Thorkild Jacobsen. 1953. "Enmerkar and Ensukušširana." *Or* NS 23:232–34.

Majidzadeh, Y. 1976. "The Land of Aratta." *JNES* 35:137–44.

———. 1982. "Lapis Lazuli and the Great Khorasan Road." *Paléorient* 8:56–69.

Michalowski, Piotr. 1983. "History As Charter: Some Observations on the Sumerian King List." *JAOS* 103:237–48.

———. 1988. "Mental Maps and Ideology: Observations on Subartu." Pages 129–56 in *The Origins of Cities in Dry-Farming Syria and Mesopotamia in the Third Millennium B.C.* Edited by. Harvey Weiss. Guilford: Four Quarters.

———. 1989. *The Lamentation over the Destruction of Sumer and Ur.* Winona Lake, Ind.: Eisenbrauns: .

———. 1995. "Sumerian Literature: An Overview." *CANE* 4:2279–91.

———. 1999. "Commemoration, Writing, and Genre in Ancient Mesopotamia." Pages 69–90 in *The Limits of Historiography: Genre and Narrative in Ancient Historical Texts*. Edited by Christina Shuttleworth Kraus. Leiden: Brill.

Renger, Johannes. 1972–75. "Heilige Hochzeit. A. Philologisch." *RlA* 4:251–59.

Römer, Willem H. Ph. 1981. Review of Adele Berlin, *Enmerkar and Ensuhkeshdanna: A Sumerian Narrative Poem*. *BO* 38:338–343.

Römer, Willem H. Ph., and Dietz Otto Edzard. 1993. Pages 507–39 in *Mythen und Epen 1*. Vol. 3.3 of *Texte aus der Umwelt des Alten Testaments*. Edited by Otto Kaiser. Gütersloh: Mohn.

Roth, Martha. 1983. "The Slave and the Scoundrel: CBS 10467, A Sumerian Morality Tale?" *JAOS* 103:275–82.

Sauren, Herbert. 1972. "Les épopées sumériennes et le théâtre classique." *OLP* 3:35–47.

———. 1974. "Der Weg nach Aratta: Zur tieferen Erschliessung der sumerischen Literatur." *AAASH* 22:137–44.

Tinney, Steve. 1996. *The Nippur Lament: Royal Rhetoric and Divine Legitimation in the Reign of Išme-Dagan of Isin (1953–1935 B.C.)*. Occasional Publications of the Samuel Noah Kramer Fund 16. Philadelphia: Samuel Noah Kramer Fund.

———. 1998. "On the Curricular Setting of Sumerian Literature" *Iraq* 61: 159–72.

———. Forthcoming. "A Literary Temple Archive from Nippur." *OLP.*

Van Dijk, J. J. A. 1970. "La 'confusion des langues': Note sur le lexique et sur la morphologie d'Enmerkar, 147–155." *Or* NS 39:302–10.

Vanstiphout, Herman L. J. 1987. "Joins Proposed in Sumerian Literary Compositions." *NABU* 87.

———. 1983a. "Problems in the 'Matter of Aratta.'" *Iraq* 45:35–42.

———. 1983b. "Een Sumerische Stadsklacht uit de Oudbabylonische Periode. Turmenuna, of de Nippurklacht." Pages 330–41 in *Schrijvend Verleden: Documenten uit het Oude Nabije Oosten vertaald en Toegelicht.* Edited by K. R. Veenhof. Leiden: Ex Oriente Lux.

———. 1984. "Inana/Ishtar As a Figure of Controversy." Pages 225–38 in *Struggles of Gods: Papers of the Groningen Work Group for the Study of the History of Religions.* Edited by Hans Klippenberg. Religion and Reason 13. Berlin: de Gruyter.

———. 1986. "Towards a Reading of 'Gilgamesh and Agga.' Part II: Construction." *OLP* 17:33–50.

———. 1990a. "Enmerkar's Invention of Writing Revisited." Pages 515–24 in *DUMU-E$_2$-DUB-BA-A: Studies in Honor of Åke W. Sjöberg.* Edited by Hermann Behrens, Darlene Loding, and Martha T. Roth. Occasional Publications of the Babylonian Fund 11. Philadelphia: University Museum.

———. 1990b. "The Mesopotamian Debate Poems. A General Presentation (Part I)." *AS* 12:271–318.

———. 1992a. "The Banquet Scene in the Sumerian Debate Poems." *Res Orientales* 4:37–63.

———. 1992b. "The Mesopotamian Debate Poems. A General Presentation. Part II: The Subject." *AS* 14:339–67.

———. 1992c. "Repetition and Structure in the Aratta Cycle." Pages 247–264 in *Mesopotamian Epic Literature: Oral or Aural?* Edited by Marianna E. Vogelzang and Herman L. J. Vanstiphout. Lewiston, N.Y.: Mellen.

———. 1994. "Another Attempt at the 'Spell of Nudimmud.'" *RA* 88: 135–54.

———. 1995a. "The Matter of Aratta: An Overview." *OLP* 26:5–20.

———. 1995b. "On the Old Babylonian Edubba." Pages 3–16 in *Centres of Learning: Learning and Location in Pre-modern Europe and the Near East.* Edited by Jan Willem Drijvers and Alasdair A. MacDonald. Brill's Studies in Intellectual History. Leiden: Brill.

———. 1996a. "Disputations." *COS* 1.180–183:575–88.

———. 1996b. "De Heilige Lugalbanda." *Phoenix* 42.1:35–53.

———. 1997. "Why Did Enki Organize the World?" Pages 117–34 in *Sumerian Gods and Their Representations.* Edited by I. L. Finkel and M. J. Geller. Groningen: Styx.

———. 1998a. *Helden en goden van Sumer: Een keuze uit de heroïsche en mythologische dichtkunst van het Oude Mesopotamië.* Nijmegen: SUN.

———. 1998b. "Reflections on the Dream of Lugalbanda: A Typological and Interpretative Analysis of LH 322–365." Pages 397–412 in *Intellectual Life of the Ancient Near East: Papers Presented at the 43rd Rencontre Assyriologique Internationale, Prague, July 1–5, 1996*. Edited by Jirí Prosecký. Prague: Oriental Institute.

———. 2000. "A Meeting of Cultures? Rethinking the 'Marriage of Martu.'" Pages 461–74 in *Languages and Cultures in Contact: At the Crossroads of Civilisations in the Syro-Mesopotamian Realm*. Edited by K. Van Lerberghe and G. Voet. OLA 96. Leuven: Peeters.

———. 2002a. *Het Epos van Gilgameš*. Nijmegen: SUN.

———. 2002b. "Sanctus Lugalbanda." Pages 259–89 in *Riches Hidden in Secret Places: Ancient Near Eastern Studies in Memory of Thorkild Jacobsen*. Edited by Tzvi Abusch. Winona Lake, Ind. Eisenbrauns.

———. 2003. "The Old Babylonian Literary Canon: Structure, Function and Intention." Pages 1–28 in *Cultural Repertoires: Structure, Function, and Dynamics*. Edited by G. Dorleijn and Herman L. J. Vanstiphout. Groningen Studies in Cultural Change 3. Leuven: Peeters.

Veldhuis, Niek. 1997. "Elementary Education in Nippur: The Lists of Trees and Wooden Objects." Diss., Rijksuniversiteit Groningen.

———. 2001. "The Solution of the Dream: A New Interpretation of Bilgames' Death." *JCS* 53:133–48.

Westenholz, Joan Goodnick. 1997. *Legends of the Kings of Akkade: The Texts*. Mesopotamian Civilizations 7. Winona Lake, Ind.: Eisenbrauns:.

Weissbach, F. 1934. "Enmekar." *RlA* 2:395.

Wilcke, Claus. 1969. *Das Lugalbandaepos*. Wiesbaden: Harrassowitz.

———. 1987. "Lugalbanda." *RlA* 7:117–32.

Zólyomi, Gábor. 1995. "Speaking Cow or Mooing Sorcerer? A Note on Enmerkar and Ensuhkeshdanna l. 173–4 (186–7)." *NABU* 3.

Glossary

The following glossary provides information on geographical names, divine names, proper names, and Sumerian terms used within this volume. A greater-than sign (>) indicates a cross-reference to another listing in the glossary; capitals are used when an exact reading is unknown or in doubt.

a-ankara. Unidentified weapon of >Inana.
Abzu. Sweet-water "ocean" beneath the earth; abode and realm of >Enki.
Akalag. An otherwise unknown region called the "meadows of >Dumuzid"; apparently very good pastureland.
Akkad. Northern part of Babylonia.
Ama-ušumgalana. Name or epithet of >Dumuzid.
An. Supreme god. City god of >Unug, together with >Inana.
Anšan. Region in southwestern Iran; stage on the road to >Aratta in ELA and LB II.
Anuna. Collective name for the great gods.
Ansigaria. Chancellor of >Aratta in EE.
Anzud. Lion-faced mythical bird; guardian of the mountain ranges between >Sumer and >Aratta. *See also* IM.DUGUD.
Aratta. Unknown, probably mythical, city supposedly situated beyond the Zagros Range to the east of >Sumer; known only from literary references, where it is consistently said to be under the aegis of >Inana.
A.RU. Reading and meaning unknown. Possibly it is the Akkadian word *aru* "leaf (of the date palm)."
Aruru. One of the great gods; goddess of childbirth.
buru-az. Precise meaning unknown; a kind of bird.
Dilmun. Present-day island of Bahrain; over long periods the main transhipment area for Mesopotamian maritime trade; in other traditions the place where culture originated.

Dumuzid. Shepherd god; legendary ruler over >Unug; lover and husband of >Inana, later betrayed by her. *See also* Ama-ušumgalana.
Eana. Main temple (of >Inana) in >Unug.
Egara. Palace of >Enmerkar in EE.
Egipara. *See* Gipar.
Enki. God of wisdom, cleverness, and technical invention; city god of >Eridug.
Enlil. Chairman/leader of the divine government.
Ensuhgirana. Lord of >Aratta in EE.
Enun. A shrine in >Eridug.
Ereš. City in the neighborhood of >Unug, dedicated to >Nisaba.
Eridug. City in the extreme south of >Sumer, then at the edge of the Persian Gulf; city of >Enki.
ešda. A type of metal containers for liquids.
Euphrates. Westernmost of the Twin Rivers; >Unug is on the Euphrates.
Ezagina. Palace of >Ensuhgirana in EE.
gamgam. A kind of domestic fowl; possibly chicken or guinea-fowl.
Geštinana. Goddess of wine.
Gipar. Room (bridal chamber?) in the >Egara at >Unug and the >Ezagina at >Aratta; also >Egipara.
girin. Grass, herbs, flowers.
girsiga. Temple servant; low-ranking priest.
GIŠ.ĞEŠ. Exact reading unknown. A kind of fish, possibly mythical.
gizi-ešta. A kind of dough; possibly pastry dough.
Hamazi/u. Unknown city to the northeast of >Sumer.
hašur. A type of tree, probably related to cedar and cypress.
hirin. A plant with long sprouts.
ildag. A type of wood.
ilu. A type of song.
IM.DUGUD. Spelling consistently used in our poems for >Anzud. Although there is a broad consensus that the sign complex(es) used for writing this name should be read as Anzud, I am convinced that in these poems IM.DUGUD ("heavy cloud, storm cloud" and therefore with the determinative [mušen] indicating a bird, "Thunderbird") is what the scribes intended us to "read" or "understand" also, as an underlying metaphorical reading.
Inana. Goddess of war, strife, and sexual love; city goddess of >Unug and >Aratta.
išib. Purification priest.
Iškur. God of storm and rain.
kalam. The term for "Land," meaning civilized country, state, nation, and ultimately Sumer.
KAL.KAL. A term in LB I line 456; reading and meaning unknown.

kib. A waterfowl.
kin-tur. Unidentified kind of fish; it seems to feed on acorns!
Kulab. Often mentioned together with >Unug as twin cities. Probably originally a part (temple quarter?) of Unug.
lahama. Protective spirits coming up from the >Abzu.
lidga. A type of container used as a liquid measure.
ligidba. Balm, oil.
Lugalbanda. Son of >Enmerkar. Hero of LB I and LB II.
Lulubi. Mountain range; part of the southern Zagros, in front of >Anšan; possibly nearly identical to >Zabu.
lumah. Ecstatic.
Martu. (Semi)nomadic tribes living in the Syrian Desert along the middle reaches of the >Euphrates; also their eponymous god.
Mašgula. Shepherd of >Nisaba in EE.
MES. Exact reading unknown; unidentified kind of tree.
gudu. High-ranking priest.
Namenatuma. Chancellor of >Unug in EE.
Nanna. Moon god.
NIM. Kind of lion.
Ningal. Wife of >Nanna.
Ninguenaka. *See* Ninkasi.
Ninhursag. Goddess of birthing and of the hills.
Ninkasi. Goddess of beer; also known (in LB II) as >Ninguenaka.
Ninlil. Wife of >Enlil.
NinTABKULIBIR. Otherwise unknown divinity who wields the sideral battle-mace in LB I.
Nintud. Goddess of birth. Identical to >Aruru and sometimes to >Ninhursaga.
Ninurta. God of warfare and husbandry.
Nirah. A snake god.
Nisaba. Goddess of grain, administration, and writing.
Nudimmud. Name/epithet of >Enki.
nu-gig. Sacred prostitute.
pirig̃. A kind of lion.
Sagburu. Wise Woman (or good fairy?) in EE.
sagkal. (1) A kind of snake; precise meaning unknown; (2) a kind of stone.
Suen. Akkadian name for >Nanna.
suhur-maš. Unidentified kind of fish.
Sumer. Southern part of Babylonia.
Šakkan. God of the animals of the plains.
šar. "Legion"; actually the number 36,000.
Šara. Son of >Inana.
šatam. An official, usually responsible for trade.

šenu. An unidentified tree of which the leaves are browsed by buffaloes and goats.
šimgig. A type of wood, apparently aromatic.
Šubur. Region to the north and northeast of Babylonia.
šulhi. A kind of reed of which the leaves apparently are used for packing.
Šušin. Region in southwestern Iran; between the Zagros and >Anšan. Its central city was Susa.
Tigris. Easternmost of the Twin Rivers.
U. Precise reading uncertain; a marsh bird, possibly the pelican.
ug. A kind of lion.
Unug. >Sumerian name of the city otherwise known as Uruk, situated in the south of >Sumer; capital city of >Sumer in the period referred to in the stories translated here; ruled by Enmerkar. >Inana is the effective city goddess.
Uraš. Goddess; in some traditions the wife >An; mother of >Nisaba.
Uredina. Shepherd of >Nisaba in EE.
Urgirnuna. The evil sorcerer in EE.
Utu. Sun god.
zabalum. A type of fir.
Zabu. Mountain region in the southern Zagros; *see* Lulubi; Zubi.
Zangara. God of dreams.
Zubi. Probably identical to >Zabu.

CPSIA information can be obtained
at www.ICGtesting.com
Printed in the USA
BVHW031824230921
617420BV00005B/90

9 781589 830837